THE TAURUS METHOD

MICHAEL CHISHOLM

Author

Published by Windsor Books
P.O. Box 280
Brightwaters, N.Y., 11718

Manufactured in the United States of America

TABLE OF CONTENTS

PREFACE TO THIS EDITION

    Probably no single field of investing has so much profit-
making potential as trading in commodity futures. Yet, at the
same time, there are few ways for an investor to lose huge
sums of money as trading in commodity futures.

    As with so many other aspects of life, the commodity futures
investor can approach the markets from a complex perspective,
utilizing sophisticated mathematical formulae and esoteric computer programs, or he may approach the commodity futures markets using as simple and straightforward a set of techniques as
is possible and yet, at the same time, pragmatic. Unfortunately,
or so it seems, the majority of commodity investors use the former and not the latter approach. Perhaps this is why the best
available statistics we have seen estimate that somewhere in the
neighborhood of 90 percent of all commodity futures investors
either lose their speculative capital entirely or a sufficiently
large portion of it that they are forced to cease trading by the
end of their first 12 months in the market place.

    What is it about the remaining 10 percent, those commodity
investors who do make money in the market place year after year?
We believe the answer is twofold and that the first half of the
equation lies in the fact that they approach the markets in as
simple a way as is workable. The other half of the equation,
so we believe, that constitutes the characteristics of the

consistent winners in the commodity futures markets is their psychological make-up. They have winning psychological components to their personalities.

It is not the purpose of this book to examine the psychological differences between winners and losers in the commodity market place. We thoroughly covered that subject in our earlier book, Games Investors Play. The purpose of this book, The Taurus Method, is instead to separate the myths of commodity trading from the realities, to at once and at the same time examine the most effective, the simplest and the most pragmatic approaches to trading commodity futures contracts profitably.

In going over the original text of The Taurus Method in preparation for this new edition, we discovered that the concepts we expounded upon in the earlier editions of The Taurus Method have not only continued to be valid approaches to a simplistic market methodology, but in many respects have actually been working more profitably than ever in the months immediately preceding the publication of this edition.

Genuine and valid principles in virtually all fields remain true over the test of time. The principles expounded upon in this edition of The Taurus Method have met and continue to meet this test of time criterion. While no approach--whether it be highly sophisticated and highly complicated, as our approach is not, or whether it be elegantly simplistic and pragmatic, as our approach is--will work all of the time in all of the markets. It has been our experience, however, that the basic bedrock methodology that we have developed in The Taurus Method will assure the commodity futures investor the highest degree of probable success that he or she can find in this investment medium.

The inherent beauties of trading commodity futures are many. First, there is the excitement of watching the volatile and rapid market action either make money or lose money for a trader.

Closely connected to this is the acceleration of appreciation
(or depreciation) of a trader's investment capital. Other than
the race track or the casino, there is no faster way to accumulate a large fortune in a short period of time--or to become
totally bankrupt--than by trading in the commodity futures market arena.

Another very important consideration--and advantage--of
commodity futures markets is the ease with which profits can be
made regardless of inflation or deflation, rising or falling
interest rates, or any one of a dozen other variables that can
adversely affect an investment in such other investment mediums
as real estate, collectables, fixed instrument investments and
so forth.

Commodity investing, then, can be a rapid way to make large
sums of money in relatively short periods of time regardless of
whatever economic climate exists at any given time.

We would urge the would-be trader to keep in mind that
since the markets are fluid and changeable and since no technique or set of techniques in commodity investing--or any other
type of investing--works 100 percent of the time, that he invest
in the commodity markets only with capital which he considers
to be of a speculative nature and that he can afford to lose
without significantly affecting his lifestyle in an adverse
fashion should he happen to enter the markets during a period
of time when they are behaving in an eccentric fashion.

Even should this latter occurrence take place, by following
the principles outlined in our chapter on "money management,"
he tremendously reduce his probabilities of financial ruin, and
he should be able to withstand the most severe market onslaughts
and still have enough equity left in his account to recoup his
earlier losses as the markets return to more tradable and pre-

dictable behaviors--which they always do.

Now, let's embark on what will be an exciting adventure in the techniques of profitable and successful commodity futures trading. The bottom line--what the commodity futures trading game is all about--is making money. And the methodology in this book is intended to show the prospective trader in a clear and concise way exactly how to do that.

We hope our readers find our approach to their liking, our explanations clear and easy to understand and our methodology beneficial to them. We hope our readers come to find that using the techniques in this book will make them consistently profitable participants in the commodity markets.

M.P.C.

CHAPTER 1

CHART READING

Unless a commodity trader is a dyed-in-the-wool fundamental analyst, he will spend a <u>good</u> deal of time studying chart action, and very likely a <u>great</u> deal of time. Charts to a commodity trader are what the Daily Racing Form is to a horseplayer. They are a visual representation of past history and their study is based on the hope that in the face of the past, the future may be discerned even if dimly through a veil. Probably not even the strictest fundamentalist foregoes peeking at charts, though he may be loath to admit it. Professional traders of all types live with their charts, because no matter how reliable their memories are, there are simply too many commodities and too many delivery months for anyone to keep all this information accurately in his head. Occasionally, one hears of a trader who specializes in only one commodity, and in that case, we suppose it is possible for him to memorize all the important chart information. But such traders are rare indeed, and as some of the market experts have said: commodity trading is merely following a series of lines across a piece of paper; it doesn't matter whether the lines represent the prices of tulip bulbs or of moon rocks. While we don't agree with that point of view because it ignores the importance of fundamental considerations, the most powerful tool in any professional trader's equipment is undoubtedly his set of charts. Whether they are from a commercial chart service, or of his own construction;

1

whether they appear on a logarithmic scale or as optimized point and figure charts, they are his key to success, limited only by his ability to interpret the information they contain. Charts in the hands of a commodity trader are much like a violin in the hands of a musician; whether a beautiful melody is produced or only random noise depends upon the skill of the musician. In this chapter we will try to help you play your own beautiful music.

Beginning with the assumption that almost all readers realize the importance of charts in commodity trading, and before we explain how the experts read charts, we shall discuss the different _types_ of charts that are used, and the sources from which they may be obtained.

There is a multitude of good chart services available, but they vary in their usefulness to the trader. Some charts come in large format, measuring eleven by fourteen inches each; others are sometimes as small as three by five inches. Some chart services provide weekly and monthly charts, some show moving averages over different lengths of time, some have relative strenght indices, some include optimized or non-optimized point and figure charts, and most of them give Volume and Open Interest figures. Taurus subscribes to a number of different chart services, for different reasons that the trader should be familiar with. First, we feel it is mandatory to have both weekly and monthly charts available. We look at moving averages, and sometimes use them, but we normally figure our own, so their availability from a chart service is not that important to us. Since we use both optimized and non-optimized point and figure charts, we find receiving them helpful, although we have to update our own during the week. An important feature which as we said is provided by most chart services, is Volume, and even more importantly Open Interest figures. Also desirable is a graphical representation of the average Open Interest figures over the past years for comparison with this year's Open Interest. But major reason that we subscribe to more than one service is that we find it absolutely necessary to keep our own charts current at the end of each day's market action. This is most easily accomplished on the larger size charts, but the relatively smaller charts often provide a more readily discernible pattern of price movement, and cyclical movement is often easier to pick up on the smaller charts too. Not every professional trader may agree with us, but this has been our experience. Regardless of which chart service you decide on or whether you take several different ones, we believe it is imperative for you to mark your charts up on a daily basis. Whether or not you are in the markets, IF you have an account open with a brokerage firm, and are serious about pinpointing trades that will be profitable, you must keep your charts current; and this includes, at the very minimum, the Volume and Open Interest figures, in addition to the daily price range and close. To do less is to delude yourself about the seriousness of your intentions in trading the markets. Trading without keeping your charts up to date is like a doctor operating without knowing the results of current x-rays and lab tests. You might succeed occasionally, but sooner or later, your lack of diligence will catch up with you. We believe this is also true of the longer range weekly charts, but we do not feel that the average trader must keep current, up-to-date monthly charts. When time is a consideration, as it is for most traders, it is necessary only to keep one or two month's charts updated for each commodity's daily action: those of the nearby month and those of the next contract month. We believe that equal opportunities for profit exist with most commodities, but we suggest that you ignore the less actively traded commodities unless you have a special interest in them and sufficient time to deal with them. These include the Canadian markets, Broilers, Commercial Paper, the Mexican Peso, Eggs, Palladium, Sunflower Seeds, and possibly even Platinum, Potatoes, and Orange Juice. Most major financial newspapers and major city dailies like the Washington Post also give Volume and Open Interest figures that can be plotted at the same time.

4

We assume that you are familiar with how to post prices on bar charts, and on point and figure charts too, if you are interested in them.

If you are involved with point and figure charts or want to use them in conjunction with or instead of conventional bar charts, it has been our experience that the optimized type which are described in several books) and provided by at least one charting service, regularly outperform the standard non-optimized point-and-figure charts. For those unfamiliar with the difference between the two, years ago a certain point value was arbitrarily assigned to each block on a point and figure chart, a different point value for each commodity. While these work reasonably well, a number of later computerized studies discovered that the traditional figures for the different blocks representing the various commodities could be changed to improve their predictive value. One school of thought believes that these improved or optimized figures should be continually changed for each commodity to reflect the changing conditions in the marketplace.

Unfortunately, only those traders with sophisticated computer systems could even attempt to use this approach. So our recommendation is that if you use or are intending to use point and figure charts, to go with the optimized type for superior performance. We will not return to the subject of point and figure charts again except to say now that virtually everything we state about conventional charts also applies to point and figure charts. Where there are any exceptions, we will note them at the time.

Having discussed the different types of charts, we would like to re-emphasize their importance. There may be exceptions somewhere in the world, but we have yet to run across a truly professional trader, that is, a trader who has made his fortune in the markets who has done so without carefully mastering, studying, and utilizing charts. They are the key to understanding market psychology, knowing what other traders are doing, recognizing cycles, seeing the effects of fundamentals, placing stops, picking tops and bottoms, and understanding almost every other aspect of the market, thereby enabling the trader to have the best chance of predicting future market action. If it sounds like we are dwelling excessively on the value of charts, it is not by mistake, as we really want to impress you with their importance.

The major reason we keep our own moving average charts and watch the published ones, is that so many traders use them and rely upon them for their trading decisions. From this standpoint, they do have a lot of predictive value because their widespread usage by so many traders actually results in creating market moves partly on their own. Decades ago, before moving averages were in general usage, they had much less predictive value than they do today. While different chart services provide somewhat different time lengths of moving averages, the important ones to watch are those of the largest chart services. You can bet when a major

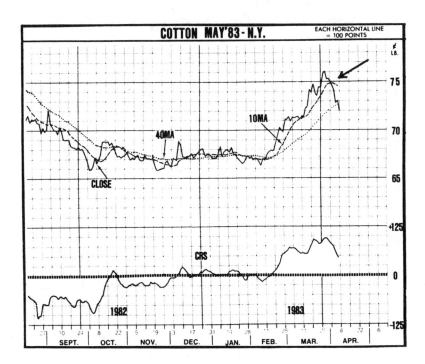

Figure 1

chart service which plots a 40-day moving average against closing prices, shows one line crossing the other, that scores of investors are either closing out or initiating positions. see Figure 1. The professional trader, if he has time to keep track of these developments, can use the information to his own advantage. This may be done in two ways, and the following examples illustrate how. If a professional trader feels that a bull market is on the verge of topping out, and a longer range moving average, say a 40-day one as published by a major charting service, appears ready to be broken on the downside by the closing price of the particular commodity, then this alerts him to a perfect opportunity to close out his long positions and institute new short positions before the bulk of the other subscribers to this service do the same thing. This is not a major method of increasing profits, but it does add points to his winnings. The second way is just the opposite in that if the professional trader's other indicators show him the market is destined to reach much greater heights regardless of what the moving averages show, and the moving average from a major chart service flashes a sell signal, then that is the time the pro moves his stops a bit lower or puts them in on a close only basis to protect his position from the reaction that will take place from the horde of subscribers to the chart service acting on the sell signal. Simultaneously, if he chooses, he can increase his long holdings at an advantageous price. The professional can take these actions, however, only when the real direction of the market is confirmed to him with a fair degree of validity by his other indicators, such as Cyclical action, Volume and Open Interest figures, Committments of Large Speculators, and Contrary Opinion. If these other indicators do not confirm his original position, and instead are indicating a genuine market reversal, in conjunction with the moving average indicators, he will bail out of the market rapidly and reverse his position, for he knows that the tremendous number of positions taken by the moving average followers will increase the magnitude of the market reversal. The effect of moving averages in causing market changes themselves is also due to the fact that some large advisory services utilize computer-generated signals that are variations of moving average techniques. Since some of these services are so popular and have so many subscribers, they actually have quite an effect on market action. So while the professional trader seldom uses moving averages as a method by itself, he is generally aware of the tremendous influence exerted on the markets by all the followers of these methods, and by watching the moving averages himself, he can often combine his other methods either to protect himself or to ride with the crowd of moving average advocates.

Much the same is true with point and figure charts, though not now to the degree it once was in past years when point and figure charts were so popular among commodity traders that the signals generated by them, whether genuine or false, often caused market movements by themselves, even when it was not justified by the fundamentals. Since the followers of point and figure charts are relatively far fewer now than they used to be, the influence generated by point and figure chart signals themselves is not as significant. This is even more true now with the different types of optimized and non-optimized point and figure charts being used, because most of the time the signals they produce are at different points, and sometimes are even contradictory. So, unless you are a point and figure chartist, you can generally safely ignore point and figure charts for their own influence on the markets. This comment is not meant to deprecate point and figure charting, because some of the best professionals we know use this method either instead of or in preference to bar charting. We only mean to say that point and figure charting is not as relatively popular as it used to be, and as a result cannot influence market action on its own as much as it used to.

We have briefly mentioned keeping one's own weekly charts, where each bar, or line, represents the high, low, and close for

8

the entire week's price action. These are very important to the
professional, as are monthly charts, for they show long-range
trends more clearly than the daily charts, as well as the levels
of price support and resistance. They also illustrate the long-
range cycles much more clearly, and we will discuss that later
when we go into using charts for cyclical analysis. Weekly charts
are constructed from the price action of the closest or most
nearby contract month, so when the spot month expires, the line on
the weekly chart for the next week's price action moves to the
next contract month, which is now the closest. This procedure,
which really is necessary since every contract month by its very
definition has a limited life span, creates some unusual gaps as
the weekly charts change from one contract month to another.
These gaps must be taken into account, and generally where gaps on
weekly charts appear, they are indicative of a change-over from
one contract month to the next. Normally these gaps do not affect
the construction of trendlines on weekly charts, since the gap

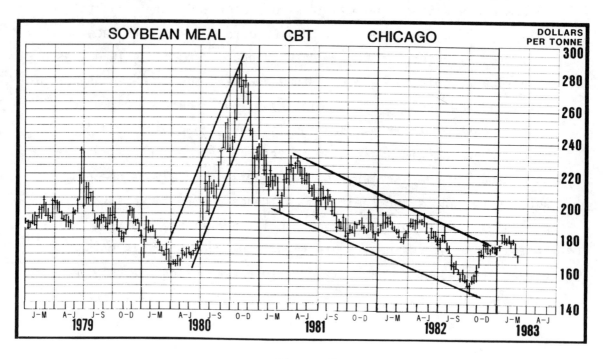

Figure 2

action is usually in the direction of the major trend move and
does not form a point that would appear on the trendline.
Trendlines on weekly charts are usually much more important than
trendlines on daily bar charts, see Figure 2, because they combine
an entire week's price action into one line, and therefore smooth
out irregularities that appear on the daily charts. The same is
true to some degree with monthly charts, but in their case the
smoothing action is so great that often significant trends that are
less than major ones disappear into the chart itself. With the
exception of determining long-range trends that are sometimes
obscured on the daily charts, short-term traders often find that
they have little use for the weekly and monthly charts.
Nevertheless, we strongly recommend that all traders, whether they
consider themselves to be short-term, intermediate-term, or long-
term traders, keep or at least consult weekly charts if not also
monthly ones. Weekly lows for a bull trendline or weekly highs for
a bear trendline show up much more clearly on these charts than
they do on the daily ones. When prices violate the weekly trendlines, it has especially strong significance. A number of different
trendlines can be drawn on a weekly chart, with different angles or
degrees of steepness. Short-term traders usually consider the
steepest of the trendlines as the most significant to them, because
if it is violated at all, they are stopped out, since their stops
traditionally rest just below this steepest of trendlines. Many
sophisticated short-term traders will therefore place their stops a
bit further below the steepest trendline, trying to "outguess" the
bulk of traders in order to stay in the market, because very often
a reaction will move to where a large number of stop-losses are
clustered, touch them off, and then reverse and start moving back
up again. Long-term traders use trendlines on weekly charts in a
somewhat different way. Their protective stops are placed just
below the least steep of the trendlines in order to keep them in
the market through moderate reactions, as long as they believe the
overall trend is still in their direction. They do this until they

10

see other signals that indicate the market may be peaking, and then they start switching their stops to just below the <u>steepest</u> of the trendlines so as to maximize their profits. The most successful long-range traders will normally place their stops on a close-only basis when using the <u>least steep</u> trendlines, and on a regular basis when they switch to the steepest trendline. Long-term traders are the most conservative of traders, even though their profits at the end of the year generally far surpass the profits realized by the more aggressive short-term traders. The rationale behind this is more fully explained in other chapters in this book on Long-Range Trading.

Another advantage of weekly charts is that they make trading-range formations more visually apparent, since weekly charts are usually drawn to a smaller vertical scale than daily charts. See Figure 3. pros look more for trading-range formations than for any other type of chart pattern because of their extreme profit poten-tial. From our research we have determined that a trading range must usually last a minimum of 5 weeks in order to have a great deal of validity, although in rare instances a 3 or 4 week trading range works. What exactly constitutes a trading range? Basically, it is a horizontal movement of prices across the graph. It can be a wide swinging trading range where for a year prices for copper may bounce back and forth between $1.00 per pound and 80¢ per pound. This type of trading range does not excite the average pro-fessional too much, unless he is attempting to sell near the top of the trading range and buy near the bottom. That technique is fraught with difficulties because trading ranges are always in danger of being violated, yet the risks are minimized since protec-tive stops can be placed relatively near the entry points. The type of pattern that excites the professional trader most is a tightly packed trading range; that is, one whose upper and lower boundaries are as close as possible. In the case of Cotton, as in Figure 3, a 3¢, range would excite the professional trader, and a 1¢ or

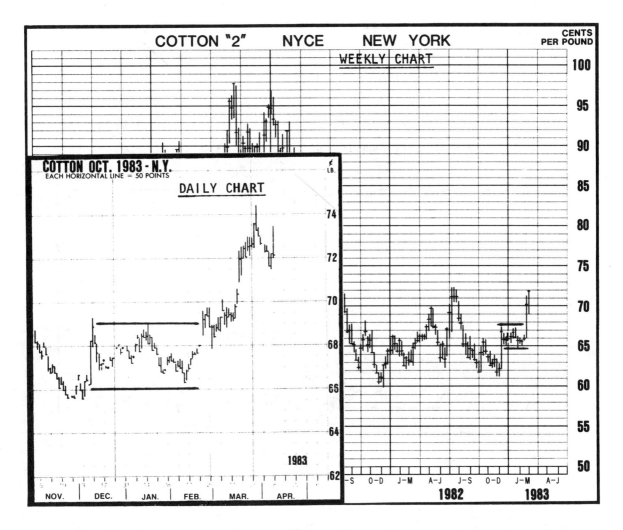

Figure 3

2¢ range would have him champing at the bit. The reason these
trading ranges excite the professionals so much is that very often
when they are broken out of, the resultant move is quite substantial, as is the case here with Cotton. This is especially true for
a resultant bull move if the trading range is either at a relatively low price level or at an important historical support level.
When the trading range is at an intermediate level, somewhere in-
between historical highs and lows, then the move, of course, may be
in either direction, but the magnitude of the move is inherently

12

limited by its starting point. It is far less frequent to see a
trading range take shape near historical highs, but when it does,
the normal resultant move is on the downside; again, as with a bull
move, with a lot of potential. Often these trading ranges will
take the shape of what is referred to as a "coiling action," as in
Figure 4, which simply means that the trading range magnitude, in
height, gets relatively smaller and smaller as time progresses.

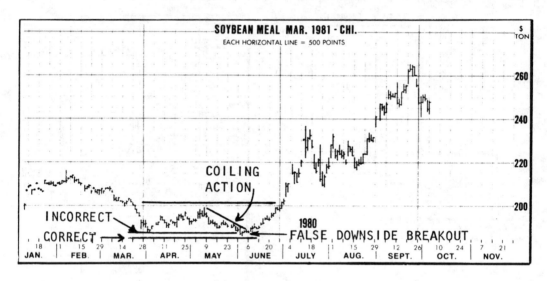

Figure 4

This formation, though not too frequently seen, is one of the most
profitable to trade. Many novice traders buy or sell on the first
break-out of a coiling pattern depending upon which way the market
first moves, having drawn trendlines that are not horizontal but
that get constantly more narrow. Thus the upper trendline slants
downward from left to right and the lower trendline slants upward
from left to right. This is NOT the method that the professionals
have found to be the most reliable. Generally when a market forms
an ever-tightening coiling pattern, it begins with at least several
weeks that can often be bounded above and below with perfectly
horizontal lines. Then, as time passes and prices compress, the

amateur disregards these original horizontal lines and draws tighter
trendlines, forming a very extended pennant shape. The professional trader, with one exception that we will mention in a
moment, does not do this, and instead waits for the original horizontal line, either the upper or lower one, to be broken in order
to indicate conclusively to him the upcoming major trend. He waits
because very often during the formation of a coiling pattern, there
will be a false breakout of the coil, only to have prices reverse
and go in the other direction. The professional has learned from
years of observation that it is better to sacrifice a few points of
potential profit than to jump into the market too quickly. Many
traders, and advisory services that do not have daily updates, utilize O-C-O orders in handling trading ranges. The O-C-O stands for
One Order Being Filled Cancels the Other, and simply means the
trader places two orders simultaneously with his broker: to buy if
the market breaks on the upside of the trading range, and to sell
if the market breaks on the downside. The first order being filled
automatically cancels the other order: O-C-O. Many professionals,
however, do not use O-C-O orders and rely instead upon other indicators on their charts, or on other signals. The two most important of these are: Committments of Large Speculators, and Contrary
Opinion (sometimes called Market Sentiment). If a market is in a
trading range, and the Committments of Large Speculators indicates
over the weeks that the big-money traders are gradually (or not so
gradually) switching over to more long than short positions, and if
Contrary Opinion is below 30%, then the professional trader will
place his open buy orders just above the trading range. He will
not enter the market until the trend starts as a final verification
of his analysis. The converse is true in that if the market is in
an extended trading range, the Committments of Large Speculators is
growing on the short side, and Contrary Opinion is above 70%, then
the professional will position his short orders just beneath the
horizontal line bounding the trading range on the bottom. Rarely,

if ever, will a professional trader pass up a trading range opportunity, because even if he is wrong two times out of three, the one
time he is right will be profitable enough to more than make up for
the two losses. Statistically, however, the percentages are much
better than this, increasing to over 80% accuracy when all of the
signals point in the same direction. It should also be mentioned
that of the two confirming signals used by professionals,
(Commitments of Large Speculators, and Contrary Opinion), if one
are neutral and one is strongly indicative of a move in one direction, that is generally enough to assume that the one indicator is
correct in predicting the next major move of the market. When
entering positions like this, the professional will place his initial protective stop EITHER just outside the horizontal line in the
opposite direction of his order, or (in the case of a coiling
pattern), above or below the angled line bounding the coil, even
though the horizontal line rather than the angled line, is used for
his entry point. The only time he uses the angled line to set the
initial protective stop is when the dollar risk between entry point
and initial protective stop point is greater than he is willing to
assume if the horizontal line were used.

Waiting for trading pattern formations takes a great deal of
patience, but the professional trader is willing to let months
pass without a trade in order to find these types of patterns.
Often, too, he will pyramid his positions by adding more and more
positions as the move proceeds in his direction. Detailed information on this is contained in another chapter in this volume, on
Pyramiding.

Occasionally the charts for different commodities will show
several different commodities forming trading ranges all at the
same time. Often a trader will want to trade all of them, but will
vary the amount of money, or number of contracts, he commits to
each commodity. There are a number of ways to determine how best
to do this, and we will examine them one by one. The first, and
most obvious way is by the amount of risk involved in assuming

each position, and this is a function of the height of the trading
range and the point value for that commodity. While risk is an
important consideration, it is by no means, THE most important.
The second determinant is how positive the information is that is
provided by the confirming signals of Committments of Large
Speculators, and Contrary Opinion. These data are also valuable in
distinguishing between the relative merits of different potential
trading range positions; but to the professional, the most important factor everything else being relatively equal, is the length
of time the commodity has been in its trading range. It has been
statistically verified that the longer the period of time the
trading range pattern has existed, the greater the potential move

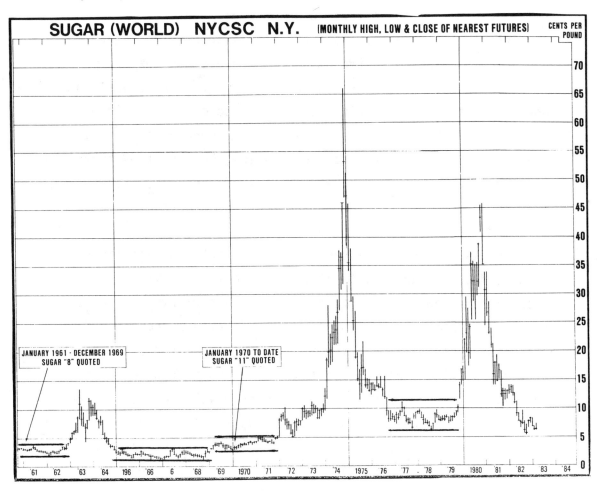

Figure 5

16

in price. Again, since one seldom sees protracted trading ranges
at high price levels, this is normally true at lower price levels
before a commodity makes a major bull move. Some commodities spend
years, as in Figure 5, in protracted trading ranges before making
their moves, and in these cases, assuming the trader trails his
stops properly, huge fortunes can be made once the move begins.
The other indicator of the magnitude of the coming move is whether
or not a coiling pattern is forming within the trading range
itself. When a coiling pattern takes place, it amplifies the
distance in which prices will move. Obviously, the best combination is a very long range trading pattern with a coiling action
taking place toward the end of it. This is one of the most
reliable patterns to indicate a huge price move.

Charts are also used by professional traders to determine
cyclical price action. Even though there are many expert publications and advisory services on price cycles for individual commodities, the professionals often prefer to measure their own as
an adjunct to their trading. They use the weekly and monthly
charts to show them the long range cycles, because they prefer to
trade on the same side as the direction of the longer-range cycles
then in effect. Depending upon whether the expert prefers short,
intermediate, or long-term trading, he will visually calculate and
mark on his charts the distances in weeks between significant
highs and lows. While it is true that most commodities have
traditional-length short, medium, and long term cycle lengths,
these vary from year to year due to fundamentals and other factors
affecting price action in the market. So the most accurate way to
predict upcoming cyclical lengths for several months or longer in
the future is to measure what the cycles have been over the past 6
to 12 months. These are most easily identified on the charts that
are relatively small, as provided by some of the major chart services. We will not go into a great deal of detail here because
this subject takes an entire chapter by itself to cover thoroughly,
but we will touch on the major points. In a bull market the pro-

fessional analyst will make his own measurements of important cycle lengths from low to low to establish optimum entry points for long positions and stop-loss points. The opposite approach is used for dealing with cycles in a bear market. Suffice it to say at this point that the trader can make his own cyclical measurements, and often do so more accurately and effectively than by using those available from sources that specialize in them. Many times the trader will not be able to see or mark <u>any</u> discernible cycles; or they will be so irregular they are of little use. Since the professional uses cycles as only one of his many tools, at such times he will let the commodity in question pass entirely. The alert professional will also be referring to <u>seasonals,</u> and for those who are not familiar with seasonals, they simply are calendar-year cycles that exist for all perishable and many non-perishable commodities. Their existence is due to supply-and-demand considerations, planting-harvest aspects, cycles in home construction and automobile manufacture, and so forth. The most knowledgeable traders actually mark these seasonal tendencies on the same charts they are using; so when they look at their Wheat chart, for instance, they see that the normal seasonal tendency for Wheat is to reach its yearly, or <u>seasonal</u> high, in the December to January period, and its seasonal low in the May to June period. By having this graph marked with a different color, on their own price graph, they can readily see how closely prices this year are following the normal seasonal tendencies. Sometimes they don't coincide with the expected seasonal cycle at all; but more often than not, they do, although they are often skewed, or moved forward or backward in time by a few weeks up to a couple of months. Using Wheat as an example, if the seasonal low was a month late, at the end of July this year, the odds are that the <u>high</u> for this year will also be skewed forward in time by a like period. There is no absolute guarantee of this, but the odds of going short a month later than normal, in February instead of in the December to January period, offers a far better chance of success. It is rare that an expert

18

will be buying Wheat when the normal seasonal cycle is due to the
topping unless he is looking for a very short-term gain, and then
the volatility would keep most professionals out of the market so
near a potential seasonal top.

Many experts also keep a graph on their daily chart for each
commodity, that indicates the Market Sentiment or Contrary Opinion
percentages. This can be done in a very small amount of space,
and has the advantage of putting the information on the same page
with the price information. Obviously, it increases the amount of
time that must be spent maintaining charts, but it is the best way
to have all the data at one's fingertips. Market Sentiment
figures are available from several sources, and normal seasonal
tendencies of commodities are published in a number of different
books on commodity trading.

One last item that the professionals keep on their daily
charts is a running graph of Commitments of Large Speculators.
This information is available from different charting services as
well as from the Commodity Trading Futures Commission. Because of
the time required to obtain it, we suggest getting the information
directly from one of the charting services that offer it. The
data are presented as how Open Interest is broken up, and are
divided into three categories: the commitments of Large Hedgers,
Large Speculators, and Small Traders. In our experience the only
figures of real use are the Committments of Large Speculators.
This information is further sub-divided into the absolute number
of Large Speculators who are long at the end of the previous
month, the number who are short, and the "net" number or positive
or negative difference between the two. Unfortunately, these data
are available only on a monthly basis, so they are most useful
during the first part of the month following the report. The
experts who graph this data do so in the following way usually:
they have a scale somewhere on their chart of from say plus 20 to
minus 20, and every four weeks record the "net" number of positions
as reported by Large Speculators. This shows how the Large

Speculators, or in most cases, the smart-money traders, are changing their positions from month to month. So, since most of them are long-range traders anyway, the fact that these figures appear on a monthly basis reduces the disadvantage of not having them weekly. For an example, let's say Wheat has been showing a "net" figure for the past several months of plus 5, plus 7, plus 5, and the new report shows the "net" holdings of Large Speculators as minus 5. That piece of information, combined with all the professional's other tools, gives him a valuable indication that the Large Speculators, while not always right in their predictions, are betting that the market is going down and starting to establish short positions to prove it. For our purposes the figures given for the Committments of Large Hedgers cannot be used, and those listed for Small Traders are relatively useless, as even in the midst of most bear markets, they are usually overwhelmingly bullish.

Much has been made of individual day's price action or movement as being indicative of continuation of or reversal of a trend. Such price movement is called intra-day and includes such patterns of price action such as island, reversals, gaps, etc. After considerable research, we have come to the somehwat controversial conclusion that in many cases such intra-day movement is meaningless to the expert investor. It does sometimes confirm other signals, and occasionally will herald a new trend or change in direction, but so will the breaking of a trendline, changes in Open Interest, etc. These intra-day signals are far more important for the short-term trader than for the long-term trader, and since most of the successful professionals do not <u>trade</u> on a short-term basis, we will restrict our comments on intra-day signals to those that may be useful. The two most useful applications we have found of intra-day price movement have been <u>gaps</u> when a market has been in a trading range and not yet broken out of it, and <u>island rever-sals</u> in heavily traded markets. In the first case, when a market has been in a trading pattern and a gap appears before market has moved out of the trading range, the probability of the market's finally moving out of the trading range in the direction of the gap is very high indeed, so high that many professionals take their positions then rather than wait for the trading range itself to be violated. By so doing, and placing their initial protective stops just on the other side of the trading range, they significantly reduce the amount of their initial risk.

Island reversals in heavily traded markets indicate a reversal in trend of significant proportions well in advance of the trendlines being broken, and present only a small risk for the professional trader to place his orders the next day with his protective stop just beyond the island reversal, without waiting for the trendline he is using to be broken. Once his trendline is broken, he often adds to his position at this point.

Seasonal probabilities and Open Interest may have tipped off the professional trader to a new trend or change in trend before either of these other signals appear, in which case gaps and island reversals merely add a confirmation to the direction he is already predicting.

There are as many possible chart formations as there are analysts to discover them, but the ones we have discussed seem to us to be the most significant ones. A trader can get caught up in so many details that he genuinely cannot see the forest for all the trees. The only other patterns we believe to be worthwhile considering are pennants and flags. Since virtually all chartists and traders are familiar with these formations and since the descriptions themselves are self-explanatory, we will not describe them further. It is a well-known fact that when prices enter a pennant or a flag formation, the direction they break out in indicates the next leg of the existing move, or a reversal of the previous move. In this respect, a flag or pennant is similar to a trading range, but is usually much briefer in duration. Many veteran traders use flag and pennant formations as points to set their stops beneath or above and as a signal to place open orders to add to their positions if the breakout is in the direction they are already holding positions in. One little-known method used by the professionals is to look for flag and pennant formations on weekly charts, since they exist there too, but are often much less visible on the daily charts. When a flag or pennant is formed on a weekly chart, a breakout from it is _far_ more powerful than a breakout from a flag or pennant formation on a daily chart. Generally stops have to be placed a bit further, but with the increased chances of profitability, the risk is worth it. The magnitude of the resulting move, when the flag or pennant is on a weekly chart, is generally _far_ greater than the move from a daily chart. In summation: We recommend to the serious trader that he keep his own _daily_ charts of the nearby month and the next month of all the major commodities, as well as keeping his own _weekly_ charts of the nearby contract month. The daily charts should be kept up to date with Volume figures and particularly with Open Interest figures, and if possible they should also show the average Open interest graph for the previous five years. Trendlines should be drawn at all times, preferably with different colored pencils which make an easily erasable mark. The chartist should acquire, from one of the services that offer them, both Market Sentiment figures, and show them as they change from week to week on his daily or weekly price chart. The same should be done with the "net" position holdings for Committments of Large Speculators. Cycle lengths should be measured and marked on daily, weekly, and preferably on monthly charts too, so that the trader is aware at all times of the major, intermediate, and minor cycles. Also marked on the graphs should be the typical seasonal cycle for whatever commodity is under consideration, so the trader can see whether this year is following the typical pattern, whether it is skewed somewhat, or whether it is not reliable. Flags and pennants should be looked for, especially on the weekly charts; and gaps, islands, and limit days should be noted as significant in heavily traded markets and during trading ranges. Above all else, the chartist should look for trading ranges, and examine their significance as outlined in this chapter.

CHAPTER 2

UNDERSTANDING FUNDAMENTALS

Fundamentals can either be one of the most frustrating and confusing aspects of commodity trading, or they can be one of the richest, most rewarding, and easy to understand.

While some of the subjects covered in this book have had very little written about them, fundamentals in commodity trading are quite different in that there has been a great deal written about fundamentals. In fact, virtually every book on commodity trading gives at least a chapter to fundamentals, and there have been entire volumes written on the subject. Magazine articles on fundamentals appear monthly in popular magazines on commodity trading. Yet with all this abundant information available on fundamentals, fundamental analysis appears to be the least well understood of any type of commodity analysis. Recently we conducted an informal poll among 20 of our subscribers. Though we had no "set format", it became obvious from the conversations, that while many of these people were quite sophisticated when it came to discussing technical analysis, only two of the 20 seemed to have some grasp of fundamental analysis.

Why is there so much confusion and mystery around fundamental analysis? In essence, there are really only two basic approaches to commodity analysis when it comes to forecasting prices: technical analysis and fundamental analysis. Most technical analysis, but not all, is done with price charts, curves, trend lines, moving average graphs, point and figure displays, etc. What do all these types of technical analysis have in common? They are all primarily <u>visual</u>. Research has proved that the majority of the people in our society are visually oriented in the way they perceive, store, and recall information. Fundamental information is also presented in a visual form, in terms of tables, production and consumption figures, and government reports, but this is a different type of visual representation. Most of us have brains that are "wired", so to speak, in such a way that the technical <u>pictures</u> of graphs are much easier for us to comprehend and analyze than a series of numbers and figures. Hence, this seems to be the major reason that even though there is so much available information on fundamental analysis, it is still so difficult for most of us to comprehend it in a way we can utilize.

While there is no easy way for us to convert most of the aspects of fundamental analysis into the more easily understood graphic form, although it is possible to do so if you have enough time, we will try to explain the different aspects of fundamental analysis in this chapter in such a way that they are more readily understandable to most traders.

Anyone who wishes to be successful in trading commodities, if you are doing your own analysis, must master either the <u>technical</u> method of analyzing and forecasting price movement or the <u>fundamental</u> method, or preferably <u>both</u>, because a good working knowledge of both methods enables you to use each one against the other in order to cross-check and validate your conclusions. Many of the most successful traders we know will not initiate a trade unless both their technical and fundamental analyses agree. This approach makes the most sense as it allows the trader to bring more information to bear on his decision.

What then <u>is</u> fundamental analysis? Strictly speaking, it is the study of the factors that will probably influence prices, and basing one's trading decisions on this study. Technical analysis on the other hand, is concerned with the actual movement of prices themselves, not with the underlying reasons behind the moves. Another way to think of the difference between fundamental and technical analysis is to look at fundamental analysis as the "content" of price movement, and at technical analysis as the "process" of price movement. Technical analysis has many different aspects, including Volume and Open Interest, and moving averages; fundamental analysis also has many different parts. The most important components of fundamental analysis include: normal seasonal price trends, supply and demand statistics, domestic government farm programs, comparison of present prices to past prices under similar conditions, international commodity agreements and price cartels, general deflationary and inflationary tendencies that currently exist, political considerations, and labor union considerations.

The basic idea that underlines fundamental analysis is that when you compare the available supplies of any given commodity with the real or expected demand for that commodity, this comparison is what determines in which direction prices will move in the future. If supplies of any given commodity are low relative to the demand or need for that commodity, the scarcity that results will drive prices upward. The degree of severity of the scarcity will determine the extent to which prices increase. The length of time the scarcity exists will determine not only the length of time during which prices increase, but also to some extent the amount they increase. Conversely, if supplies of any commodity are abundant or super-abundant relative to the demand for that commodity, its producers and suppliers will cut prices in an effort to move the commodity, and prices will fall as a result.

This is the basic method of fundamental analysis: to compare supply and demand to determine whether there will be a shortage of the commodity or a surplus; and then to position yourself appropriately in that market, preferably in a distant month, because these types of trades are usually long-term. By careful and constant analysis of this supply and demand balance, the fundamentalist is able to take full advantage of major price moves. The one most important advantage of the <u>fundamental</u> method of analysis over the technical method is in the prevention of being whipsawed by erratic market action. The technician who is using his methods to determine his entry and exit from the market, will, during a period of erratic market action, find himself being whipsawed by the market; that is, forced to take a number of positions first one way and then the other, as his methodology changes course repeatedly. The fundamentalist, on the other hand, does not have this happen to him since he has established a long-range view about the course of price action; and once he has taken an initial position, he simply holds on to it until the fundamental factors themselves change.

Since fundamentals, like the supply and demand ratio, normally change slowly over a period of time, he is able to take this long-range approach. There are times, however, when these supply and demand factors are not so kind to the fundamental trader and change virtually overnight, due perhaps, to a revolution in a foreign country, an unexpected move by the Federal Reserve Board, a sudden freeze or flood, or a surprise strike by a particular union. If any of these factors directly affects the supply and demand balance, then the change in fundamentals becomes very dramatic and rapid.

Most expert fundamentalists do not ignore the technical aspects of the market altogether, but instead use some technical tools to confirm their fundamental analysis; just as the expert <u>technical</u> traders try to seek confirmations for their analyses from fundamental information. The accomplished fundamentalist gives careful consideration to actual price movement, and thereby is often able to improve the timing of his entry and exit from the marketplace.

Once a trader learns how to interpret fundamental data, he will often find himself using that approach more frequently in his

26

trading decisions, especially if he is interested in long-term
trading that reduces the amount of day-to-day surveillance of the
marketplace that is required by detailed technical analysis. The
true technical trader will often reject the fundamental approach by
arguing that all fundamental factors show up in price movement
anyway, and that the market seems to have the knack to anticipate
changes in fundamental situations before they become public
knowledge. While this is often true, it is not always so, and
hence the ideal approach to the markets is the combination of both
technical and fundamental analysis.

Fundamental analysis depends upon studying the basic, or fundamental, market factors. These factors, when compared with past
market behavior, should result in predictions about how the market
will move in the future. In addition to the supply and demand
balance, the other factors a fundamentalist normally considers
include seasonal price tendencies and price levels. The basic
information required by the fundamental analyst differs in nature
for all three of these areas, and often has to be obtained from
different sources.

First, we'll look at the factors which affect the supply and
demand balance and which can be used in making fundamental decisions. We begin with the supply and demand balance because it is
the most important factor in determining future price movement for
any given commodity. In order to analyze the supply and demand
balance, your most important source of information is governmental
statistics. The majority of statistical reports come from the
United States Department of Agriculture, and are called official
reports. They are the government's best estimates of total
upcoming supply, and indicated potential demand. These reports
may be obtained directly from the U.S.D.A. by writing them in
Washington, D.C. Their zip code is 20250. Other sources of similar statistics available to the fundamental trader are reports
from the United Nations, from producing associations, and from

private forecasters. Most, but not all, of these statistics are
reported on in The Wall Street Journal, The Journal of Commerce,
Barron's, Commodities Magazine, and many major daily newspapers in
the financial section.

For the statistics that are more difficult to locate, especially for those commodities that are not reported on by the
U.S.D.A. and are less heavily traded, the importance of your
broker cannot be over estimated. In another chapter in this
book titled "You and Your Broker", we deal with the question of
how to find your own broker who has the capabilities you want.
Taurus also maintains a list of brokers who have been recommended
to us over the years, and we will be glad to recommend one to any
of you who requests it from us. A professional broker will either
have access within his own firm's research department to these
supply and demand statistics, or he will be able to get them
elsewhere quickly, whether the request is for Wheat or for
Palladium.

One point needs to be made clear: and that is, the supply and
demand figures normally refer not to a calendar year but to a
marketing period or crop year. A crop year starts on the first of
the month of the date closest to the harvest time. It is assumed
in these figures that any new crop is fully available for
marketing at the start of the new crop year, which in fact, is
plainly not the case. In order to make any sense out of the
supply side of the supply and demand balance, the trader needs to
take three different factors into account. You need to know first
what the new crop estimate is, then how much of the old crop is
considered to be available as a carry-over, and third the amount
of that commodity that will probably be imported from foreign
countries. Added together, these three figures give you the total
supply of the commodity.

"Old crop carry-over" refers to the amount of last year's
crop or production that is, in effect, in reserve or in inventory.

Some commodities are not storable, such as live cattle and hogs, so there are no carry-overs for these commodities. Some that you would not normally expect to have a carry-over, such as orange juice, pork bellies, and iced broilers, are capable of being stored, so they will have inventory figures available.

After you have these supply figures in hand, you need to determine the demand side of the equation. Sometimes this is referred to in articles or reports as "utilization" or "disappearance". We prefer the term "consumption" and will use that term mainly in this chapter. Under consumption, there are only two factors to consider, that of domestic consumption and that of exports or foreign consumption. These two figures are normally readily available in estimate form. Before determining whether or not there will be a shortage of the commodity or a surplus, there is one adjustment that needs to be made for five commodities, which, coincidently, are among the most popular ones traded: Corn, Cotton, Soybeans, Oats, and Wheat. These five commodities, and one other not traded on the futures market, are supported by the U.S. Government by its Price Support Program. Often substantial amounts of these crops are owned by the government or are under government loan.

You will often run across the term "impoundings" when looking at this data. Impoundings are merely the amount of the current crop that is placed under government loan. So whatever the total figures are for these five crops, under government loan, support, or impounding, they must be subtracted from the original supply figures in order to come up with an accurate, adjusted figure. This figure is often referred to as the "free" supply-and-demand balance. Therefore, in order to compute the total supply, you simply add together the total new crop estimate, the amount of estimated imports, and the carry-over stocks; and subtract the amount under government loan to arrive at a total figure. From this figure, you subtract the total estimated consumption, both domestic and foreign, to determine the estimated surplus or deficit for any particular commodity.

The second factor to be examined is the Seasonal Price Tendency; and here, with graphics, the utilization of information becomes somewhat simpler, as shown in Figure 6.

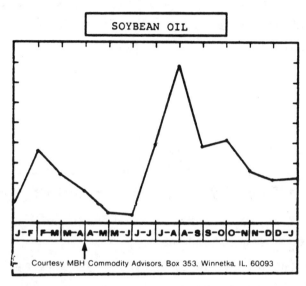

SOYBEAN OIL

J-F F-M M-A A-M M-J J-J J-A A-S S-O O-N N-D D-J

Courtesy MBH Commodity Advisors, Box 353, Winnetka, IL, 60093

Figure 6

There is usually a tendency for most commodities to have some type of seasonal pattern, or seasonal cycle. In fact, this is the key to large-cycle cyclical analysis. Excellent work in this area has been done by several analysts, notably Jake Bernstein of M.B.H. Advisors and Walt Bressert of H.A.L. Commodity Cycles. Articles frequently appear in Commodities Magazine discussing different cycles. For our purposes, however, it is important to distinguish between cycles in general and seasonal price tendencies in particular. Cyclical analysis covers a multitude of time frames, from short periods of time to cycles that extend through decades. Fundamental analysis is more particularly concerned with the repetitive twelve-month price cycles that are generally called seasonals.

It should be obvious for many commodities why this seasonal cycle takes place, in that there is a new crop or slaughtering time at approximately the same period every year. It is less obvious, but equally important that seasonals exist for a number of other commodities too, such as plywood and lumber being affected by the seasonality of home-building due to weather conditions throughout the United States. Still less obvious, and less understandable seasonals appear to be at work in the Financial Instruments, Foreign Currencies, and Precious Metals.

Regardless of the reason for their seasonality, even these commodities show some evidence of responding to seasonal factors; but in general, for these commodities, the seasonal tendencies must be viewed a bit more skeptically, and not given as much weight. It is important to remember, too, that no matter how reliable the seasonality of a commodity, it can be disrupted by sudden, unexpected occurences such as unusual weather patterns, labor problems, overnight trade embargoes and wars.

The third factor in fundamental analysis is referred to as "price levels". The true fundamental analyst will not take a position before dealing with the price level question regardless of what his supply and demand balance shows him or what the seasonality indicates. Some different considerations need to be made in this area. First, look at the current price level compared to previous years when a similar supply-demand balance existed.

For example, if the commodity in question is Wheat, and there appears to be a moderate shortage of it in the upcoming crop year, if Wheat is currently selling, say for $4.00 a bushel, and in former years when a similar shortage was estimated, it was selling for $2.50 a bushel, it certainly does not look like as good a "buy" at the current price level of $4.00. Conversely, if Wheat, under similar circumstances, normally is selling at $5.00 a bushel, the fundamental analyst would consider today's wheat at $4.00 to be an extremely good buy. The opposite conclusions of course, would be drawn if wheat showed a surplus rather than a shortage. So to use fundamental analysis properly, it is necessary to look at all the previously mentioned factors, combine them, and then by using your own judgment as "colored" by past price behavior, determine how the major moves of the market will be in the coming months.

Obviously, a large deficit or scarcity in any commodity will be very bullish. The extent of the deficit, when compared to the current price levels and adjusted for the seasonality of the commodity, will all help determine the degree of bullishness. A large surplus, on the other hand, will be very bearish for a commodity, again considering current price levels and seasonal factors.

If Cocoa, for example, is currently selling at $1000 a ton on the futures market, and the supply-demand balance shows there will be a huge surplus of cocoa over the next twelve months, while seasonally you are at the time of year when Cocoa normally declines in price, the conclusion you would have to draw, looking at long-range monthly charts, is that Cocoa should not be sold short, or indeed that any action at all should be taken; both because the $1000 level is a very long-range support area, and also given the fact that regardless of all the fundamental factors in existence, no commodity drops to zero under any conditions. True, at times a given commodity may drop very low, even below its historical price support levels; but price support levels are very stubborn points which usually hold price declines, just as resistance areas usually blunt price advances.

There is one fundamental condition that needs to be examined carefully, and that is called an "indicated free supply scarcity". This is an apparent or artificial shortage resulting from the government's programs designed to stabilize prices. The way this occurs, is that under U.S. Law, authorized by the Congress, the United States Department of Agriculture may make loans to farmers

at a specified loan rate, and take the farmers surplus inventory
to hold as collateral. By so doing, when there is a great surplus
of a commodity on the marketplace, Uncle Sam can retain some of
the surplus until prices go up enough to justify selling it on the
open market.

Only certain commodities are considered eligible for the
loans, and then for only a specified time after the harvest. This
time period is called the "impounding deadline". The loans themselves are called "nonrecourse loans" due to the fact that the
farmer is granted the choice of defaulting without penalty, or of
paying the loan off before it matures and redeeming the commodity.
So the apparent scarcity is in reality an artificial one since adequate supplies actually exist, but due to the loans, not all of the
commodity is readily available to go into the distribution pipe-
line.

This type of scarcity is bullish, but within limits, and not
nearly as bullish as a genuine scarcity. When farmers apply for
these government loans, they pledge a certain percentage of their
crops as collateral for the loan. This takes out some of the
supply from the open market. If enough of a particular crop becomes tied up this way, the supplies that are still free, not owned
by or pledged to the government, will become scarce, though artifi-
cially, and prices will rise as a result.

After cash prices go higher than the loan rate, to a figure
where the farmer can get more money by selling on the open market
than he can get from the government, the farmer may redeem his
loan. He then removes his crop from the loan program, markets it
at the higher cash price, and pays off his note. If the cash
market prices do not increase higher than the loan price before
the deadline for redeeming, the farmer, instead of making the
redemption, simply delivers the crop to the government. The law
requires the government, in most situations, so as not to upset
the open cash markets, not to sell the commodities it has acquired

from loans which have been defaulted on, except at a certain
price. This generally is true only for the domestic market and
does not ordinarily apply to government export sales.

Therefore, when free supplies are insufficient to meet the
anticipated demand side of the equation, prices will normally go
up to the government selling price in order to pull in the
necessary supplies. When Uncle Sam has enough inventory on hand
to sell at its price, it will supplement the supplies that are
available on the free market to satisfy demand. Therefore, the
government sale price may actually become a ceiling beyond which
cash prices cannot advance. When it happens that the government
doesn't have enough inventory to take care of demand, then prices
will generally increase until the less important portions of the
demand sector are withdrawn, and the supplies that are available
are sufficient to take care of the more important demand
requirements.

Now we will turn to some other fundamental aspects that must
be considered as part of the total picture of fundamental analysis. First, consider what takes place when, due to weather,
disease, or other causes, there is damage to a crop that is not
yet harvested, or if the threat of such damage appears to exist.
In this case there is what we call a sudden fundamental change, in
that it is out of the ordinary by the very fact of its occuring
within a shorter time frame. This is a very bullish situation,
especially when the existing supply and demand balance or seasonal
factors or price levels or any combination of these factors are
also bullish.

As a rule when there is a situation of this nature, the
extent of the bull move is far greater than usual because there is
widespread publicity given to a situation like this and the market
feeds upon itself, drawing numerous small speculators and even
large investors and advisors who don't want to miss out on such a
good thing. While the advance in prices may be greater than

usual, the reversal and crash that results happens more rapidly than usual also. Hence, when dealing with a market like this, it is extremely advisable to alter your method of determining where to place your protective stops or where to take profits. More information on this can be found in the chapter on "Stop Placement". Suffice it to say here, that when markets are more volatile, more caution and different methods must often be put into effect.

There is little question that the overall state of the national and world economy has a significant fundamental influence on commodity prices. With the inflation we have experienced until recently at home and world-wide, most commodities were selling at higher prices than the supply-demand balance would seem to warrant. During times such as these, price levels must be adjusted accordingly since what was a high level in 1976 may today be a resistance area that is sliced through rather easily, due only to inflationary forces. When the economy is in a period of deflation, which it will surely experience again, then the bottom level price support areas also become more vulnerable to being violated.

It is important to realize the inter-relationship of all the factors mentioned so far, because using any one of them by itself can be disastrous, whether or not you are also using technical analysis. An astonishing number of traders and advisors trade solely on the basis of seasonal price tendencies. This is very foolish without taking the other fundamental factors into consideration. It is true, that Corn, for example, generally bottoms in the fall or early winter and moves up to its seasonal highs during the May-July period. This is especially true when a normal supply-demand balance does not exist, and due to the bullishness or bearishness caused by the supply-demand balance, normal seasonal tendencies fly right out the window and are totally useless. It is also important to consider price levels compared to seasonal price tendencies. For example, if it is November, a period during which Corn can normally be expected to make its seasonal low, and say for the past several years the normal seasonal low has been in the $1.80 to $2.20 level, and that this year the low is $1.50 with normal supply-demand figures, you can expect that the upside move will be far more extensive than usual.

The converse is true when the low appears to be at a higher than usual point; then the percentage increase to the top of the move is less than usual. The dollar amount of the move may be the same, but the percentage of the move will be less than in previous years.

Seasonals can be very difficult to work with because of so many other factors influencing the marketplace, but a good general rule to follow is not to buck the seasonal tendencies unless you have a wealth of reasons to do so that give an indication that there is a good probability of the seasonal tendency not working out this year. For example, it would take a number of unusual occurrences in order to want to be long Corn in November. It would require, say, a bullish immediate supply-demand balance and possibly depressed price levels too.

Now that we have explained fundamental analysis and its different aspects, let us turn to some specialized applications of fundamental data. There are times when it is best to ignore fundamental news entirely, and we want to examine them. If a market has been in a definite trend for some time, as Sugar was in late 1980, fundamental news finally runs out of power to influence the major trend. Sugar had been rising steadily since the middle of 1979, except for one major reaction during the Spring of 1980. As it formed an asymetrical double-top during the summer of 1980, most analysts were calling for prices to continue up, up, and away.

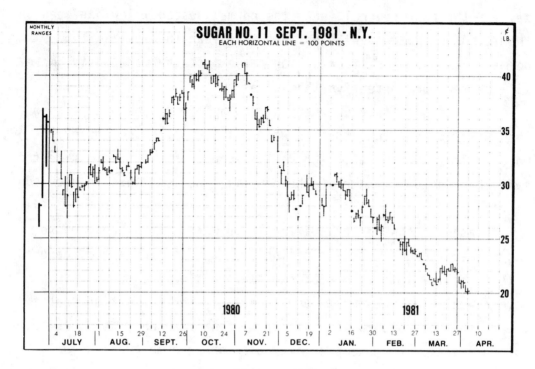

Figure 7

Some were talking of seeing the 60¢ per pound level, and a
few were even talking of $1.00 a pound Sugar by year's end. The
news in the media, such as The Wall Street Journal, seemed to support this view by reporting almost daily some expert's prediction
of greater than anticipated crop losses in Eastern Europe, or predicting increased consumer demand, etc. Unfortunately, for those
holding long positions in Sugar, the Sugar market itself mustn't
have been reading the papers and reports. The market had become
so overbought, and bullish sentiment figures were running so high,
that no piece of fundamental news was able to prevent the market
from running out of steam and crashing down. As you can see in
Figure 7.

The point we want to illustrate here is that all of the
bullish fundamental news in the world was not able to support

such an overbought market. The one time to ignore fundamental news entirely is when market sentiment is extremely bullish or bearish, depending upon the direction of the move and the nature of the fundamental news, and to be extremely wary of those markets where the open interest is increasing greatly to very high levels. When either of these situations occurs, it makes little difference what type of fundamental news breaks, as the market is generally either topping or bottoming out. There are exceptions to the overbought/oversold rules and the market sentiment rules, but they are so infrequent that it is advisable not to break the rules without genuinely compelling reasons to do so. One way to avoid getting "caught" in these markets is to keep track of the amount of news being reported by the media about different commodities. If, for example, you cannot pick up a paper or listen to a newscast without hearing something about how high sugar prices are, or how tight sugar supplies are, then this is a News Market; and if you feel you must trade it, at least do so with your eyes open, being aware that this type of market experiences sudden and dramatic reversals just when all the news and all the experts say it will go on forever. So, even if you are a pure technician and decide to ignore the fundamental analysis at all times, it would benefit you to keep an eye on this overlap of technicals and fundamentals, and to avoid the markets that are riding along on the news they generate.

Another specialized fundamental tool to work with is the report that is released by the U.S.D.A. on the 10th of each month called the Commitments of Traders in Commodity Futures. This report shows the holdings of large and small traders, identified as such, and whether they are long or short. The Commitments of traders figures are also published by various other Chart Services as illustrated in Figure 8. Generally, you can bet that the large traders are on the right side of the market from the long-range standpoint, and that the small traders are on the wrong side of the market, again from a long-range perspective.

38

COMMITMENTS OF TRADERS—LARGE HEDGERS, SPECULATORS AND SMALL TRADERS											
Open Interest Positions Shown in Percent (Rounded) as of February 28, 1983											
MARKETS	LARGE HEDGERS				LARGE SPECULATORS				SMALL TRADERS			
	Long	Short	Net	△	Long	Short	Net	△	Long	Short	Net	△
Cattle (Live)	22	32	-10	+ 2	16	4	+12	+ 2	58	60	- 2	- 4
Cocoa	35	64	-29	+ 7	25	5	+20	- 9	39	29	+10	+ 3
Coffee	49	49	0	- 4	3	16	-13	0	47	33	+14	+ 5
Copper	19	64	-45	+15	19	8	+11	+ 3	58	23	+35	-18
Corn	45	50	- 5	+ 8	11	3	+ 8	- 1	39	43	- 4	- 8
Cotton	33	66	-33	-13	14	3	+11	+10	52	30	+22	+ 3
Gold (Comex)	42	58	-16	+15	10	11	- 1	- 9	38	21	+17	- 6
Heating Oil #2	57	23	+34	+ 3	3	26	-23	+ 1	34	45	-11	- 4
Hogs	30	12	+18	+ 6	13	20	- 7	-18	53	64	-11	+13
Lumber	12	44	-32	+ 4	11	5	+ 6	- 8	76	50	+26	+ 4
Oats	22	51	-29	0	3	7	- 4	- 3	74	42	+32	+ 3
Orange Juice	47	55	- 8	+24	4	9	- 5	- 4	46	33	+13	-20
Platinum	14	56	-42	+29	20	12	+ 8	-17	60	26	+34	-13
Pork Bellies	17	13	+ 4	+ 6	20	29	- 9	- 2	56	51	+ 5	- 5
Silver (Comex)	14	40	-26	+ 8	9	11	- 2	-13	68	40	+28	+ 4
Soybeans	33	46	-13	+19	5	8	- 3	-13	53	38	+15	- 6
Soybean Meal	59	60	- 1	+16	4	6	- 2	-18	30	27	+ 3	+ 1
Soybean Oil	40	54	-14	+18	6	6	0	- 6	43	29	+14	-11
Sugar "11"	57	84	-27	- 5	13	9	+ 4	+ 5	29	6	+23	0
Wheat (CHI)	17	27	-10	+29	8	22	-14	-19	69	44	+25	- 9
Wheat (K.C.)	62	59	+ 3	+ 6	6	3	+ 3	0	31	36	- 5	- 5
Wheat (Minn)	29	40	-11	+ 1	*	*	0	0	71	60	+11	- 1
Ginnie Maes	54	66	-12	+ 1	12	6	+ 6	+ 3	21	15	+ 6	- 4
T-Bills (90 Days)	38	73	-35	-18	29	4	+25	+11	30	19	+11	+ 9
T-Bonds	43	61	-18	-13	16	6	+10	+10	24	16	+ 8	+ 3
NYSE Composite	27	20	+ 7	+21	23	20	+ 3	- 4	35	44	- 9	-17
S&P 500	19	15	+ 4	+ 4	35	33	+ 2	+11	38	44	- 6	-15
Value Line	4	2	+ 2	+ 3	23	27	- 4	- 3	57	57	0	- 1

* Less than .05%.   △ Change in % Net from Previous Month.
(Plus - increased long or decreased short. Minus - increased short or decreased long).
Positions do not equal 100% because intermarket spreading statistics are not included.

Figure 8

These figures are useless for the short-term trader if for no other reason than that they are reported only once a month. In general the large traders are right far more often than the small traders; after all, that's how they got to _be_ big traders, in most cases anyway, and they have developed methods, whatever they may be, of being right more often than being wrong in determining the long-term trades. More big traders are into long-term trading too than small traders are, so the Commitment of Traders figures are more indicative of the long-term trend than of the short or intermediate-term.

One other fundamental method that is sometimes thought of as a technical method, is what is called premium spread analysis. Actually, this method uses technical data to interpret the moving fundamental forces in the marketplace. Normally when you look at commodity prices, all for the same year, you will find that the June contract month is priced higher than the March contract month and that the December contract month is priced higher than the June. This is the typical way prices run, with the more distant months selling at a premium over the nearby months. We refer to this situation as POSITIVITY. Occasionally you will look at prices only to see that this is not the case, and that the nearby months are selling at a premium over the more distant months, which we call NEGATIVITY.

What this really means is that there is definite need right now for the commodity in question, very often to store in anticipation of increased prices in the future. The only people who do this are the commercials, those firms and individuals who must have the product now or who wish to take delivery now and store the product for future use. The commercial interests are very similar to the large traders, and in many cases, are one and the same. They generally either know where the markets are heading or have a pretty good feel for the ultimate market direction.

One source has reported investigating all major bull markets over a period of years, and while we have not independently substantiated their report, their conclusion was that there had been virtually no major bull markets without a premium spread or positivity, being evidenced at some point prior to the start of the bull move or during the beginnings of the move itself.

40

Another interesting aspect that we would like to consider is the relationship between Open Interest and fundamentals. Open Interest is one of the simplest ways we know of to confirm other fundamental data. It is a well-established fact that small traders tend to go long much more often than they are willing to sell short. This tendency seems to be due to some inherent psychological trait on the part of small traders, where they can see unlimited potential on the upside for moves, and only limited downside potential, since nothing can drop down to and through zero. There also seems to be a psychological component for small traders in that it feels okay to them to buy a commodity, but somehow it doesn't feel right or normal to sell the same commodity.

For these, and possibly other reasons, the majority of small traders are long at any one time. Since the Open Interest in a market is the sum total of all the long or short positions in the market, the Open Interest will go down only when short sellers are covering their shorts. Conversely, Open Interest will rise only when short sellers are increasing their short positions. Due to the fact that the large traders are the smart money traders, and that they are the ones who do the bulk of the short selling, then when Open Interest increases, the smart money traders are throwing a bearish cast on the marketplace.

And when Open Interest decreases, generally the large, smart money traders, many of whom are the commercial interests, are showing that the market forces at work are bullish. While this is generally accurate, it is not infallible. We mention it here to draw your attention to the fact that if your other fundamental indicators are forecasting a move in one or the other direction, it is wise to double-check what the Open Interest is doing. If the supply and demand balance, seasonal tendencies, and price levels are all very bullish, and yet at the same time you notice on the charts that Open Interest is increasing greatly, it would be wise to re-consider establishing a long position, or at least if you do so, to know that you are going against the commercial interests in your prediction.

The commercials are not always correct in their analysis, but when you are trading against them, it is better to exercise more caution. One of the best times to use this Open Interest indicator in conjunction with fundamental analysis is when a commodity has been in an extended trading range, of perhaps 5 weeks or more. If in this case your other fundamental indicators are calling for a move in one direction and you get a confirmation from the Open Interest figures, your odds of having a successful trade are greatly enhanced.

For example, say you have determined that seasonally, Cotton is due to decrease in price; your data on the supply-demand balance indicates there will be a surplus of available Cotton during the time frame you are examining, and Cotton is at historically high price levels. If at this time you see that Open Interest is rising, and the price of Cotton has been see-sawing back and forth between, say 80 and 90¢ for five weeks or more, you have all the appearances of a real winning trade. On the other hand, if all of the previous factors are present but Open Interest is declining, it means if you establish a short position in Cotton, you are betting that you are correct and that the smart money commercials are wrong.

Often you may be right, and they may be wrong; but with so many trading opportunities in commodities every week, you may want to ask yourself if it is worth taking the risk, and if you do find yourself taking such positions consistently against the Open Interest indicators, you may want to do some serious psychological soul-searching about whether or not you have a subconscious wish to lose your money. If that possibility seems to be a factor, you may want to read carefully another chapter in this volume "How Your Mind Affects Your Trading", in order to learn how best to approach this problem.

To summarize the keys to using the fundamental approach in analyzing your own commodity trade selections: first, determine the supply-demand situation and compare it to previous years to appraise its significance to the future direction of the market you are interested in. Make the necessary adjustments for any crops which are being held by the government. Look at the seasonal price tendency for your particular commodity and see whether or not there are any factors present at the current time that have disrupted or may disrupt the normal seasonal patterns.

Then examine price levels on long-range charts to see if the commodity has much room to move in the predicted direction, or if it is already so high, or so low in price, that the market has already discounted the supply-demand balance and seasonal factors.

Next, you should look at any real or potential crop damage to the commodity, and judge what, if any effect that may have on price direction. Then, notice if there are any impending labor negotiations or strike deadlines or transportation problems or international unrest that might adversely affect the position you are considering. True, there will be many times when the changes in fundamentals are sudden and unpredictable. But there are many times when they signal their occurrence, and it is wise to consider these instances seriously before initiating your position.

Then, consider whether it appears the economy is going to be in an inflationary or deflationary posture over the coming months during which you will be holding your trade. If you are using the fundamental approach for initiating long-range trades, then learn more about the technical aspects of trade selection, and you will greatly improve your entry and exit points, thereby greatly increase your profits.

Also, check the data, if available, for the commodity you are considering, on Commitments of Traders, to see where the commercials are betting their money. Remember, they are wrong at times too, but more often than not, they are right. Lastly, check the

Open Interest figures to confirm the wisdom of your position or to decide not to initiate the position if the Open Interest contradicts your other analysis.

CHAPTER 3

CYCLICAL AND SEASONAL ANALYSIS

Cycles are one of the most fascinating aspects of commodity trading, as well as many other aspects of business, politics, and life itself. There have been numerous books written on different types of cycles from the cycles of political upheavals to the cycles of mating patterns of animals. Virtually everyone is familiar with the effect of the cycles of the moon and the seasons on all aspects of our life here on earth, and many people are familiar with the results of cyclical sunspot activity. There even is an institute for the Study of Cycles with its regular publication reporting on new findings on different types of cycles, many of which involve research in commodity price cycles and stock market cycles.

One major commodity advisory service bases the majority of its recommendations on a number of cycles of different lengths for different commodities, and at least one other major advisory service has published a wealth of information about cycles of a long-range basis and seasonal cycles. Biorhythm experts and astrologers base their predictions for individual behavior on the use of different types of cycles.

It seems then that there exists a tremendous fascination among the public with cycles, for if events do not occur randomly, but do take place in a cyclical nature, then the future, to some degree, is in fact predictable, and whether the object being studied for cyclical activity is a racehorse or a commodity, the potential exists for realizing profits from using any method that has degree of validity in predicting the future.

There is such a wealth of information, and often misinformation surrounding this subject, especially as it applies to
the commodity markets and to individual investors themselves, that
it sometimes seems impossible to sort out all of the conflicting
information and make a coherent whole out of it.

The real reason cycles exist in commodities, and in many
other fields too, is actually based upon supply-demand considerations. Whether the commodity be one that is perishable like
Wheat or one that is storable, like Copper, there are fairly predictable and regular fluctuations in the supply of and the demand
for virtually every commodity known to man. Much long-range
research has been done to validate the existence of such cycles.

An English statistician did a study showing the cyclical fluctuations of Wheat over a five century period. While the cycle
discovered for Wheat on such a long-term basis could be correlated
quite directly with the political upheavals and wars during this
five hundred-year period, it is immaterial which came first, the
chicken or the egg, as to whether a cycle in war-making resulted
in the cyclical price changes in Wheat over a long-term period or
whether the cyclical price of Wheat somehow caused the European
powers to wage war.

As strange as this may sound at first, it is well-known by
historians that food supplies or the lack thereof often are
responsible for internal revolutions, wars between neighboring
haves and have-nots, etc. The purpose here is not to determine if
shortages of Wheat create wars but to point out that virtually all
cycles have their basis in shortages and oversupplies of some product or being.

Well-known cycles in the breeding patterns of insects, micro-
organisms, and mammals and birds have been determined to result
from a shortage of the specie, followed by an adequate number,
followed by an overabundance, and then the cycle repeats itself.
This is seen most clearly in perishable commodities on a seasonal

46

basis where shortly after harvest, crops are normally abundant, stocks on hand rise, supplies glut the market, and prices fall. As the year progresses, the supplies normally are used up, become in tighter and tighter supply as the next harvest period approaches, and reach a peak in prices due to generally constant demand concurrent with diminishing supplies as harvest time approaches.

Obviously, there are a multitude of other factors that affect such a simplified example. A drouth may seriously affect the supply of the harvest, preventing the post-harvest glut in supplies. An international trade embargo may disrupt exports to the point where demand is tremendously reduced. An actual or expected war may increase demand over and beyond normal expectations. A shipping strike may disrupt distribution of supplies after the harvest, preventing prices from dropping.

As the reader will probably understand by now, cycles are subject to all types of interruptions by external fundamental events. This is one of the major reasons why interpreting cycles can be so very, very difficult for the commodity speculator who is attempting to utilize cycle theory in the selection of his trades. Just from mentioning a few of the possible occurrences that could affect the price of Wheat, and thereby alter the normal cycle, it can be seen that the trader who depends solely on established cyclical information without taking into account other factors, will very seldom be successful in the commodity markets.

In addition to this problem of constantly changing fundamentals that affect cyclical action, the existence of overlapping cycles of many different lengths at times makes interpretation of cycles difficult. Your author recalls that many years ago, when he first became fascinated by cycles, he began using them in his charting of Stock Option prices. While a great deal of success was accomplished, it was at this time the multitude of cycle length importance really became evident. For individual groups, or complexes, of stocks, it was found that there were readily discernible cycles of a few weeks, that varied by a fairly constant plus or minus days. Then it was discovered that within those weekly cycles there was a shorter cycle, and inside that a shorter cycle still.

Upon further study, there were found to be a number of longer cycles, until seven different lengths of cycles were found that ranged from a few days to several years. It was noted that even longer cycles existed for the stocks in question, but they were not examined as their practicality in calling market turning points was not deemed sufficiently important to warrant the additional study.

In order to utilize these different cycles, all of which had different frequency, or lengths in time, and all of which had different amplitudes, or price magnitude, it was necessary to create an "envelope concept" where the different amplitudes of the various cycles were graphically represented, proportionately showing their corresponding frequencies and combining the differing frequencies and amplitudes in order to be able to predict prices over several months into the future.

This, even though it proved to be quite accurate, took literally dozens of hours per stock, and periodically had to be re-computed and updated. Despite all of this effort in combining, calculating, projecting, and updating these cycles, the ultimate results were sometimes disappointing, as prices often did not behave in the predicted fashion, despite there being very strong evidence that they would do so.

Upon very careful examination in an attempt to discover why prices had not moved as anticipated, it was found that invariably there was some external, or fundamental, occurrence that temporarily distorted the frequency or amplitude of one or more of the cycles under investigation, usually the shorter or near-intermediate frequency cycles. It is not our intention to deprecate or debunk cycles or their use. Quite the contrary. We believe that cyclical analysis of commodites is an important adjunct to every commodity trader's portfolio of methods.

We simply want to point out that cyclical analysis is not as simple as it may seem on first glance, nor is it immune from being affected by a multitude of external factors. If cyclical analysis were in truth so simple and uncomplicated, all of the cyclical analysts would be retired from the marketplace.

We will not attempt in this chapter to go into the already established cycle types and lengths, as a multitude of excellent work on this subject has been done by many contemporaries in the field of commodity analysis, such as Jake Bernstein and Walter Bressert. Any reader who is seriously interested in getting into

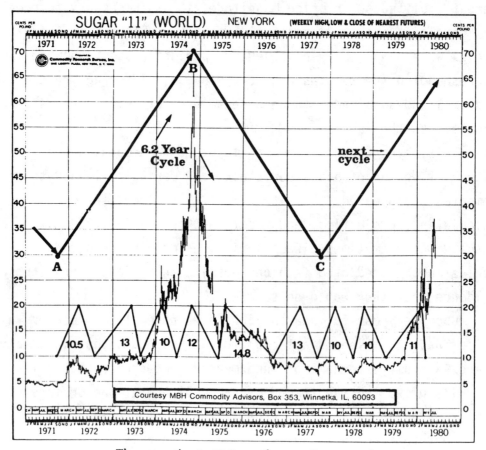

The approximate 12.5 month sugar futures cycle 1971–1980.

Figure 9

the intricasies of cyclical analysis is recommended to their writings.

What we will be attempting to provide in this chapter are some useful guidelines that can be utilized by all commodity speculators, especially in conjunction with other methods of analysis.

Whatever the degree of importance you place on cyclical analysis in your commodity trading methodology, the first aspect that must seriously be considered is what cycle or combination of cycles to use in your trading program. Since there are different of cycles with different lengths and amplitudes as shown in Figure 9, how can the average trader make any sense out of them, or at least understand them enough to use them?

Fortunately, the answer to this is quite simple, unlike many other areas of cyclical analysis. The individual commodity trader's own "style of trading" provides the answer to this question. By style of trading, we are referring primarily to whether it is his preference to make short-term, intermediate-term, or long-term trades. The type of trade he prefers will be one of the most important factors in how he decides to use cyclical analysis.

Obviously, a trader whose preference is short-term trading will be most interested in cycles with the shorter frequencies. And fortunately, these are relatively easy for him to use. If a trader knows that, say, Cocoa has a short cycle that normally lasts 22 trading days, plus or minus 3 days, as in Figure 10, it is relatively easy for him to take the current Potato charts, check out to make certain that this cycle is currently exhibiting itself, and time his trade entry and exit accordingly. We say that it is necessary to see if that cycle is currently exhibiting itself, because while all cycles are always present, they are often distorted by other cycles, both longer and shorter frequency ones, combining in such a way as to apparently eliminate the particular cycle in question.

50

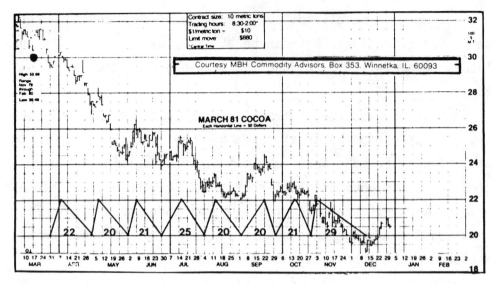

Figure 10

If a trader prefers to make long-term trades, say those
ranging from 3 to 8 months, then longer cycles assume much greater
importance. The long-term trader may still wish to use the shorter
cycles to "fine-tune" his entry and exit points in order to pick up
some additional points of profit, but his primary interest will be
in the long term cycles. It is important to note at this point the
similarity and the difference between long-term cycles and seasonals. Seasonals are simply calendar-year cycles that exist due to
relatively predictable changes in supply and demand based upon the
seasons of the year. So when someone speaks of Seasonals, they are
simply talking about a 12-month calendar Year Cycle.

Seasonals are one of the most reliable and most important
cycles, and will be discussed thoroughly later in this chapter.
For the long-term trader, since he is looking at months at a time,
Seasonal Cycles assume much more importance than they do for the
short-term trader. They are important too for the short-term
trader from the standpoint of giving him the information as to the

direction the major trend of the market should be moving. Many
short-term cyclical traders have brought themselves to ruin by
overlooking the Seasonals or other longer cycles and depending
solely on the short cycles that appear to them to be of prime
importance.

For example, let's take our hypothetical trader with his
22-day Cocoa cycle. He has verified not only its overall
existence but the fact that it is currently exhibiting itself.
Being like the majority of traders, our trader prefers to trade
the long side of the market. So disregarding longer cycles, the
seasonal cycle, and any other fundamentals that may be present, he
initiates his trade, and since this looks like such a sure thing,
he splurges and buys as many contracts as he can at the bottom of
the 22-day cycle. Unfortunately for him, he does this during the
latter part of February or early part of March when the Seasonal
Cycle for Cocoa normally drops, as seen in Figure 11.

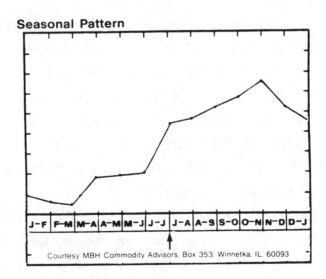

Seasonal Pattern

J-F | F-M | M-A | A-M | M-J | J-J | J-A | A-S | S-O | O-N | N-D | D-J

Courtesy MBH Commodity Advisors. Box 353. Winnetka. IL. 60093

Figure 11

Of course, given his predisposition to certainly trading with this
cycle he has so much faith in, he doesn't place any protective
stops. His 22-day cycle tops in two days from the low point at

which he purchased, instead of the 9 days he was anticipating and starts down. The chances are that now he believes he mis-timed his entry point due to the plus or minus factor that exists with all cycles and hangs on while prices plummet toward the lows of the 22-day cycle. Before long, he is out of the market and no longer trading.

While this example may seem ridiculous to some, we have heard variations of it repeated time after time, and want to emphasize it to demonstrate the importance of either not using cyclical analysis without other methods, or if one does use cyclical analysis solely, as do many very successful traders, to become expert in all its intricasies before risking ones money. While it can be important at times for the long-range trader to be aware of the shorter cycles in order to improve his results or to confirm his other indicators, it is mandatory for the short-term trader to be very cognizant of the long-term and seasonal cycles if he has any hopes of succeeding.

Many professional traders ignore all of the published data on seasonals and cycle lengths and utilize their own methods of cyclical analysis, though often they are either not aware that this is what they are doing or choose to refer to it by some other name. The best of these professionals, however, do not ignore seasonals, but take them into account in conjunction with their own method. Their method, quite simply, is to take current charts of the commodity they are interested in.

A good example is that of 1981 delivery Wheat. Wheat typically bottoms out seasonally in price in the May-June period, and hits its peak in the November-December period. Since cycles, as we have mentioned, are not perfect, March, 1981 Chicago Wheat, as shown in Figure 12, formed a double-bottom in April and June, closely hitting its normal bottoming time period. Subsequently it topped in late October-November, again just a bit off from its expected topping action.

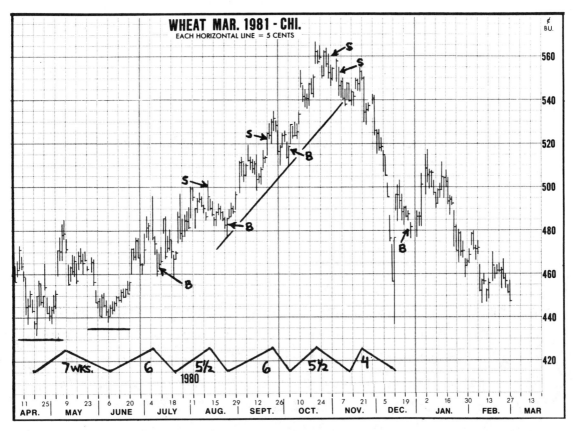

Figure 12

So, most professional traders would be trading Wheat from the long
side from the May-June period up until the expected peak in
November, at which time if they were trading Wheat, they would
reverse and normally only trade from the short side. During the
period from June 6th, 1980 through November 10th, 1980, Wheat
made almost 4 perfect cycles of 5 and one-half weeks each between
low points as it climbed from its seasonal low to its seasonal
high. Prior to its bottom, two more 5 and one-half week cycles
were evident between lows, though the first of the two was not
quite as evident due to the sharp downmove that was taking place.

However, the professional trader would have noted that cycle as possibly being 5 and one-half weeks, watched the bottoming action that was starting to take place and noted that there was a 7 week cycle between the lows of the double-bottom. Armed with his seasonal information now that prices should be going up over the next 6 months, he would wait 5 and one-half weeks and institute his first long position.

When he took this position, he would also have noted that prices for this first 5 and one-half week cycle peaked at about the fourth week into the cycle, then slid for a week and a half. So, after buying Wheat at about $4.65 per bushel, he sells his position out 4 weeks later, at which time prices are about $5.00 per bushel, a nice return of 35¢ per bushel or $1,750 profit on his original investment of $1,500, a net gain of 117% of original margin. He then waits a week and a half and buys another position at about $4.85 per bushel. He waits four more weeks and with prices at $5.25 a bushel, sells for a profit of 40¢ per bushel or $2,000 per contract. He now waits another week and a half and buys another contract with Wheat prices at $5.15. After four weeks pass, he sells his position out again with Wheat at $5.60, a profit this time of $2,250 per contract. Three trades, total profits of $5,750.

Does he now continue to buy and sell on this regular basis. No, for now it is late October and since the seasonal pattern exhibited the yearly low coming about a month earlier than usual, the seasonal high is getting far too close for comfort to assume any more long positions. Besides, some of his other indicators are showing signs of a top possibly being formed: major trendlines are in danger of being violated, Market Sentiment is extraordinarily high, and Open Interest has reached an extremely high level, being almost double the average Open Interest for the years 1974 to 1979.

If our professional trader is of an aggressive nature, what he will now do is assume a small position on the short side, say at $5.55 in hopes of catching the market top, since he only has to place his stops just about the then-contract highs of about $5.67, a minimal risk of 12¢ or $600. Well, his analysis of both the seasonals and the cycle length were right on the button and he sells around the middle of December when the 5 and one-half week cycle should be at its lows. Unfortunately for him, the cycle was distorted, for whatever reasons, and actually bottomed in about 4 weeks instead of five and a half weeks. It bottomed at $4.40, and when he gets out the market is at $4.80. Instead of making $5,750 as he might have if the cyclical length had held, he instead nets $3,750 for an initial risk of $600, or a return of 625%.

Sound unbelievable? Well, it's not. Just check the charts for March, 1981 Chicago Wheat and see how clear these moves were. When we said that this professional probably assumed a small position when he felt there was a good chance of the market topping out, we meant in relation to the positions he took along the way of the bull move. An average professional would probably have gone long 5 contracts on his first trade, 10 on the second, and possibly as many as 20 on the third, especially since he was using the market's money at this point, and not his own. By so doing, starting with his original $7,500 margin for his first 5 contracts, at the end of the bull move, he has profits of over $73,000, not to mention the additional $18,750 for his small short position. So, by calculating his own cycles, and not depending upon the published ones as to what Wheat should be doing, except on a seasonal basis, the professional trader has made nearly $100,000 on an original investment of $7,500 in a 5 month period!

Instance after instance of these types of trades can be seen going over old charts, and while what occurred in the past may not be exactly replicated in the future, the concept itself will be.

Wheat also may have a 4 week cycle or a 7 week cycle, but you can bet that careful examination will show that it does have a predictable cycle. The reasons for these variations in cycle lengths is not critical to our discussion, but as already mentioned, it can occur either due to overlapping of much longer cycles or fundamental events taking place in the world. The reasons why cycle frequency vary from year to year are interesting to speculate on and to determine if one has the desire to, but they have little bearing on the end results or outcome of your trading.

Some cyclical analysts insist that there are no reliable cycles for certain commodities, especially those that are non-perishable in nature, such as the financial instruments, foreign currencies, precious metals, etc. as well as some of the perishable ones such as Orange Juice. They base this on the fact that the cycles that have been exhibited over the years these commodities have been traded on the exchanges are either too few in order for the statistical data to be statistically significant or due to the fact that the commodity seems to exhibit no reliable pattern of cyclicality over the years they have examined it. Often the unique method used by professionals to measure their own cycles does not work as perfectly on non-perishable commodities, but then it often does not work as perfectly in the perishable ones either.

To further illustrate the point as to how the professionals utilize cyclical analysis in their own, somewhat unconventional way, we randomly decided to turn to the Financial instrument section of the same issue of charts and pick one chart at random to see if we could further illustrate our point see Figure 13. The first chart that caught our eye was for June, 1981 T-Bills, a period that saw record-breaking interest rates drive the financial futures market down suddenly and steeply. Certainly, how could any type of cyclical pattern exist in such an instance. In measuring between lows during the violent downslide, we found that

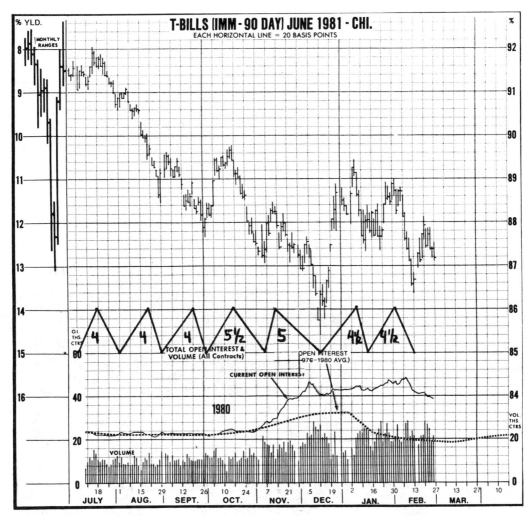

Figure 13

from the low just following the fourth of July, down to the low of
mid-December, the low points were spaced 4, 4, 4, 5 and one-half,
and 5 weeks apart. Not perfect, but amazingly cyclical for a supposedly non-cyclical commodity during an unusual period of time
for interest rate futures. The cycle preceeding the first four-
week low cycle just mentioned was also four weeks, so any trader
who bought his short positions out every four weeks on the

downslide, and having gone long about every two weeks into the cycle would have made very substantial profits.

Again, these methods are not absolutes, due to intertwining of cycles of different frequencies and fundamental occurrences, but this method, used by professionals, of calculating their own cycles, especially when taken into account with other factors, is a highly reliable and profitable approach to commodity trading.

Every professional trader we have spoken with who utilizes cycles in some way seems to have a similar approach to that we just described. However, they differ in some other aspects that should be mentioned. Many of them find the charts published by chart services that are relatively small the best to work with when looking for and calculating cycles. Others find the larger the chart the better for their similar needs. We suspect that this is due to the different ways that different people are able to visualize the same information when presented in different visual formats. Because of this, we would suggest that a trader get some samples of all the different available chart services and start looking for and measuring his cycles on each of them. By doing so, it will become rapidly apparent which type of charts are easiest for that particular individual.

Another important aspect the professionals utilize are long-range charts, usually weekly ones, but sometimes monthly ones also. The reason for this is that the long-range cycles are only readily apparent on these types of charts, and many professionals will not trade against a long-term cycle. Let's say upon examination that it is determined there is a pretty reliable 3.6-year cycle in Pork Bellies. They are normally on the ascent for say 1 3/4 years and on the descent for the next 1 3/4 years. The professional trader, having established that they are presently in the latter year of their 3.6-year cycle, would not normally trade the long side during Potatoes' normal seasonal rise from November to August, but

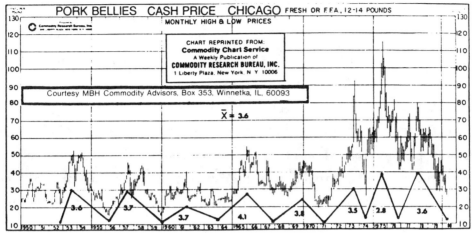

The 3.6 year cycle in cash pork bellies.

Figure 14

instead would wait and trade the short side during Bellies' normal seasonal decline from August to December.

The simple reason for the professional wanting to combine the long-range cycles with the normal seasonal trend and his own calculated cycles that exist for Pork Bellies for that particular year has to do with the amplitude of the cyclical moves. Amplitude referring to the amount of price movement. Whereas by trading the short side of the seasonal cycle during the downside of the longer range cycle, he might pick up an average of 10¢ profit per trade, whereas if he traded the long side during the seasonal upmove while the longer term cycle was down, not only might his profits only average 5¢ per trade, but from experience he would know that his calculated cycle length for that particular year would be more valid for the seasonal bear move due to the influence of the long-term cycles that would be affecting the market.

The real experts trade whenever possible so that all of the cycles, or as many of them as possible, are going in the direction in which they are holding their positions. With so many different markets, exhibiting so many various long-range, short-term and

season cycles, it makes little sense to the professional to trade
the long side of Pork Bellies as in the example above during, say
June, when Bellies are normally going up since he would be trading
against the long-range cycle, than perhaps in October, when Bellies
are normally going down, and Bellies are also in a long-range cyclical downmove. With so many possible choices it makes the most sense
to pick the best possible candidates for the largest profits. One
other way professionals utilize their own special method in addition
to the previously mentioned considerations is by examining all commodities at all times to see which ones are showing the most regularity of cyclical action.

The important point about examining all, or as many different
commodities as possible at any given time is that some will simply
not show any cyclicality or the cyclicality they do show will be
so irregular as to make it impractical to use in making trades.
To explain this, we again have to return to the reasons discussed
before: overlapping of cycles of different frequencies and
overriding fundamental considerations. If a five-year and seasonal cycle are bottoming at the same time that a 50-year and 21-day
cycle are topping, and all of these points coincide fairly closely, it will distort tremendously the regular cycles the professional is looking for. And possibly added to that might be an
unexpected strike, flood, freeze, embargo, or whatever else that
is unexpected in the fundamental arena, then cyclical predic-
tability goes "out the window", at least for a period of time.

So, when looking to establish your own cycles for trading purposes, if the cycles are not apparent on the charts or seem too
irregular to use, attribute it to one of the previously mentioned
factors and move on to another commodity's chart. There are
plenty of commodities, and you only need one at a time that is
exhibiting good cyclicality in conjunction with its seasonality in
order to make big profits.

Some traders discount the need to take into account the long-
range cycles, and they often succeed regardless of what the long-

range cycles are showing. We would recommend ignoring long-range cycles as determined on your weekly and monthly charts ONLY if time is a factor and you simply do not have enough time to go into this detailed analyses. No effort was made to determine how many of the 30 to 40 different commodities in the chart service we picked up to give examples from were exhibiting such good cyclicality, but suffice it to say, that if the first two we selected at random were showing it, a large number more would also be so exhibiting it.

The use of long range cycles can be of extra, added importance in the profitability of positions you take by helping you pick tops and bottoms more accurately. The first way to use them to do this is by combining them with seasonals, and when you see a commodity is due to bottom, in say February, start watching the cycles you have measured, say a 5 week one. Given that seasonals vary a bit from year to year, only one of two 5 week cycle bottoms should be the low for the year. Many pros will look for this every year and make their purchases of long positions, half at the bottom of the first 5 week cycle closest to the seasonal bottom, and if prices close them out, or as is more often the case, move sideways, institute the remainder of their positions at the second 5-week period point.

As mentioned before, when combining cycles with seasonals, it is very important if the commodity in question has been behaving typically this year in terms of seasonal movement instead of atypically. One veteran trader told us that he looks for just one commodity each year, sometimes two, to hedge his bets, that for the past twelve months has been following its typical seasonal cycle within a month or so, and that has measurable cycles. He then invests in these and only these commodities and rides the cycles through just like our investor did in our previous Wheat example.

He did note too though that he looks for the long-range cycles, as we have discussed, to confirm that the moves he participates in will be of good magnitude. All the while he is doing this, he is monitoring the other commodities he had eliminated, watching for any to start showing their typical seasonality and predictable cyclicality for other potential investments. In fact, he said this is the only type of trade that can come up, that is, another cyclical trade following its seasonal pattern, when he has all of his available capital tied up in these one or two other trades, that will persuade him to use borrowed money to trade with.

There is a certain degree of psychology that goes into the creation and utilization of cycles. With a number of large advisory services utilizing cycle information on which to base their recommendations, and with other advisors and the news media picking up on this, often the trader will hear that "Gold is due to hit its 5-year high within the next couple of months," or "Soybeans are due to hit their seasonal lows this month". With such information receiving widespread distribution, it only adds to the validity of the cycle turning point coming to pass. In effect, such pronouncements act as self-fulfilling prophecies and can on occasion turn the markets on their own regardless of whether the cycle being referred to has been skewed or not.

Let's take Wheat as an example to see how this works. With Wheat normally making its seasonal low toward the end of June, beginning in May these advisory services, some of the major brokerage house newsletters, and some of the news media that cater to the commodity trader all start discovering reasons to justify why Wheat will be reversing and heading up soon. It may be that there are rumors of increased export sales, a poor Canadian crop, bad weather in the midwest, or whatever. Then they will all add in that Wheat is not only nearing its seasonal low but that "X", "Y", or "Z" cycles indicate also that Wheat is due to increase in price.

In fact, at any given time, with any commodity, a case can

be made with either technical data or fundamental information to predict a move in EITHER direction. This is most frequently seen in news accounts the day AFTER some relatively significant price action. The commentators and analysts always have a reason. The market was oversold or undersold; there was a rumor one way or the other; or any one of dozens of other reasons. This is most evident in listening to the nightly national news commentators "explain" why the stock market went up or down that particular day. We don't want to belabor the point, but what is important is that all of this information about a seasonal low or a seasonal high being due is acted upon by many, many small traders hoping to capitalize on a big move.

The large speculators are well aware not only of the seasonal tendencies but also of the actions of the small speculators. Combining all of these forces together virtually guarantees, that barring some really major, unforeseen fundamental event, the market will act as predicted. This is not to say that the masses create cycles, for these cycles and seasonal tendencies existed before they were popularized. It is to say, however, that they often force a cycle to occur when it might otherwise not do so because of the longer-range cycles.

Understanding cycles can be very useful too in stop placement once into a move or even for placing initial protective stops. For initial stop placement, one of the best methods, having identified the primary cycle that is being shown, and having checked out the longer-range cycles, is to place your stop, on a long position, just a bit below the last cycle low. Very, very seldom, if the long-range cycles are up, and the seasonal cycle is up, will the measured exhibited cycle low that was previously established be violated unless there is something really drastic occuring that affects the markets in general or that particular commodity.

The same principle applies to moving one's trailing stops after entering a position with a measured cycle. Once, upon visual observation, it becomes apparent that the cycle low has been established, stops can be moved to a point just beyond the cycle low. Since cycles do have their variances, a trader should wait several trading days after the apparent cycle low has been established to make certain it really is the cycle low. Frequently, say in the case of a 4-week cycle, prices will go up for three weeks, and then start down the fourth week. At the start of the fifth week, prices will go up the first day or two, indicating that probably a cycle low was established at the end of the fourth week. However, often, due to other factors, prices will drop for a day or two then, breaking through the low set at the end of the fourth week and then starting up again.

Seasoned cyclical traders know to watch out for this, and since most of them are longer-range traders anyway, will often wait a week after a supposed cycle low to move their stops if they are holding onto their position through a number of cycles. The cyclical trader who is attempting to buy at the bottom of the cycle will normally not do this as the small amount he might save by missing a false cycle bottom will in the long run be eaten up by the cycles he misses entirely.

Instead, the cyclical trader who wants to sell at the cycle peaks and buy at the cycle lows, will more generally use a certain day on which to buy and sell. The day, based upon his measured calculations, that is the one most likely to be the high or low for the move of that cycle. He will not squeeze out the maximum possible profits by doing this, but it is a far better way than trying to guess the frequency variance and enter and close out positions in that manner.

We are often asked about Moon Cycles and whether they really work or not. For those of you who are not familiar with moon cycles, the theory is that when there is a new moon, a sell signal is given for most commodities, and when a full moon occurs a buy signal is generated. One popular writer has devoted an entire chapter in one of his books to validating how well this works. Since the charts used in those examples were some years old, we picked at random a set of 1978 charts to see how playing the moon worked that year. Taking moon phases by themselves, without using anything else, was disastrous.

Interestingly enough, though, since the moon cycle is 28 days, it coincides pretty closely with a well-recognized 4-week trading cycle. The question as to whether the moon cycles create the 4-week cycle or whether the opposite is true is immaterial to our discussion. The question is not whether there is some agreement between the moon phases and a 4-week cycle, but can it be utilized by the average trader. Strangely enough, the answer appears to be yes, as long as other indicators are also taken into account. When a seasonal and long-range cycle are both pointing up for a commodity, and the measured exhibited pattern approximates a four week cycle, the appearance of a full moon, though not perfect, is as good a time to enter a trade as any as long as your other signals are pointing to the establishment of a bull position. Conversely, a good time to go short or to close long positions out, WHEN your other indicators are confirming such action, is to do it on the day of a new moon.

We suspect that in addition to the coinciding with a 4-week cycle, the popularization of moon cycles adds to their effect, again becoming a self-fulfilling prophecy. It is a well-established fact that the moon affects many things on this planet, from the tides to the amount of anti-psychotic drugs that must be given institutionalized patients, so it is not so far-fetched to conclude that maybe, just maybe, moon cycles involve more than a self-fulfilling prophecy. Whatever the reason, they do work to some degree, and the serious trader who wishes to devote the time to marking his charts up with indications of when the full and new moons will appear, should improve his results sufficiently to justify the additional effort.

A fascinating exercise too, is to take a set of old charts and an almanac for that year, and go through all of them marking them up to indicate the full and new moons, and then comparing those points with changes in Open Interest, seasonals, moving averages, momentum oscillators, etc. Not nearly enough research has been done yet in this area, and at some point we suspect an enterprising researcher will check all of this out with a computer.

In the meantime, let us conclude with the observation that we have not found moon cycles to be limited to any one commodity or complex of commodities as has been stated by other researchers; rather, we have found a rather universal reliability for any and all commodities. One last point we have noted in our studies of moon cycles is that they work better for some years than for others. Whether this is due to a longer-range moon cycle or some other phenomena, we do not know. But if we were to utilize them, we would want to check and see how they have been working over, say, the past 6 months, before depending upon them in the present. They seem to work either for almost all commodities at the same time during the same year, or to be very imperfect for all commodities at the same time. Hence, the suggestion to check out how they have been doing recently before depending upon them now.

Of course, with a name like Taurus, an astrological sign, we are often asked if we use astrological signals. The answer is "no". It is a long story how Taurus got its name, but it has nothing to do with astrology. However, over the years, astrology has become somewhat of a personal family hobby, and normally we can tell a person's astrological sign after a brief conversation with him or her, just because of so many similarities that seem to exist for certain signs. But to use them when trading? It may be possible, but we doubt if they can be used for individual trading decisions. Too many other factors enter into them.

Some signs, like Capricorn, which typically exhibit a bit more patience than some of the other signs, may lend the Capricorn trader to be more adept at long-range trading, which requires an extra amount of patience. Certainly typical characteristics of other astrological signs MAY have some bearing on a trader's technique, but we feel these as to be so incidental as to not be worthwhile to consider.

The one exception, however, is the trader who is deeply involved in astrology, not so much in the selection of an individual trade or a period of time during which success in financial matters is predicted for him, but in terms of personal characteristics. The Leo trader who genuinely believes he is courageous like most Leos, may very well exhibit that trait in his trading, and we believe his psychlogical make-up will determine whether he uses this successfully or unsuccessfully. Much more depends upon a person's psyche, in our estimation, than upon his astrological sign.

Another rather controversial area that we would like to cover in this chapter is that of biorhythms. It is difficult to pick up some magazines or supermarket newspapers without being innundated with biorhythm calculators, charts, etc., and as a result, biorhythms themselves are sometimes looked on as being a hoax. However, considerable scientific study has been made of them, and without going into the details of these studies, we have examined them carefully and can only conclude that biorhythms have a great degree of influence on an individual's life.

For those of you who are unfamiliar with biorhythms, the theory goes that at the moment of an individual's birth, three cycles of different lengths, or sine waves, begin. One is for the person's physical body, the next for the psychological state, and the longest for the intellectual level of functioning. The simplest way for one to determine their own biorhythms is to purchase an inexpensive electronic calculator, called a Biolator, which is available in most stores that sell calculators. Not only have we read most of the research, pro and con, on biorhythms, but we have spent considerable time going into the past and checking biorhythms for individual family members for dates we knew significant occurrences had taken place on.

The results were almost uncanny, in terms of successes and disasters. We do not believe that biorhythms have predictive abilities per se, but rather predisposition tendencies instead. A person is much more likely to have an accident when his physical biorhythms are critical or low than when they are high. As a result, we recommend that if one is interested in a bit of "fine-tuning" of his life, to consider taking his own biorhythms into account. We would not avoid fixing the roof just because our physical biorhythms are negative, BUT we would be a bit more careful. Nor would we decide not to initiate or close out a trade because our intellectual biorhythms were "bad", but when they are, we might double-check our computations for errors. This may sound like a minor point, but we have caught errors on a number of occasions that otherwise would have passed unnoticed, solely due to keeping track of our biorhythms. If this chapter seems an unlikely place to hear about biorhythms, remember that they are cycles too, your own individual cycles, and there appears to us to be an overwhelming amount of evidence as to their validity.

We have attempted in this chapter to take some of the mystery out of cycles, and to emphasize the really important aspects of them, which to us are the seasonal cycles, long-range cycles, and measurable exhibited cycles, and to understand how fundamentals and psychology cause these cycles to some degree, and how often they become self-fulfilling prophecies.

While there undoubtedly are many traders who rely on cyclical analysis solely, it is our opinion that it is only one of an important set of tools to use in commodity trading. These other tools are discussed in the other chapters of this book. Even if a trader can successfully trade by only using one method, or tool, if he can obtain better results by combining two, three, or more tools, using each of them to confirm or validate the others, assuming he has sufficient time to do so, it makes the most sense to use everything that is available. We do not believe, however, that it is necessary to spend countless hours analyzing all of the different cycle frequencies and amplitudes in order to successfully use cyclical analysis.

The important things to remember in cyclical analysis are: first, determine from long-range charts what the long range cycle is predicting for a given commodity. Second, determine if the commodity is following, at least to some degree, the seasonal tendencies it normally exhibits. Next, see if there is a visually measurable cycle on the charts that should have predictive value. If a commodity is difficult to read on any of these counts, pass it; there are many more to examine. And lastly, if you have the time, combine this cyclical analysis with other important technical and fundamental methods in order to get the best results.

CHAPTER 4

VOLUME & OPEN INTEREST

Volume and Open Interest are two very specific technical
tools. When they are fully understood, especially the significance of the interrelationship between them, they can be one of
the most useful and profitable methods of selecting which commodities to trade, when to enter a trade, and when to exit a
trade. Many books on commodity trading have sections or chapters
on this subject, but much of the material in them is misleading,
difficult to understand, or in some cases, downright erroneous.
This chapter, on how professional traders really use Volume and
Open Interest.

Before getting into the most successful use of Volume and
Open Interest in your own trading, it is appropriate to explain
fully what the terms mean so that no confusion exists later on
when we show how to implement them. Volume and Open Interest are
two different statistics that are primarily the concern of the
technical analyst, but they are also used by the expert fundamental analyst either to confirm or to question the conclusions
the fundamentalist draws from his data. So, regardless of whether
you use technical or fundamental analysis, or some combination of
both, Volume and Open Interest can be vitally important tools to
you either to confirm your own predictions or to use by themselves
if you are looking for a relatively simple method of making market
selections.

The Volume of trading is defined as the sum total of purchases or of sales. It is not the sum total of sales and purchases
combined. every time someone buys a contract, there has to be a

seller who sells the contract, so the total of all sales is equal
to the total of all purchases. If Volume were defined as the
total of purchases plus sales, the figure would be double the one
that is conventionally used. This figure for the Volume of
trading is determined from the reports on every commodity, showing
all sales and purchases, which are submitted daily to the commodity exchanges by the exchange clearing members. The exchanges
merely summarize these figures, and report every day what the
total volume is for each commodity. By plotting these figures on
a graph, normally in the form of a bar graph showing each day's
volume, a visual representation of the Volume is given. This bar
graph is usually shown at the very bottom of the graph for the
commodity itself, below the Open Interest graph, as seen in Figure
15.

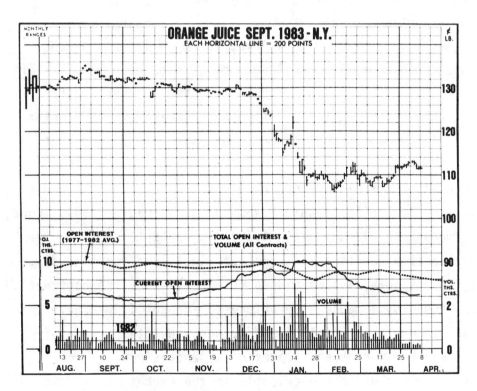

Figure 15

Many sophisticated chartists feel that instead of showing the Volume in a bar graph form, the visual representation of using dots for the total figure, to form a curve, is more understandable and easier to interpret. Since all the commercial chart services we know of use the bar graph, we will refer to that type of format throughout this chapter, realizing that some of our readers who keep their own Volume charts will be using the other representation.

Volume is a figure that changes daily, and that is the key difference between it and Open Interest. While Volume is a figure representing the total number of either sales or purchases for any given day, Open Interest is the total number of all futures contracts that either have been liquidated by an off-setting transaction or have not been fulfilled by delivery. All the open contracts for any given day, which may represent the Volume or portions of it for many of the preceeding days, is the Open Interest. Just as with Volume, the Open Interest figure is the total either of all open long contracts or of all open short contracts, since each figure equals the other. Open interest, by convention, is not the sum of all open contracts, both long and short; if it were, it would simply be double the figure that is currently in use.

One important difference between Volume and Open Interest is illustrated by the fact that if you buy a contract of say, Sugar, from someone who already owns it and now wants to sell it, then the transaction counts as one contract in Volume for that day. But it counts nothing toward Open Interest, since the contract wa already owned by someone else before you bought it. However, if you want to buy a contract of Sugar, and you obtain it not from someone who had purchased it previously and is now selling it, but from someone who was not previously in the market at all and now wishes to go short a contract, then this transaction shows up not only as one contract in Volume for that day, but also as an increase in Open Interest of one contract for that day, because this particular contract of Sugar was not owned by <u>anyone</u> prior to the day you bought it. The Open Interest was, in effect, created by your desire to buy a contract and a corresponding desire by another trader to sell a contract that he did not already own.

Two points of interest should also be made clear here. The first is that because of the time needed to compile the data on Volume and Open Interest, there is a two-day lag in reporting the market information; the figures given in financial papers always refer to the transactions of two days before. These figures are properly identified both in the financial papers, and on the graphs. Most financial papers do report on "Estimated Volume" and on "Estimated Open Interest changes" for the day before, but often these estimates are highly unreliable and should be used only with great caution.

The second point worth noting concerns day trades. Since day trades do not cause any changes in the Open Interest at the end of the day, because these contracts closed before the close of the market, no day trade transactions appear in the Open Interest Figures for that day. Ordinarily this is of no great consequence, but there are times when day-trading is so exceptionally heavy that it can have some significance. Even though these day trades do not appear in the Open Interest figures for any given day, they do show up in the Volume for that day.

Most storable commodities show a fairly predictable pattern of seasonal changes in Open Interest, due to shortages in the product before harvest or slaughter, and surpluses after harvest or slaughter. Woods and metals show somewhat the same tendencies, but these are due to seasonal cycles in areas like homebuilding and industrial production. Many chart services show a graphical representation of the average Open Interest curve for the past five years, plotting along with the Open Interest Curve for the current year as shown in Figure 15.

While there are many ways to interpret the difference between
this year's Open Interest, and the Average Open Interest of the
past 5 years, we know of no studies that have conclusively come up
with exact rules on how to utilize the information gleaned from
the observed differences. Perhaps the best approach is to notice
if there is a divergence from the average pattern, either in the
direction of the curve, or in the rate at which it is declining or
increasing; and if so, to realize that something is taking place
in the market this year to distort the normal seasonal pattern of
Open Interest. Then examine the existing fundamentals to try to
determine what is happening, whether it is significant, and
whether or not you can use this information in your trading decisions. There are some slight seasonal tendencies in Volume, but
our studies indicate that they are of no usable significance to
the average trader.

In order to make the concepts of Volume and Open Interest
more understandable to the listener, we would like to discuss what
significance any changes in Volume and Open Interest indicate, so
as to make what follows in this chapter clearer. On the one
hand, Volume gives us a measurement of the level of intensity with
which traders feel the need to take positions, whether long or
short, at the price level where the market is ranging on that particular day. Most trades are initiated because traders feel that
a particular commodity is either cheap or expensive at its current
price; so when volume increases for any given day, it indicates
that a large number of traders see that day's price as a good opportunity to go long or short, depending upon their analysis. On the
other hand, the Volume also indicates the intensity felt by those
traders who view their positions as being in jeopardy because the
market is moving against them.

When prices are in a trading range, as shown in Figure 16,
Volume normally dries up to a great degree, because the traders
who are not yet in the market are waiting to see what happens, and

those traders who are already holding long or short positions are
content to wait and see which direction the market will take after
it breaks _out_ of its trading range.

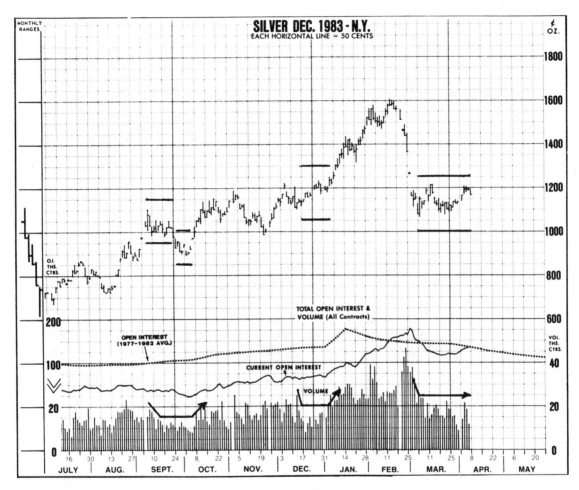

Figure 16

But, if prices move out of the trading range, and at the same time
Volume _increases_ dramatically, it means that those traders holding
positions in the opposite direction are bailing _out_, while new
traders are anxiously getting _into_ the market. If prices move out
of the trading range and at the same time Volume changes only
slightly, it indicates that those already in the market do not
believe the move to be a genuine one; and neither do those traders
who are not already in the market want to _get_ in.

VOLUME, then, is a measure of urgency. OPEN INTEREST, on the other hand, is not a measure of urgency; it is a measure of the overall desirability of a particular commodity to traders, as a whole. With between 30 and 40 commodities being traded at all times, not counting those on the Canadian markets, these commodities are, in effect, competing for investors' money. As an example, if the Open Interest on any given day for Cocoa is 20,000 contracts, while for Hogs it is 40,000 contracts, in essence what that indicates is that Hogs, at that particular time, are about twice as popular with commodity investors as Cocoa is.

Margin requirements play a part in determining how much interest, or Open Interest if you will, there is in a commodity; yet margin requirements alone do not solely determine the popularity of a given commodity, as witnessed by the usually low Open Interest in some low-margin commodities such as Eggs, Broilers, and Oats. News factors, such as droughts, freezes, political developments, and embargoes, often focus investor attention on a particular commodity or group of commodities, thereby funneling money to those commodities and driving their Open Interest up.

With regard to Volume, it is important to note that the reason Volume dries up in a trading range is that the fundamental supply and demand factors have come into some semblance of balance. When there are no fundamental reasons for prices to move out of their trading range, there is no reason for traders to be trading. As a result, Volume remains low until there is a change in the fundamentals to drive prices out of their trading range and thereby increase volume. It must also be noted that Volume is a highly specific measurement for each commodity; the daily volume in Gold for instance, will be many times that of Platinum. What the technician is looking for is not the absolute figures showing the Volume for many commodities, but rather for changes in the Volume figures of one particular commodity over a period of time. As long as the daily Volume for a given commodity remains relatively constant, it is of little interest. Only when the volume changes, in one direction or the other, does it become a significant factor.

Volume occasionally increases very rapidly within a given day because of the pit scalpers who initially buy or sell contracts as stops are hit, and then re-sell or re-buy them later in the day. This action by scalpers to accommodate the needs of the market sometimes causes a single contract to change hands many times in a given day, especially when the market action is frantic; and at times the Volume for a given day may actually be greater than the Open Interest itself.

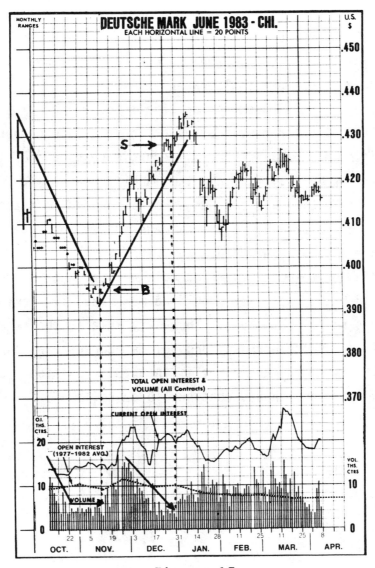

Figure 17

Volume increases dramatically when a cluster of stop-points is hit; it stays high as the weak traders are removed from the marketplace and then it dries up. When this situation occurs, it generally means that the market is about to reverse itself and go in the direction opposite to its last move. A cardinal rule to follow with Volume is NEVER to short a market after a price drop if the Volume dries up; and conversely, NEVER to go long a market after a price rise, if the Volume dries up. In both cases, the market is almost certain to reverse itself. One of the things that many professionals do is to profitably trade this cardinal rule, as shown in Figure 17. If there has been a sharp price drop and volume becomes quiet, they go long; and if there has been a sharp price run-up and volume becomes quiet, they short the market. This one rule has been responsible for many millions of dollars made by professional traders.

Volume is the slowest acting of all the technical indicators, in that it will often remain stagnant for significant periods of time. Months may pass with no discernable changes in volume for a particular commodity. Suddenly the market comes alive with great increases in Volume, and the fundamental reasons that account for it are of no consequence to the average trader, because the Volume figures are already exhibiting their effects.

There are two more important rules concerning Volume, and they are so basic that they should be memorized by every trader who decides to follow Volume. The First Rule is that when Volume increases as prices increase, and Volume decreases when prices decrease, this means the market is in a bull position; technically it is moving up and should continue to do so.

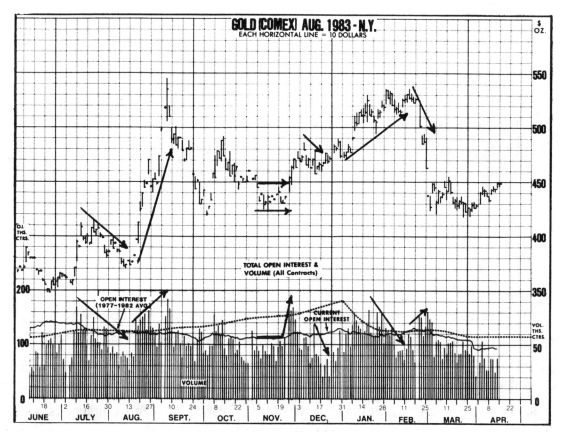

Figure 18

The Second Rule is that when Volume increases as prices decrease and Volume decreases when prices increase, then the market is in a bear position; technically it is going down and should continue to do so. These are not infallible rules, but they are good guidelines to the direction of the market as can be seen in Figure 18; and when they are combined with an analysis of Open Interest, these rules assume even more validity. Neither changes in Volume nor in Open Interest nor in the two combined have any validity, as a rule, unless viewed in conjunction with what price action is doing at the same time.

One of the best definitions of Open Interest is that it is a measure of the willingness of both the shorts and the longs to hold different positions in the same market. Another way of looking at it is that Open Interest in a commodity is a measurement of the differing opinions that exist between traders about the direction that prices will move for that particular commodity. When Open Interest is going up, either current holders are increasing their positions, or new traders are joining them on both the long and short sides of the contract. The numerical difference of opinion about the direction of price is increasing.

When Open Interest remains relatively constant, either new traders are entering the market to replace those who have gotten out, or strong traders are assimilating the contracts of weak traders who are giving up their positions because they have turned into losing positions that are too large for them to handle.

When Open Interest decreases, weak contract holders are closing out their positions either because the price movement is going against them, or because they have become impatient at the lack of market action, or at what they perceive as the lack of market action. The positions they liquidate, whether long or short, are acquired mainly by traders already holding contracts on the other side. As a result, the willingness of both longs and shorts to hold their different positions in a particular market is decreasing.

While there are two basic or cardinal rules for interpreting moves in Volume, there are four rules for interpreting changes in Open Interest, as illustrated in Figure 19 because these rules are tied in to the price action of the market itself. Again, while there are exceptions at times, these rules are valid enough to be carefully memorized by all traders regardless of the type of analysis they are following.

When Open Interest is increasing, it means that new trades are being initiated. Trades by new sellers and by new buyers are outnumbering trades by old sellers (who are buying back their contracts) and by old buyers (who are selling out their contracts). Since an increase in Open Interest shows both new

selling and new buying, the fact that prices are advancing shows
both that the buyers are more aggressive than the sellers and that
the market is technically strong. Hence, the First Rule of Open
Interest is: If Open Interest increases while prices are
increasing at the same time, then the market is strong and should
continue to advance.

Figure 19

The Second Rule of Open Interest is that if Open Interest
increases while prices are decreasing at the same time, then the
market is weak and prices are getting ready to reverse and go
down. Whenever Open Interest increases it means that new
contracts are being established in the market. But, since in this
case, open interest is increasing while prices are decreasing, it
means that the shorts are stronger than the buyers, which shows
that the market is definitely weak and ready to start down.

The Third Rule of Open Interest is that when Open Interest
decreases while prices are also decreasing at the same time, then
the market is strong and is ready to turn around and advance.
This happens because obligations by old sellers and by old buyers
are greater than the commitments by new sellers and new buyers.
Prices going down simultaneously with Open Interest going down
means that the old buyers, who are now sellers, are more forceful
in getting rid of their long positions that the old sellers, who
are now buyers, are in covering their positions; and this indicates the market is getting ready to go up.

The Fourth Rule of Open Interest is that when Open Interest
decreases while prices are increasing at the same time, then the
market is weak and will decline in price. Since Open Interest is
decreasing, it means that old sellers and old buyers are closing
out their positions. But, since prices are increasing, it means
that the old shorts, who are covering themselves by buying back
their contracts, are much more aggressive than the buyers; hence
the market, from a technical standpoint, should begin to head back
down again.

Normally, the only time the professionals ignore Volume and
Open Interest is when the graphs of either or both of them are
running across the page in a virtual straight line, as can be seen
at different points in Figures 18 and 19. This also makes them
consider whether they even want to enter a market like this, due
to the lack of action. But the professionals will watch these

markets carefully looking for a gradual or sudden change in either Volume or Open Interest, which will be a signal to them to start looking at all the other variables to see if they wish to initiate a trade.

What they particularly look for is a <u>sudden</u> change in Open Interest rather than a gradual change, because this is more indicative of a sudden move upcoming. If the move is large as well as being sudden, it has even greater significance. When this type of change occurs, it is almost a sure sign that the market is about to make an abrupt change in direction, usually because of a sudden change in opinion by the large-money traders and commercial interests.

Figure 20

84

The professionals look closely at the difference between
this year's Open Interest and the average of the past 5 years. We
mentioned this briefly before, but now we want to show how the
professionals interpret such changes. They look for two distinct
patterns to alert them to possible positions. When the current
Open Interest is much lower than the 5-year average, as seen in
Figure 20 and declining at the same time, this often triggers them
to initiate a long position, or at least to look at all the other
factors that might justify taking a long position.

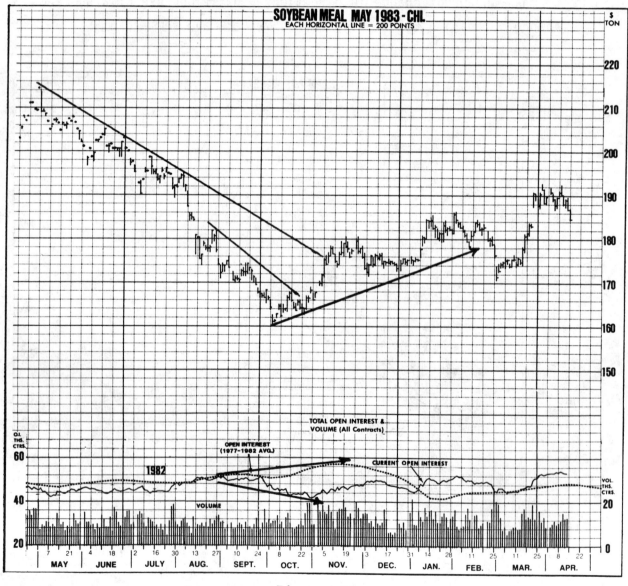

Figure 21

The other pattern they look for shows this year's Open Interest declining when the 5-year average indicates that it usually is increasing as illustrated in Figure 21. This is a potential long situation if confirmed by other technical factors.

The perfect way to combine Volume and Open Interest is by the use of the Two Rules previously given on Volume and the 4 Rules given on Open Interest, using one set to validate the other. Thus, if Volume is increasing, Open Interest is increasing, and prices are increasing, you are using Rule One for Volume and Rule One for Open Interest to cross-check each other and strengthen your prediction that a bull move is either underway or about to take place. However, if Open Interest is increasing, prices are increasing and Volume is declining, there is no cross-validation between the sets of rules, and a stand-aside posture would be in order unless there are some other facts that cause you to take a position.

There is little question that psychology affects Volume and Open Interest, and while that fact in itself is not of much use to the average trader, it _is_ useful to understand how this takes place. As we mentioned before, Open Interest in any commodity is the result of competition between the different commodities for an investor's money. If the news media, brokerage house letters and advisory services, among others, get keyed in on one or several commodities, that becomes "news". If everyone is talking about damage to the Sugar crop in the United States and Cuba, and a low sugar content in the sugar beets of Eastern Europe, this type of news tends to feed on itself and by creating _investor_ interest, that is, every investor wanting to get in on a "hot thing", money that might otherwise be invested in Wheat or T-Bills gets diverted to Sugar, thereby pushing up its Open Interest and Volume. There is nothing wrong in this, and the resulting Volume and Open Interest statistics will be just as valid as at any other time, since they are a function of fundamentals anyway.

We want only to point out that "news markets" help to accelerate or decelerate the moves in Volume and Open Interest. Man being basically a greedy animal, the trader wants to get on the bandwagon and get his share of the market, too; so the news feeds upon investor psychology, which in turn creates more news and more investor interest in a never-ending cycle until the market runs out of steam and either tops or bottoms.

This psychology that affects Volume and Open Interest is also fueled by many brokers and brokerage houses who want to get their clients in on a good thing or into an interesting market with a lot of action. They want either to please their clients, or in some cases to get them in markets that are wildly moving so that the client may have to get into the market several times, thereby creating several commissions for the brokerage firm.

Another way to double-check your conclusions on Volume and Open Interest is to consult Contrary Opinion Market Sentiment or Bullish Consensus (all three terms are used interchangably) figures. These figures are published weekly by a couple of different firms, and if you do not know how to obtain them, you may write to Taurus Corporation and we will be happy to send you the names and addresses of those firms. For those of you who are not familiar with Bullish Consensus, we will give a brief description. Bullish Consensus is expressed in terms of percentages of bullishness. A compilation is taken every week of all the advisory services and brokerage house newsletters, and a figure is expressed indicating how many of them are bullish on any given commodity.

For example, in a given week, Wheat may have a Bullish Consensus of 70%, which means that 7 out of 10 of these advisors and brokerage-house newsletters believe Wheat will increase in price. On the other hand, if the figure for Cocoa is 20%, it means that 8 out of 10 believe Cocoa is headed lower and only 2 out of 10 expect higher prices. On the face of it, this appears to be an excellent way to predict the future direction of prices. However, research has indicated that when the Bullish Consensus figure is 70 to 80% or greater, the market is seriously overbought and due to either correct or reverse itself.

Conversely, when the Bullish Consensus figure is 20 to 30% or lower, the market is seriously oversold and due for a rally or a reversal in trend. Now, the professionals, just as you do, want to be able to wring every point of profit out of a market that they can. If prices are in a bull move, the pros expect some reactions along the way, but what they really want to be tipped off to, is a complete reversal of trend so they can liquidate their long positions, and either take to the sidelines or establish short positions.

With Bullish Consensus running at 85% for Wheat, the trader holding a long position is faced with the question of whether to get out of the market or just ride out a reaction. By using Volume and Open Interest, this problem can be solved most of the time. If Bullish Consensus climbs up to the 70 to 80% and above figure, start watching the Volume and Open Interest figures. If prices are continuing to climb, and Volume starts to decrease at the same time Open Interest shows a sudden, even if slight, upward spurt, it is time either to take profits or to move stops in much closer.

If while the prices are going up, Volume stays steady or increases, and Open Interest either stays the same or increases gradually or slightly, you can generally disregard the Bullish Consensus figures. The Bullish Consensus figures are based on the theory that when too many people all believe the same thing about the market, they are wrong. And this is generally the case, but not unless it is confirmed by the changes in either Volume or Open Interest, or both, that we have just discussed. It is also true if you are holding a short position and the Market Sentiment drops to 20% or lower. If prices are still going down, and the Volume is high or increasing, and the Open Interest is steady, you

88

can disregard the Bullish Consensus data as not being valid from
the standpoint of indicating a change in trend. During all
sustained moves, however, there are minor rallies and reactions
along the way. How can one distinguish a minor rally or reaction
from a bottom or top being formed?

Usually when a market is topping or bottoming, the Bullish
Consensus figures will be very high or very low. As we have
noted, the fact that these figures are high or low is not in
itself necessarily indicative of a top or bottom coming up. What
needs to be examined next are the figures for Volume and Open
Interest, using the rules we have been discussing. In the bear
market of the previous example, if prices start up, and market
sentiment is at 20%, and Volume goes up quickly, then the chances
are good that you are _not_ seeing a brief rally, but that the
market is either going to go into a sideways trading pattern or
that the market may be getting ready to reverse itself completely.
In either case, it is a prudent idea either to take profits at
that point or to move your stops in close.

At this point we would like to note some other conditions
that do not occur frequently in the marketplace, but are well
worth looking for and taking advantage of when they do occur. The
first is when Open Interest increases dramatically in markets like
Eggs or Broilers or Oats which are usually lightly traded. When
this happens it means that large amounts of money are pouring into
these markets, and something is afoot. Despite the illiquidity
these markets normally exhibit, the increase in Open Interest
changes all that, and makes them potential trading candidates.
The second observation follows the first in that it is almost
never a good idea to trade _any_ commodity where the Open Interest
is relatively low. A good rule of thumb is to exclude any commodity
for which the current Open Interest is less than 10,000 contracts
unless other reasons for trading this commodity are particularly
strong. Such Open Interest encourages bad fills, and often makes
it difficult to liquidate your positions when and where you want
to.

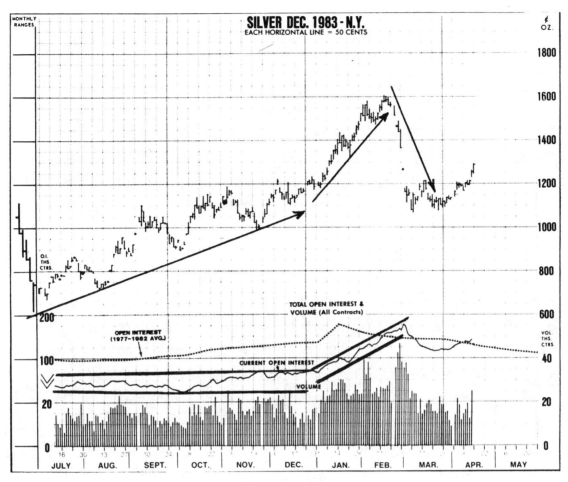

Figure 22

One of the best types of bull markets to get into, and which
can generally be entered safely even mid-way through the move, is
one in which Open Interest remains relatively flat during the
increase in prices as can be seen in Figure 22. This indicates
that the commercials are unwilling to assume new short positions,
and is a very bullish signal. When this occurs, the time to get
out of the market, or at least to keep one's stops very close, is
when the public starts getting into the market, as evidenced by
sudden increases in the Open Interest.

Following Volume and Open Interest figures can be a very

90

important element in the management of your trading capital. Let's assume you have been following three different commodities, all of which for various technical and fundamental reasons convince you that they are ready to begin bull moves. Again, let's say all three of them are in protracted trading ranges, at relatively low price levels. You may decide to commit your money equally among all three, positioning yourself to enter all three markets when they break out on the upside of their trading ranges.

However, being a student of Open Interest, you are watching their Open Interest figures carefully too. Simultaneously, all three break out on the upside, but two of the commodities show no change in their Open Interest, while the third shows a slight but sudden decline in Open Interest. For good money management, you have a number of options available to you. You could pass the first two trades entirely and triple-up on the third trade; or possibly better yet, since Open Interest signals are not infallible, you could allot your capital so that you entered all three positions, but concentrated your capital more heavily, in more contracts, on the third position. You would invest in the same way if the signals were opposite; that is, the opposite would be true if you were expecting a _bear_ move and you got a _rise_ in Open Interest in one of the three commodities.

It might be well to point out here that the rules for Open Interest given earlier in this chapter are general rules, and need to be modified slightly when prices are in a protracted trading range. We said earlier that when Open Interest increased and prices increased, the market was bullish. This is true for most situations, but not for when prices are in an extended trading range. When prices are in a trading range, and Open Interest increases _before_ prices move much in either direction, the signal is extremely bearish and is predicting a decline in prices. Volume is generally useless when prices are in a trading range of this nature since the movement of prices will not be significant enough to mean much, and in any case, volume is normally relatively light during trading range formations.

The opposite rule modification applies too. If prices are in an extended trading range, our previous rules about the market being bullish if Open Interest decreases while prices are decreasing, and the market being bearish if Open Interest decreases while prices are increasing, does not hold. Rather, when prices are in a trading range, anytime Open Interest decreases suddenly or significantly, it is an advance warning that a bull move is about to come, because prices are reamaining relatively neutral.

Supposedly some large-money traders make their fortunes year after year simply by watching for trading ranges and buying or selling accordingly when there is a sudden change in Open Interest one way or the other. An interesting study that we have made and which you may wish to make, is to take a collection of old charts that have Open Interest Graphs on them and examine them carefully to verify this connection. Our studies have indicated that generally it takes a trading range of at least five weeks for these principles to hold true.

Many professionals utilize Volume and Open Interest for their stop placement, and we would like to discuss how they do that. Once they have initiated a position that is going in their direction, many professionals use a conventional stop-loss method for trailing their stops, such as either a bit below the previous week's low, or just beneath a major trendline, in order to lock their profits in from sudden reverses.

However, they follow the Volume and Open Interest figures carefully, and in the case of a bull market, if Open Interest suddenly spurts up or if Volume starts to decline on days when the market is advancing, they then go to a tightly-drawn trendline, instead of the major trendline they had been using before, and place their stops just below it. A careful examination of old

92

charts will reveal countless times where volume is extraordinarily
high on increasing prices the week <u>before</u> a top is made; and then
the following week, when the top is being made with still rising
prices, volume sinks way down. When combined with Bullish
Consensus, especially if there has been a rapid rise in Open
Interest during those two weeks, this is an excellent signal that
a true top has been formed.

Another topic that should be covered here because it is so
intimately related to Volume and Open Interest, is the
"Commitments of Traders". This is a monthly report issued by the
Commodities and Futures Trading Commission that gives a breakdown
of the number of outstanding contracts of both small and large
traders at the close of each month. Large traders are those who
hold positions in excess of certain limits specified by the CFTC,
and who must report their holdings to the CFTC on a daily basis.
Small traders' holdings are determined by subtracting the reported
holdings of the large traders from the total of all open positions.

As we might assume, the small traders are wrong much more
often than they are right. These figures are reported in different financial journals, and are given by some of the weekly
chart services in table form as shown in Figure 8 in an earlier
chapter. The large traders reported in the Commitments of Traders
report are the ones who account for those commodities which are
receiving a lot of action. The first thing to do when examining
these figures is to look at how these large traders are holding
their positions. That is, are the bulk of them long or short? The
small trader's report you can pretty much ignore, since they are
the traders who are generally on the losing side. It is not unusual to look at such a report and find 10 commodities in a row
where the overwhelming majority of small traders are bullish, and
where in perhaps 7 or 8 of the same commodities, the largest traders are bearish.

The small traders have an inherent tendency to be bullish no matter what, at least most of the time. You must note however, that the Committment of Traders report is <u>not</u> a timing tool, due to the delay between the accumulation of data and the time that data appears in the press. It does give you a general indication, however, of where the smart money is. A trader should be very reluctant to take a position that goes against that of the large speculators, unless the large traders are fairly evenly split in their views, say 60-40, or unless the small trader has strong reasons to believe he is right. The Commitment of Traders is still another confirmation, although a somewhat delayed one, to help interpret the significance of Volume and Open-Interest figures. Using the Commitment of Traders data for large speculators when attempting to pick a top or a bottom is virtually meaningless, due to the rapidity with which such events generally take place. However, when you are looking at the extended trading range concept, and you see that the Commitment of Traders Report shows 70 or 80% of all large speculators holding long positions; then when the sudden decline in Open Interest Comes, it adds just that much more validity to your bullish prediction.

We would like to emphasize that for the average trader, using Volume and Open Interest by themselves is usually not sufficient to guarantee consistently winning trades. It is by using them in conjunction with other technical and fundamental methods of selection that they can greatly increase the average trader's rate of success.

If we were forced to pick one method and one method only of using Volume and Open Interest for trade initiation, it would be that one previously discussed that requires prices to be in a trading range, and then waiting for a change in Open Interest to predict the next major price move. Beyond that, Volume and Open Interest can help you pick tops and bottoms quite well; but this requires a bit of practice, as top and bottom picking is more of an art than a science, and one must develop a "feel" for it which can be done only by going over old charts and examining the changes in Volume and Open Interest as the tops and bottoms are approached.

As you do this, remember, you are not interested so much in the changes that take place the week <u>after</u> the top or bottom has been hit, for by then it may be too late to do anything about it; but by using the guidelines set forth in this chapter, you must be able to identify the subtle changes that take place the week <u>preceding</u> the top or bottom being formed, and the movement in Volume and Open Interest during the week the top or bottom actually takes place.

The signals put out by changes in Volume and Open Interest, especially when combined with trendlines, Bullish Consensus, and Commitments of Traders seem on the one hand remarkably simple, since they work so consistently and so well. However, since the inter-relationship of all these factors is what is so important, using them can appear quite complex unless you take the time to practice analyzing all of them simultaneously. Even though Volume and Open Interest are hard and fast figures, that is deceptive in that they cannot be analyzed by themselves without taking the other factors just mentioned, along with price action, into account.

It is somewhat analagous to learning to type: what could appear to be simpler than to hit keys on the typewriter keyboard that are plainly marked? Yet, as all typists remember, it took some practice before their brains made the necessary neurological interconnections to make everything work smoothly. Now that you can see the keys on the keyboard, from the standpoint of knowing how each of the factors we have discussed works, it takes some practice in order to blend them all together so you can understand their significance. It takes some practice and some patience too, for now that you know how and why Volume and Open Interest tip off market moves in advance, you just need to work on being able to recognize and integrate all of the factors involved.

CHAPTER 5

PLACING YOUR STOPS

During our many years of trading, first in stocks and then in
commodities, no area has presented as many difficulties for Taurus
as that of stop placement. It has taken literally years and
thousands of hours to finally make some sense out of what is probably
the most difficult area of commodity investment. The difficulty
does not lie in the fact that there is insufficient information in
the literature on commodity trading. Quite the contrary. There
is, if anything, an over-abundance of books, articles, methods,
special systems, and experts abounding in the field of commodity
speculation, all giving the perfect way to place stops.

Having examined every single published method, combined them
in different ways, and attempted to devise our own original
methods, we believe that at long last we have made a coherent
"package", of all the different methods that have been proposed
over the years. The old saw about there being a time and a place
for everything seems to fit the area of stop placement beautifully.
There are times when one method of stop placement is generally
superior to the other methods, and times when the other methods
seem to work best.

Unfortunately, as in all areas of commodity speculation,
there are no absolutes in the area of stop placement; rather there
are probabilities that certain methods will work better than
others under specific circumstances. It will be the overall purpose of this chapter to examine all the major methods of stop placement, and a few of the lesser known ones, and to specify under

which situation each seems to work best. We will also divide our approach between the placement of the initial protective stop, the trailing stop, and the stops near what appears to be the end of a market move.

By attacking the problem of stop placement in this fashion, it is our hope that you will gain a better understanding of the different methods of stop placement and when each is most appropriate to use.

Before we begin our discussion of the different methods of stop placement, it is important to distinguish between the different TYPES of stops. The first is the initial protective stop, sometimes abbreviated as I-P-S. This is the stop placed when first initiating an order. Whether the order is to be filled at the market, at a given point, or at the open or close, the initial protective stop indicates the amount of risk involved in initiating the position. Many traders, of course, do not use initial protective stops at all, or they may choose to use "mental stops", meaning that if prices reverse on them to a certain point, they will close out their positions.

For our discussion here we will assume that an initial protective stop is used. The alternatives of no stop placement and mental stops will be discussed later in this chapter. Initial protective stops establish one very important point at the inception of a trade, and that is the amount of risk the trader is willing to assume.

For instance, if you are initiating a long position in Wheat, at $4.00 a bushel see Figure 23, the point where you place your initial protective stop determines the degree of risk you are either willing or feel forced to take. With Wheat valued at $50 for every 1¢ move, an initial protective stop placed at $3.90, or 10¢ away from your entry point, involves a risk to you of $500 if the market reverses and your stop is hit.

If your stop is placed at $3.70, or 30¢ away from your entry point, you are risking $1,500. Assuming that the margin requirement for Wheat at the time of the trade is $1,500, in the first case you are risking an absolute amount of $500, or a percentage amount of 33% of Original Margin. In the second case, you are risking an absolute amount of $1,500 or 100% of Original Margin.

Figure 23

With varying margin requirements for different commodities, such as $8,000 original margin required for a contract of Coffee, you can see that 100% risk on a Coffee contract-involves substantially more money than 100% risk on a contract of Wheat. The major factor in placement of initial stops, regardless of the method involved, is the amount of risk of your TOTAL TRADING CAPITAL. If your trading account has $20,000 in it, obviously you can afford to make a lot more wrong decisions about which markets to enter if you are risking only $1,500 on each trade than if you are risking $8,000 on each trade.

   While there are no hard and fast rules about what percent of
his total trading capital is "safe" for a trader to risk per
trade, 10% seems to be an adequate figure. This permits 10 losing
trades in a row before the trader is wiped out, and if he cannot
get <u>some</u> wins during a string of 10 trades, he probably shouldn't
be trading commodities in the first place. The main reason we
suggest 10% is to allow or the unforeseen small strings of
losses, while keeping enough capital in reserve to take advantage
of new trading opportunities as they come along. We will not go
into the mechanics of how to select trading <u>positions</u> in this
chapter, but suffice it to say, when making a choice between two
commodities on initiating a trade, if all other things are equal,
then the trade with the smaller initial dollar risk should be the
one selected.

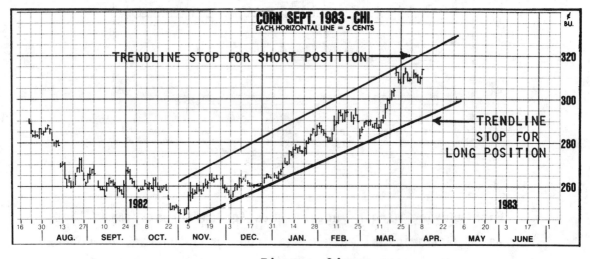

Figure 24

   In a relatively quiet market, which is not exhibiting a lot
of volatility or wide-swinging price action, probably the best
method to use to place one's initial protective stops is to draw a
<u>trendline,</u> even if it is horizontal, and place the initial stops
just beneath it for a bull position - or just above it - for a

short position as shown in Figure 24. This sounds ridiculously
simple, but in quiet markets, it seems to work better than any
other method. The trader must calculate, however, the distance
between his projected entry point and the initial protective stop
point to determine the amount of dollar risk before making the
final decision. Often, even in so-called quiet markets, the
distance will be enough that the dollar risk is excessive, and the
trader is best advised to look elsewhere for a trading opportunity.

Another method that frequently works well, is to place the
stop just below the low of the last two weeks, in a long position,
and the opposite in a short position.

Figure 25

If the trader has correctly analyzed the market, very seldom will
prices reverse and penetrate the low of the previous two weeks as
illustrated in Figure 25. The best method, however, is to use the
low of the last _four_ weeks, which may be possible in a very quiet
market. If the trader has accurately predicted the upcoming

trend, almost never will the low of the previous four weeks be violated.

Whether or not this method can be used depends again on the amount of dollar risk involved. Many expert traders are willing to assume this additional dollar risk of using the low of the last four weeks when they are convinced by all of their predictive signals that a market is going to go in their direction. a beginning trader might ask why it is necessary to place stops so far away at times if he has correctly analyzed the next trend of the market, or for that matter if he is trading with the current trend. A cursory examination of most charts will reveal that for many reasons the markets do not behave in a nice, straight, zig-zag line up or down as illustrated in the textbooks. The markets are often given to unpredictable behavior, and for this reason if for no other, stops at first must be placed sufficiently far away to guarantee remaining in the market despite a severe initial reaction or rally. Again, a quiet market is best to do this in, from a risk standpoint.

Placing initial protective stops in a volatile market is a different thing entirely. We suggest in this case to follow the procedures mentioned previously for quiet trading markets, that is to check the trendline, and the lows of the past two and four weeks, and make notes of all of these. Then, if you are con-sidering a long position in a market moving with a great degree of volatility (which we would recommend only if the market were moving sideways or already upward) compute what the distance your stop would be if it were placed one and one-half times the amount of a limit move for that commodity. In the case of Pork Bellies shown in Figure 26 the maximum daily limit is 2¢, the stop com-puted this way would be 3¢ away from your entry point, or almost 100% of original margin which would equal $1,140. At this point, compare which stop is the GREATEST distance away from your entry point, either the trendline stop, the 4-week low stop or the one and one-half limit move stop, and select the GREATEST of the

three. That is, of course, providing you are willing to risk whatever amount of money that entails. If you are not, then pass the
trade, because in a violently moving market, your stops must be
further away from your entry point.

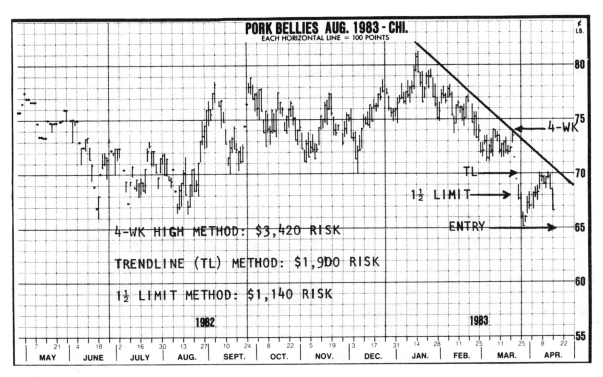

Figure 26

When considering a short position in a sideways or declining
market that is moving with a high degree of volatility, basically
the same procedure is used, but with one exception. Calculate the
initial trendline stop, then the stop above the high of the past
four weeks, and then calculate a stop that is TWO times a limit
move away from your entry point. In the case of Pork Bellies just
given, that would be 4¢ away from your entry point, or a risk of
$1,520.

Obviously, a good deal less risk is entailed in trading
markets that are quiet at the time of entry. There are a couple

102

of exceptions to initial stop placement that need to be noted at
this point. If a market is in a sideways trading pattern, at a
relatively low price point, and if the seasonal factors, Open
Interest, and other indicators are starting to point to the possibility of a bull move, then draw a horizontal line slightly
beneath the bottom of the sideways trading range, leaving a bit of
white space between the line and the bottom of the bar prices.
Place your stops just below this horizontal line, again assuming
that the risk factor computed from where you will enter the market
is not too great for you. Do not use this method if the market is
in a trading range at a middle price level or a high price level,
but revert to the other methods previously mentioned for placing
initial protective stops.

The other exception to placing initial protective stops
occurs when you have a market that has made a bull move of from 5
to 8 months duration and appears to be running out of steam. Once
you have decided that it has and you enter short positions, for
whatever reasons, then place your initial protective stop a hair
above the high of the move to that point. Normally the risk in
this case will be relatively small, and even though you may get
stopped out several times as the bull move continues past the point
you thought it would, no market moves up forever; and when a bull
runs out of gas, it generally comes down quickly with enormous profits for those who have managed to get short in time.

If a market appears to have made a double-top, and one top is
lower than the other, and too much risk is involved to place your
stops just above the higher of the two tops, but the risk is permissible if you use the lower of the two tops, it's all right to do
so IF the lower of the two tops has followed and not preceded the
higher of the two tops. When using point and figure charts, whether
optimized or non-optimized, the same basic approaches apply to the
placement of initial protective stops.

We would now like to turn our attention to "mental stops", or
the case of a trader not placing any stops at all. If we convince

you of no other point in this chapter, it would be: <u>NEVER enter a position without placing a protective stop.</u> The absence of a stop is almost a form of financial suicide, because we have seen trader after trader initiate positions without stops or with a mental stop that he fails to act on as the market starts to go against him. This is as disastrous a situation as "averaging down" on a long position.

We have known traders, who (taking our example of going long Wheat with an entry point at $4.00 per bushel) place a mental stop at say $3.85, only to see prices drop to $3.85 and yet fail to take any action. What seems to be the psychological process that occurs is that under the stress of the situation, they are unable to make a decision to phone their broker; or they are somehow convinced, or hoping, that their mental stop was "just a bit too close", and since their analysis indicated the market was going to go up, obviously if they hold on just a bit longer, the market will finally start up and their position will have been justified.

Similar but to a different degree, is the trader who refuses to move his stops up to the break-even point even when the move really appears to be risk-free, and who insists on keeping his original protective stops in place far beyond the time such action is justified, as is the trader who refuses to trail his stops in any appropriate manner once he has moved them up to the break-even point. Both traders exhibiting either a difficulty in accepting financial success or a perverse enjoyment of accepting the additional risk and danger of inappropriate behavior. Both of them are similar to a man starting an automobile trip with his gas gauge nearly on empty and not knowing where a gas station is.

Certainly few if any traders would do this, yet many of them insist on behaving inappropriately when it comes to stop placement. For your own safety, <u>always</u> place an initial protective stop. Then, following the methods outlined in this chapter, get your protective stops up to the break-even or entry point as rapidly as you can (as long as you do it judiciously); and finally, use one of our methods to trail your stops and keep locking more and more of your profits in.

One last word of warning: unless you are a successful expert in the commodity markets who has consistently been showing a profit for at least two years, never move a stop further away. By that we mean, if you have your initial protective stop on a long position at $3.85, and you entered the position at say $4.00, never lower your stop down to $3.80 or any other figure below your initial stop placement point. The same applies once you have your stop to the break-even point. Never move it from break-even to a potential loss; and the same applies to your trailing stops. The reason we prefaced this statement with "unless you are an expert of two years' standing" is that there are cases where an error in calculation has been discovered AFTER the stop has been instituted, and the expert feels the need to make a correction to protect himself. So, unless you have reached this stage, double-check your computations the first time around, and then do not tinker with your stops once they are placed.

Once you are in a position and it is moving in your direction, stop placement becomes even more difficult because now the technical and the psychological problems both increase. We shall examine the psychological aspects first. Once you have a profit in a position, it is human nature on one hand to become somewhat greedy and hope that this is the million-dollar trade all speculators look for. On the other hand there is the fear that if you do not take your profits now, they may evaporate and disappear completely. In psychological terms, this is known as an "impasse", or conflicting internal messages in one's mind.

Short of therapy, the best way to deal with this situation is to pretend you are a computer that primarily trusts the data he is seeing, and which only secondarily trusts his hunches or intuition. This can best be clarified by an example. Let's say you've gone long a Wheat position at $3.00 per bushel, and by now the price has increased, over a four-month period to $4.00 a bushel. You now have 100¢ profit or $5,000 on your initial minimal investment. One circuit in your brain is probably saying: "Hold on, prices are bound to go up to $6.00; after all, all the experts say so!" At the same time, another circuit in your brain may be saying: "Good grief, are you a pig? You've got five grand and that's the most you've made on a trade in ages. My God, man, cash your chips in before it is too late and you end up with nothing!"

We know that this sort of thing happens, not only from many conversations that have been related to us, but also from our own personal experience of many years. Now is the time to pretend you are a computer. In order to get this mind set, recite your social security number a few times, a few zip codes and phone numbers you know to activate those parts of your brain that do not deal with feelings and emotions but with facts. After doing that, look at your charts and your figures. Use the techniques that we will be describing in a few moments on how to trail your stops, and see if your stops are where they should be. Then close your eyes, take a deep breath, and wait for your intuition to "tell" you what to do.

It may take a few moments before your intuition comes through, and while you are waiting, keep your mind clear by thinking about and visualizing some favorite landscape scene or sunset. The hunch will come, and when it does, do not question it, but act on it. Do not second guess your hunches, but accept them as being the best you can do under the circumstances. Remember that they are not infallible but that they are considerably better than any decision you would have made under the stress you were wrestling with from the conflicting messages in your head. Unconventional? Sure, from a commodity trading standpoint; but this is a technique used by some of the best therapists in the country to help their clients make an important decision, and, after all, what is commodity trading but a succession of decisions, some more important than others?

Now, let's move from the psychological aspect of trailing
stops to the actual mechanics of doing it; and this is not quite
so simple as the psychological approach. We shall examine the
different methods, and evaluate them; but whichever method or combination of methods a trader decides to use, it is important for
him to decide first whether his general trading philosophy, or
just his approach to a particular trade, is of a short-term or a
long-term nature. The type of trade he either envisions or prefers has a great deal to do with the method of stop selection he
chooses.

A trader who is projecting a trade of a relatively-short
term nature, or who prefers short-term trading in general, would
be well-advised to learn the methods for long-term stop placement, because he will often find that the trade he has intended to
be of a short-term nature suddenly accelerates in magnitude to the
point where the long-term potential looks so appealing that he
wants to stay in it for the long haul. Conversely, the long-term
trader would do well to become familiar with placing short-term
trade stops, because his projected long-term trade often does not
materialize, and in order to reap maximum profits, he has to alter
his method of stop placement.

One of the most common methods of placing trailing stops is
to draw trendlines, connecting significant lows in a bull move or
significant highs in a bear move, and to change the stops as often
as necessary to keep them a slight distance away from the
trendline, so that the trendline would have to be broken in order
for the stop to be hit. While this is a fairly acceptable method,
two difficulties arise with it. First, since so many people use
this method, a market will often penetrate the trendline enough to
set off all the stops, and then resume its original course. This
is an excellent time to use close-only stops if you are using
a trendline method, so that only if the market closes through the
trendline are you stopped out.

Normally, unless the trend has reversed itself in reality, the market will move through the trendline but not close beneath it. True, sometimes it _does_, but you are at least offering yourself a better chance of staying in the move. The second difficulty with drawing trendlines, in a great many cases, is in choosing what points to connect to draw the trendline. Usually there are a number of points, especially if the move has been progressing for some time.

Figure 27

There are two rules that we believe work best in these situations. First, draw all the possible trendlines on your charts as in Figure 27. Then, if you are a short-term trader, place your stops just beneath, on a close-only basis, the STEEPEST trendline of any significance. But, if you are a long-term trader, or feel that the

move has a lot more potential, place your stops beneath the LEAST
STEEP trendline, and DO NOT place them on a close-only basis.
Based upon our calculations, these methods have the greatest degree
of success in terms of profits produced.

There is an exception here too, though, that applies only to
the long-term trader; and that is, if his signals indicate to him
that a market may be stopping (no matter what indicators he uses to
determine this) then he should immediately switch to placing his
stops beneath the STEEPEST trendline he can draw with the stops on
a CLOSE-ONLY basis. Often, using this close-only approach will
cost profits at a market top, but more frequently it will keep the
trader in the market all the way to the top of the move, which will
more than make up for any profits he might lose on a sudden key
reversal day.

In speaking of the difference between short-term and long-term
traders, it is important to note that the really successful traders
generally use different types of charts for their trendline
drawing. The successful short-term trader will generally use daily
charts, but often he will also use weekly charts in order to compare any differences in trendlines that he may discover. The successful long-term trader, on the other hand, generally begins with
trendlines drawn on weekly charts, and also draws them on monthly
charts for comparison.

Since the short-term trader frequently is trading the nearest
contract month, he has no problem with interpolating figures,
since the weekly and monthly charts are both drawn using figures
from the nearest contract month. But if he trades any contract
month other than the nearby month, he is faced with the same
problem as the long-term trader, in that the figures or trendlines
he comes up with must be adjusted to account for the more distant
month that the position is being held in. This, fortunately, is a
relatively simple matter to take care of and takes little time to
do.

Many traders believe wholeheartedly in using stops based on moving average graphs, and since there are so many possible ways to compute moving averages, whether from a time standpoint or with composite methods, or weighting procedures, we are forced to discuss the pros and cons of using moving averages in general. Moving averages DO work in stop placement, just as they do in the initiation of orders, BUT they carry the inherent difficulty of the trader's not knowing which moving average is best to use with any given market at a given time.

As a result, much confusion exists in their usage, and many mistakes ensue. To state some general principles: The use of moving averages as a method for placing stops can be really disastrous in markets that are displaying a whipsawing pattern. Of course, any stop placement is hard in this type of market, but moving averages, it has been our experience, are the worst method to use in such circumstances.

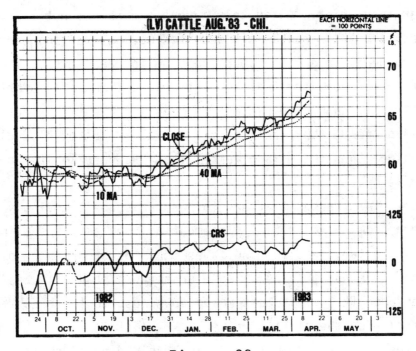

Figure 28

110

In short term trades, a 10 or-15 day moving average plotted against
the daily closing price, with the stop placed just a little away
from the cross-over point between the two, is probably the best
way to use moving averages for short-term trading stops as shown in
Figure 28. long-term trading, a 40 day or a composite moving
average applied in the same way is probably best.

If we sound lukewarm to the approach of using moving averages
in general, despite some of the results reported by the "experts",
it is because we have found in our research that moving average
methods DO work, but we have also found that other methods consistently work better, and produce greater profits. However, if
you are a devotee of moving averages and have developed a high
degree of expertise in their use, it may in fact, be best for you
to stay with them, possibly adopting the suggestions for their use
that we have just given.

Another important consideration in stop placement is when to
move your initial protective stops from their first placement to
the break-even point. Often this cannot and should not be done in
one move. The basic rules laid down for moving trailing stops
apply in general to getting your stops up to break-even. There is
one difference, however, that is worth noting. When a market has
apparently just changed direction from bull to bear or vice versa
in its main trend, the reactions or rallies are often of a different nature than those in a market that has been in its trend
for some weeks.

Hence, in a market that has topped, we suggest moving your
stops down from their initial placement as soon as a trendline can
be drawn. If the trendline indicates that the stop can be placed
at a profitable point rather than a break-even point, it has been
our experience that it is best moved down just to the break-even
point itself for the first move.

In the case of a market that has been riding along at a low
level and seems to be starting up into a bull move, we would not
place our first stop change based on a trendline method, no matter

how shallow that trendline might be. We suggest waiting for a low
point to be made after your entry, and then a second low point,
which normally will take anywhere from a couple of weeks to a
month. Once the second low point has been established, move your
initial protective stops up to either just below the first low
point or to the break-even point, whichever is the lower of the
two. Subsequent moves of the stops will be made by using the
methods detailed previously.

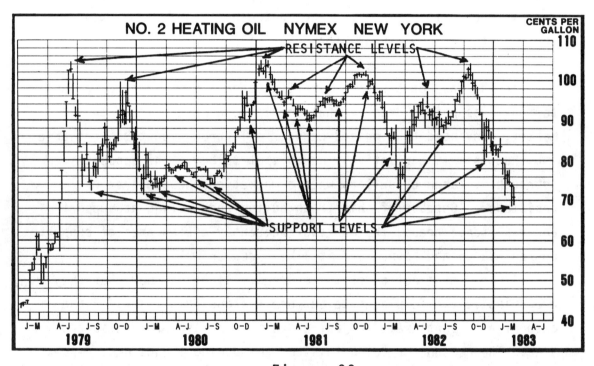

Figure 29

After a move has been in progress for some time, there are
definite support and resistance areas established. A support area
is an area beneath prices that supposedly "support" these prices
from falling through it. A resistance area is just the opposite
in that it is an imaginary line somewhere <u>above</u> the current prices
that supposedly acts as resistance to a price movement through it.
These imaginary lines are constructed at levels where prices

stalled, either on the upside or on the downside, previously in the move as shown on the weekly chart in Figure 29.

There are also historical price-support and resistance levels seen on long-range charts, and in this case there may be a number of them that show up over the years, at different points where prices ran into congestion or formed a trading pattern. Fundamental factors of supply and demand were often responsible for stalling these old upmoves or downmoves, and very possibly these fundamental factors do not apply to the markets of today. But there is so much talk in the advisory services and in the press about important support and resistance levels, that they often behave like cycles in that they become self-fulfilling prophecies.

In the case of a support area, whether a short-term or a long-term one, as prices drop to that area, fresh buyers enter the market, convinced that prices cannot fall through that support area and that this is a relatively cheap spot to buy. The opposite approach is taken by sellers when a market reaches an area of resistance. Because of this fresh buying and selling at support and resistance areas, the markets frequently hit an area of support or resistance and bounce off it like a rubber ball.

A close examination of these areas will often show that they are relatively safe places to put one's stops just <u>below</u>, in the case of a support area, or just <u>above</u> in the case of a resistance area. The reason for doing this and abandoning trendlines, 4-week lows, and other methods when this situation occurs, is that when prices go through what has been reported as an important support or resistance level, it generally means that the large speculators and smart-money traders have good reason to know the areas of support or resistance will not hold, and the market is in for a sustained move once it slices decisively through one of these zones.

For example, let's say you are long Wheat, and it has a significant reaction, back down to a level that has been named in the press, or that you can see on your charts, as an area it has had trouble dropping through in the past. If you are still in the market on the long side, it would be advisable to place your protective stops just below this support area, along with a short order to sell Wheat at 5 or 10¢ below the support zone. This way you are covered whichever way the market moves. It is not our purpose in this chapter to get into methods of market entry, but this seemed an appropriate place to make this observation. Short-term traders will find levels of support and resistance to be in general of less use in stop placement, than in the initiation of orders. Long-term traders, on the other hand, will find many more occasions to set their stops using levels of support and resistance rather than the methods already discussed.

We find some traders using their stop placement in conjunction with Bullish Consensus. It is possible to use this approach, but we will not go into detail here on its mechanics, because to be successful, it must be combined with other factors, such as chart patterns, Open Interest, and Volume, as well as Committments of Large Speculators; and we believe that the other methods presented in this chapter are both simpler to use and superior in results. A discussion of the use of all of these factors in determining trend changes in the initiation of positions is found in the other chapters in this volume.

One of the most intriguing methods of stop placement, as well as a method of adding to existing positions, that we have ever encountered is the 45-50-65 method. It is also one of the most difficult to use unless you develop a "feel" or a "skill" at sensing the proper way to do it. Though on the face of it, it sounds mechanical, in fact it involves quite a bit of art. We will discuss this method here in as much detail as possible because those of you who are given to more research and who have the time to perform it, may well be able to master this technique.

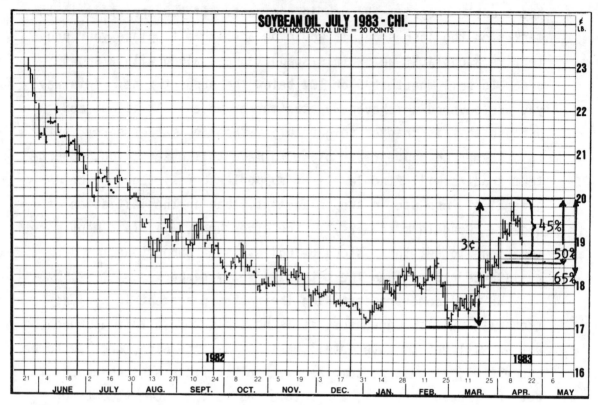

Figure 30

The basic thesis of the method is that ANY move in the market that moves <u>with</u> the trend will retrace itself by certain percentages. In our examples we will assume we are talking about a bull move. If Soy Oil has been trading as low as 17¢ a pound as shown in Figure 30, and starts up and hits 20¢, and then starts back down, the 45-50-65 Method states that in most cases it will retrace 50% of the upward move, or drop back to approximately 18½¢. The theory also states that an ideal place at which to add to your long positions is at a 45% retracement, because the 50% figure is not always hit exactly. In this case, it would recommend additional purchases at 18.65¢, a 45% reaction back from the temporary high of 20¢.

The theory further states that if the trend is a genuine one, the reaction will normally not carry back to 65% of the original move, so that point is an ideal place to put one's stops. In this case, a 65% retracement would be at 18.05¢. So, the trader using the 45-50-65 method who bought Soy Oil at a low point or at a trading range level point of 17¢, would add to his positions on a drop back to 18.65¢ and place his stops for the original and subsequent purchase at 18.05¢.

A more sophisticated variation of this requires that the stop placement at the 65% retracement level be on a close-only basis; and if you are following the market closely on a daily basis, this seems to work slightly better. Just the opposite approach would be true on a bear move, where the computations would involve adding to purchases on rallies of 45% from a low point, and placing protective stops at 65% from a low point. Often in the press or advisory services you will hear that a move made almost a perfect 50% rally or retracement.

The 45-50-65 method is based on a complicated set of theories involving supply and demand considerations, Open Interest, and how large buyers and sellers normally react to rallies and reactions. We have done considerable research on this method and have found it many times to be extremely accurate in predicting where a reaction or rally against the main trend will end. Since the method has not yet been overly popularized, we suspect there is much more here than merely a self-fulfilling prophecy. There is one major difficulty in using this approach, however, and that is in determining the point from which to take one's initial measurement when making the percentage computations.

To give an example, take the Soy Oil move just given, from a baseline point of 17¢. It goes up to 20¢, and then drops down to 18½¢, a perfect 50% retracement. Then it starts up again from 18½¢ and goes right on up to 22¢ before it starts another reaction. Now, at this point, the trader using the 45-60-65 method is faced with the problem of what point to use as the base, or reference point, to make his percentage computations. Should he pick the original point of 17¢ and set his stops at 65% back from the 22¢ high which would be at 18.75¢ or should he consider the other low point of 18½¢ as the reference point from which to measure? If he does, his stop loss point would be set at 19.72¢, and that is almost a one cent difference or $600 in risk differential from computing it the other way.

To further complicate matters, suppose the reaction stalls somewhere between the two 50% levels computed using both possible base points; in other words, somewhere between 20½¢ and 19½¢. To which point has the 50% retracement been made? To the original starting point of 17¢, or to the secondary point of 18½¢?

And next assume that Soy Oil, which dropped to 20¢, now runs straight up to 30¢ per pound. Which among several possible reference points is the proper one from which to make measurements? 17¢? 18½¢? or 20¢?

That is the kicker in attempting to use this method, as good as the results are. When the move is a _fait accompli_, after it is over, it is relatively easy to see which reference point the 50% retracement was back toward. (Hindsight always has 20/20 vision). But for predictive approaches, it is much more difficult. We believe that with further research, either by ourselves or by other traders, a more predictable way of establishing which reference points to use in various situations will be discovered; and that while this method will not be perfect, it will represent an improvement on what we now know.

Our research to this point has come up with some initial approaches. For a short-term trader, it appears to be generally best to use the _closest_ reference point both for stop-loss placement and for adding additional positions. The potential gains are less this way but so are the potential risks involved. For the long-term trader, the ideal method would be to use the _most distant_ reference point to compute his measurements from, but this entails losing an enormous amount of profit if the retracement is <u>not</u> a retracement but is a genuine change in trend.

Fortunately, we have developed some additional methods that, while more time-consuming, have greatly improved the results when using the 45-50-65 Method, and we will now go into them. First, the short-term trader should draw the steep trendlines on his charts and then compare them with where a 65% retracement would be. IF the 65% retracement is <u>above</u> the steep trendline, then we would suggest that the trader add to his positions at the 45% level, and place his stops at the 65% level. Conversely, if the 65% retracement is <u>below</u> the steep trendline, we would suggest not adding to his positions at the 45% level, and to place his protective stops at the steep trendline level.

For long-term traders, a similar approach can be utilized, using the LEAST STEEP trendline method; or different combinations can be tried, involving the 4-week low, the least steep trendline, and a 65% retracement to the lowest level where percentage calculations could begin. There are a multitude of possibilities in determining the validity of the 65% retracement-level stop placement by adding possible other validation factors such as moving averages, momentum oscillators, and Bullish Consensus changes. In fact, there are so many possible combinations of indicators to test in order to find if there is any optimum combination of validating signals, that a definitive way of using the 45-50-65 Method may never be found. For those of you like us, however, who want to research it, the possibilities are fascinating.

The way the real market professionals set their initial stops, move them up to the break-even point, and then trail them is determined by two things; by their own inclinations and by the type of the market itself. A long-range trader will use long-range type stops as we have discussed in this chapter only with those markets that appear to be gearing up for a sustained move. If the trader is a true pro, and does not see a good long-range trade, he will either pass the markets entirely or will enter into a good-looking short-range trade, and change his method of stop placement.

The professionals have two characteristics that typically are lacking in many amateur traders: patience and flexibility. Patience in their ability to wait for their types of trades, and in moving their stops the way they know from experience they should be moved. Flexibility in their ability to switch methods of stop placement as the nature of the market position unfolds itself, going from long-term stops to short-term ones or vice versa, as conditions dictate.

For either the beginner or the experienced trader, the best way to develop the skill of stop placement in different types of markets is to take a set of old charts, and move a blank piece of paper from left to right across them one at a time, day by day, and practice choosing where he would place his stops, based on what he has seen of the market action up to that point. This will give any trader a lot of experience in using all the different methods of stop placement discussed in this chapter.

But regardless of the number of methods a trader may be familiar with, stop placement is still more of an art than any other aspect of commodity trading. There are many tried and true methods of stop placement, both for initial protective stops and for trailing stops, and many good guidelines on when to use which method. In spite of all of these guidelines, there are still enough eccentricities in the marketplace that you need more than just a good grasp of the mechanics of stop placement; you must also develop the skill of using these guidelines automatically, and of knowing, or rather feeling, when to change methods.

CHAPTER 6

TOP & BOTTOM PICKING

It seems on casual observation that the quickest way to great riches in the commodity markets would be the ability of a trader to pick the absolute top or bottom in a market. It has been written many times that if a trader could do this just once or twice a year, unfailingly, that would be all he had to do to ensure his financial success. This chapter on how the professionals in commodity speculation do pick tops and bottoms, will explore the subject in great detail.

If we have seen it written once, we have seen it dozens of times in print that it is impossible to pick tops and bottoms. Virtually all authors who deal with this subject write that it would be wonderful to be able to pick tops and bottoms even occasionally. One popular author has even written that if you make twenty tries at picking a top or bottom during a year and are right only once, you will make substantial profits for the year. Of course, he neglects to mention that the ability to pick a top or bottom involves other abilities as well.

We have known a number of traders over the years who had an uncanny knack for being able to pick tops and bottoms of markets with considerable accuracy. Nevertheless many of these traders consistently lost money, despite having this ability. In addition to recognizing at what point a top or bottom in a market has occurred and entering the market near that point, a trader must also have some degree of expertise in stop placement and money management.

If a trader has picked, let's say, a bottom in Corn, at $2.50 a bushel and enters at $2.60, even if the market goes up to $3.50 a bushel (or more) he may still end up losing money, due either to poor stop placement that takes him out of the market too soon or to poor money management that returns too little profit on the trade to make up for other, losing trades. The subjects of money management and stop placement are discussed in detail in other chapters of this book. They are important to any trader who is seriously interested in using the approach of top and bottom selection trading.

One reason picking tops and bottoms has seemed impossible to so many advisors and commodity theoreticians is that most commodities make only one significant top and one significant bottom during the course of a year. On occasion, however, this is not true, as in the case of a commodity that is in an extended sideways trading pattern which appears as an almost horizontal line with little (or sometimes big) dips and rises.

These sideways trading patterns are seldom seen in commodities that have a definite life cycle, such as the Grains, Meats, Foods, Woods, and Fibers. From a theoretical standpoint, the Metals, Currencies, and Financial Instruments would be more prone to such sideways trading patterns; but given the volatility of both the domestic and the world economic situation in the eighties, it is unlikely that many of them will go into such patterns for any extended period of time.

While it is true that most commodities make only one significant top and bottom in the course of a year, this is no reason to assume that those tops and bottoms cannot be predicted with a reasonable degree of accuracy. Authors on commodity trading tend to feel that there are so many variables that affect the actual location of tops and bottoms that this multiplicity of factors in itself makes both the recognition of formations at the time they occur and the prediction of them before they occur impossible.

Nothing could be further from the truth. These authors are correct in recognizing that there are a number of factors, both technical and fundamental, that work together to bring about the peaking or bottoming in prices of a commodity. But in most cases they have failed to realize that the very existence of all these factors is in itself an advantage in determining and predicting tops and bottoms. The multitude of factors either affecting these formations or causing them to develop, contain in themselves a way to recognize and predict the very tops and bottoms that are supposed to be unrecognizable and unpredictable. And having more than one or two factors that are predictive in nature allows for cross-checking and validation of the potential tops and bottoms.

Another reason many technically-oriented writers claim it is almost impossible to pick tops and bottoms is the existence of what they see as false chart signals. Some writers have said that chart patterns are often so deceiving that the patterns which do appear in conjunction with top and bottom formations are virtually useless because they frequently appear under other circumstances too. They do, of course; but here is where having a multiplicity of other factors involved becomes critically important.

When potential top and bottom chart formations (or price action signs) take place, it is often possible to tell if they are accurate or false signals simply by considering the other factors involved and seeing whether these other factors also predict an imminent top or bottom. So even though it sometimes appears impossible to forecast accurately or to recognize top and bottom formations, it really isn't impossible. The constant and repetitive pronouncements from commodity writers about the impossibility of doing so have tended to make it a self-fulfilling prophecy for many commodity speculators.

Having shown why it appears so difficult to pick tops and bottoms while in reality it is not so difficult as it looks, we will now proceed to a discussion of when and how to recognize and

122

predict tops and bottoms.

Since major tops and bottoms, by definition, occur only once each year, the commodity speculator must examine all commodities with that in mind. In other words, he must be patient and not assume there will be a top or bottom forming in some commodity every day or every week. Since there are approximately 30.35 major commodities traded on American exchanges, and 52 weeks in the year, from a statistical standpoint there is an average of less than one top forming every other week, and one bottom forming every other week. Unfortunately, reality is not that simple; otherwise a trader could sit down and say to himself "Hmm, in the next two weeks, which commodity will form a top and which will form a bottom?"

Since many commodities move in unison, or close to it, and others move in direct opposition to one another, there exists the significant probability that several will top or bottom together. For instance, Soybeans, Soy Meal, and Soy Oil frequently top and bottom in unison. Often Plywood and Lumber do the same thing. Gold, Silver, and Platinum generally run in unison; the financial instruments do the same. Bellies and Hogs often top and bottom together. These are only a few examples of commodities that are likely to reach their peaks or valleys together.

When these commodities do not move in unison, it is generally due to some specific fundamental occurrence that prevents them from doing so; a fundamental occurrence that affects one of them but not the others. For this reason, as we will discuss later in the chapter, fundamental analysis cannot be ignored when picking tops and bottoms. The reasons that professionals can successfully pick tops and bottoms is that they recognize this uniformity of move- ment, are able to select from among the different commodities that are moving in unison the one that has the greatest probability of actually topping or bottoming, and then to single out the com- modity that has the potential for the greatest ensuing move.

For example, let's say the professional analyst determines, from the methods we will be discussing shortly, that Gold, Silver, and Platinum all appear to be forming a top. He will examine all three first from a fundamental standpoint to determine if any of the three has some particular reason that might prevent it from starting to decline in price. Let's say that among the three commodities mentioned, Gold at the particular time does exhibit such reasons. Perhaps there has been a strike in the gold mines in South Africa that appears likely to continue for some time; or a war has broken out there that will disrupt gold production seriously. Perhaps the Federal Government has announced it is suspending all gold sales for 12 months, or the Russians have entered an economic period where they will have to be using their gold reserves to purchase goods on the international market.

These are only a few possibilities, and similar possibilities could apply to any other group of commodities that tend to move in unison. So if one or more fundamental factors are occurring that might prop Gold prices up, or at least retard their decline, the professional analyst will scratch Gold from his list of precious metals that may be topping. Gold may in fact top out anyway; but with these fundamental factors weighing on the market, the analyst will look at Silver and Platinum to see if either of these is a better possibility. At this point (considering Silver and Platinum) we will not be taking into account the variance in Original Margin requirements, as these requirements will vary from time to time. We would like to note, however, that the professional will calculate his risk as a percentage of Original Margin, based on where his stop will be placed for each commodity, in order to determine if either one has a significantly higher risk factor initially.

The next thing the professional will do is to calculate the potential of the move (down, in this case). He may look at the charts, both short-term and long-range, for Silver and Platinum and

find that their patterns during the previous bull
move were somewhat different. Let's say Silver began its move up
after a period of consolidation around $6.00 per ounce, and
is now at $15.00 per ounce. The chances are that the ensuing bear
move, if a top is really forming, will stall at the support level
of $6.00. So the potential in this move is $9.00 per ounce, or
$45.00 profit. Now he looks at Platinum and finds the move began
in the vicinity of $300 per ounce and his risen to an apparent top
of $500 per ounce. He will assume that the potential downmove
will be the difference between the two, or $200 an ounce, which
would result in a potential profit of $10,000. At this point
Silver appears to be the better selection of the two because of
the greater profit potential, but at the same time, perhaps Silver
requires an initial margin of $10,000, while Platinum has an origi-
nal margin requirement of only $5,000.

So for an investment of $10,000, the professional can take
either 1 contract of Silver or two of Platinum. Assuming that the
initial risks between the entry points and initial protective stop
points are approximately equal for both metals, the two contracts
of Platinum (assuming the calculations of the potential downmove
are reasonably accurate) would yield potential profits of $20,000
for an investment of $10,000 as opposed to potential profits of
only $45,000 on a $10,000 investment in one Silver contract.
Clearly, the Silver trade offers substantially greater profits; in
fact, over 100% additional profits in this example. This is how
the professional trader might discriminate between two or more different commodities in the same complex (or in different complexes)
that are moving in unison and are interrelated in their price movement in some way.

To take a brief look at the risk factor mentioned in this
example; originally we assumed that the initial risk was identical. However, let's look at a real example to see how a professional trader would evaluate this situation. With the Silver

trade, if he saw that he could enter the market at $14.50 and place his initial stop at $15.00, he would be risking $2,500 between his entry point and stop loss placement. With the Platinum trade, if he could enter the market at $450 per ounce and place his stop at $500 per ounce, he would then be risking $2,500 in this case too. But in the Platinum trade the $2500 represents 50% of his original margin of $3,000, while in the Silver trade (because of different original margin requirements) the $2500 represents a 25% risk of his original margin of $10,000. So an equal dollar risk is not an equal percentage risk. The professional trader would then have to decide whether he was willing to accept twice as much percentage risk on the Platinum trade in order to make a potential gain of 50% less profits. Here the disparity in percentage risk and profitability is so great that the pro would definitely take the Silver trade.

Now we want to discuss how to spot the most likely candidates for a market that is getting ready to make a top or a bottom. This discussion will differ from later parts of this chapter in that here we will deal with generalities such as eliminating poor potential candidates, and narrowing the field down somewhat, while later on we will deal with the specifics of isolating the best choices from among the initial potential candidates. As a first consideration, if a commodity has not been doing much over the past several months (that is, if it has been moving either in a trading range or in a whipsaw manner), then it can be generally eliminated as a commodity that may be topping out. The opposite is true, however, for a potential bottom. If the commodity has been trading in a sideways pattern for at least a couple of months and is at an historically low price as in Figure 31, or at a price level that shows up on long-range charts as a significant support area, then it is a potential candidate for a market that is in a bottom formation.

126

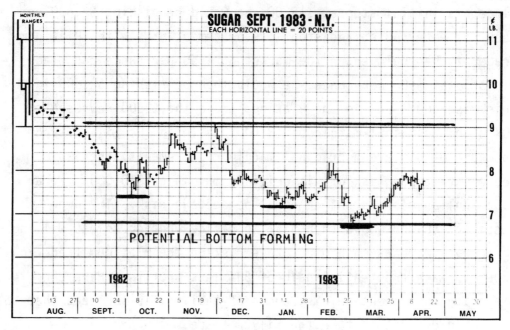

Figure 31

Commodities that fall in trading patterns in the middle and upper range of historical price action can be eliminated out of hand because they do not approach either the top or bottom price levels. After eliminating these commodities, the next consideration is Seasonal Charts. These charts show the seasonal tendencies for commodities on a calendar year basis, and are tied to the consumption, production, and demand for each commodity that varies fairly regularly on a cyclical basis every calendar year. Seasonal charts are available from a number of sources. These charts are not infallible, although many traders believe they are and trade from them religiously.

For example, Live Cattle tend to hit their highs in the July-August period as shown in Figure 32. So if it were February you would not want to discount Cattle completely as a market that might be topping out; but seasonally speaking, if Cattle do top out in February, that is unusual, and the fact would alert you to exa-

mine other aspects of this possible topping action for verification
that this year Cattle are not behaving as they usually do.

Seasonal Pattern: LIVE CATTLE

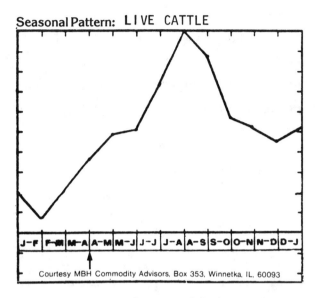

Courtesy MBH Commodity Advisors, Box 353, Winnetka, IL, 60093

Figure 32

For example, in 1980, Live Cattle topped in the October-November
period, 3 months later than seasonally indicated. Anyone who sold
in August when the market appeared to be heading down and placed
his stops any closer than 3¢ above the July highs would have been
stopped out in October when Cattle made their real high. A major
use of seasonal tendencies then is as a "warning flag" to check a
particular commodity more closely when the market, for whatever
reason, is not behaving as it generally does every year.

The simplest way to isolate a potentially topping market is
to find on your charts a market that has been going up from a low
price range for a minimum of three months. The average bull
market rises from its lows to a top in 5-6 months. The longer the
bull market has been going on, the more likely your candidate is
near a top.

The second criterion for isolating such potential markets,
after you have found one that has been going up for at least 3

128

months (and preferably for 5 months or more, is to look at
the amount of increase in prices during that time. The reason for
this is two-fold. First, if the increase has been minimal, say in
Pork Bellies a move from 45¢ to 55¢, then the chances may be that no
top is in the offing, regardless of whether it has been 5 months
in formation or not. The second reason is that even if a top is
going to form, the potential on the downside for a sustained bear
move is greatly reduced.

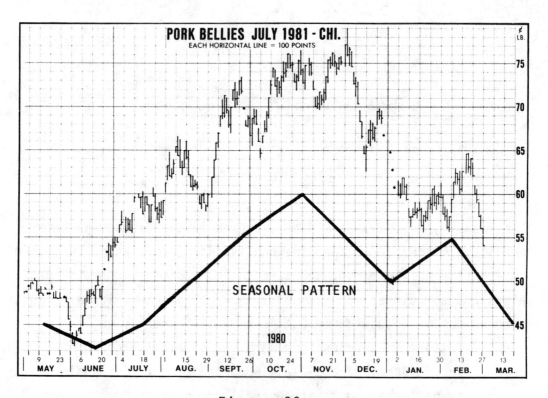

Figure 33

What would be far better is a move such as July 1981 Bellies
made over a six-month period from June of 1980 through december of
1980 which saw prices rise from 43¢ to 79¢ as illustrated in Figure
33. Here we have a sustained move time-wise and a broad move price-
wise. This is a far better candidate than the former example. So,
in a bull market, initially you will be looking for a move that has
covered a lot of time and has risen significantly in price.

Bear markets are a bit different, in that they predominantly fall into two patterns instead of one, as in bull markets, with regard to price motion. Bottoms are generally of two different types. The first, which is referred to as a "V-bottom", resembles an upside-down version of most market tops, in that prices here move violently in one direction, only to reverse themselves suddenly and head back up again. This type of bottom is not the most common, but traders should be aware of its existence in order to watch for its possible occurrence.

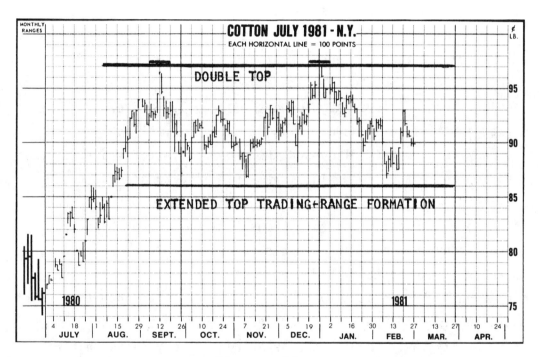

Figure 34

Most bottom formations occur a bit differently from top formations. Top formations almost never reach a top and then go sideways for any significant period of time. An exception to this rule can be seen in the price movement of Cotton from September of 1980 through at least the next 5 months as shown in Figure 34, during which time it traded in a wide-swinging trading range.

That, however, is an exception to the usual formation of tops. In market bottoms, we normally see prices decline from their tops, over a period of months, until they reach a long-term support area. One imperfect but useful rule is that often the longer it takes a market to make its top, the faster it will collapse down to that support area. Conversely, the faster a bull market runs up to its top, generally the decline down to its bottom support area will take much longer than the bull phase of the market. Again, this is generally but not always true.

Once the bear move has dropped to this long-term support area, markets generally then go sideways for at least one month and more often for two months or longer. Often this sideways pattern is not a true trading range or horizontal pattern, but rather has a slight downtrend or uptrend to it. The key point is that the rate of deceleration in prices has slowed tremendously, and even if the market is still going down, it is doing so only slightly.

Now that we have discussed the generalities of spotting potential top and bottom formations, we would like to present a more detailed technique of seeing these formations as they occur. First we will examine top formations. Nearly every trader has heard of double-top and head-and-shoulder formations, but we want to review these patterns. A double top takes place when the market has risen to a certain point, retreats down from that point and then rises to the same price level a second time, only to start backing away from it. Conventional theory holds that when such a pattern forms, it is a top, and a sell order should be placed just below the point reached when the market backed away from its first high.

This is an extremely reliable top formation, and it occurs frequently as shown in Figure 35. Just because it is discussed so often, many traders seem to have become complacent about it, evidently believing that anything that is so well-known cannot be all that accurate.

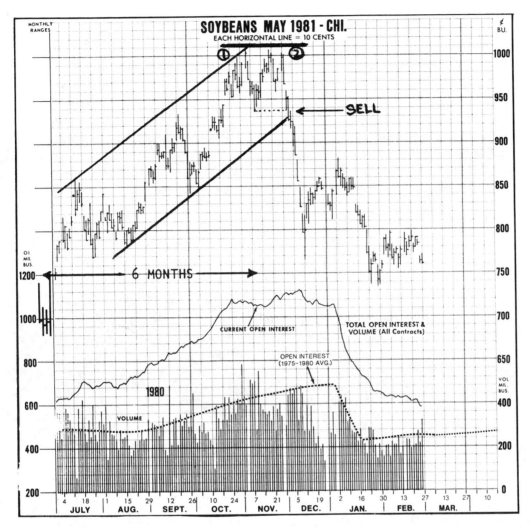

Figure 35

On the contrary, it is a good way to pick tops, especially if the
market is at the relatively high price level and has been in a
sustained up-move for a period of at least 3 months (and preferably
for five months or longer). If the time period has been less, or
the price move not very significant in scope, or if prices are not
at a relatively high level for that particular year, then the
reliability of using the double-top formation is greatly reduced.

The second most reliable top formation is sometimes called the
head-and-shoulders, and in certain cases, the triple-top as shown

132

in Figure 36. This is similar to the double top except that a third attempt to break contract highs takes place and fails, and then the market starts to decline. We have found in our research that a triple top, which is different from a head-and-shoulders formation in that all three highs are at almost the same price level (or occasionally at exactly the same price level) is much more reliable in indicating a top than is the head-and-shoulders.

Figure 36

The head-and-shoulders is different from a triple-top formation in that there are three peaks, or highs, but they are not all at the same price level, and generally the middle peak is the highest of

the three. Conventional trading practice suggests that the two
low points or retreats from the first two tops be connected by a
line, which is generally slanted down, and that the trader should
enter the market when this line (extended out in time) is broken
through on the downside.

We have found that this approach results in an unnecessary
loss of profits, and instead suggest that a sell order be placed
just a tick below the lower of the two dips unless the neckline is
sloped upward. Generally, when this level is broken through, especially on a close-only basis, that is confirmation of a bear
market's beginning. Frequently the slanted line connecting the two
dips is at somewhat of a downward angle, resulting in an entry
point significantly lower than in using our method of placing sell
orders just below the lower of the two dips.

The last major type of top occurs when the market has been
zooming upward, and then suddenly and without warning turns around
and heads down without indicating any kind of formation. Many
theorists claim that the only way to catch these sudden-forming
tops is by watching for key reversal days. In a bull market, a
key reversal day appears when prices rise significantly for the
day but close on or near their lows, and close below the lows of
the preceeding day.

Looking at the bull move in Corn from June of 1980 through its
sudden top at the end of November of the same year as shown in
Figure 37, if one had used the key reversal day concept to try to
pick the market top he would have had occasions to reverse his
position (all of them traps) and when the reversal did come in late
November, the day the market made its top was not a key reversal
day at all. There is a way to pick these tops, however, and we
will discuss that later when we cover the near-perfect yet often
overlooked method for identifying market tops.

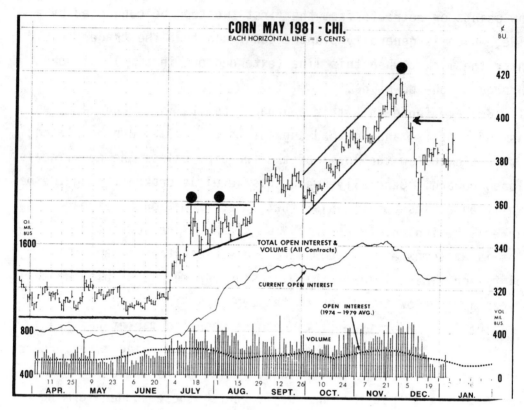

CORN MAY 1981 - CHI.
EACH HORIZONTAL LINE = 5 CENTS

Figure 37

Bottom formations have some similarities and some differences with top formations. They too form double and triple bottoms and head and shoulder bottoms (which are inverted or mirror-images of head-and-shoulder tops), and they form those sudden bottoms that are just the opposite of the sudden tops we have just discussed, and are called V-bottoms because of their resemblance to a V. These formations are all in addition to the extended trading pattern we have previously discussed which occurs at a low support level after a sustained downmove.

The major difference between bottom formations and top formations is the time it takes them to develop in. Generally, the double-top that took, in the case of the Soybean complex in late 1980 anywhere from 3 to 4 weeks, will be extended out in a double-

bottom take two to three months. Generally, but not always. For
every rule such as this, there are exceptions where a double-bottom
forms in 3 weeks instead of three months. What we are speaking of
here is the way that occurs most often.

Many traders, in their hurry to get in on a market bottom,
will prematurely identify a double bottom or an inverse head-and-
shoulders in what is really only a series of minor rallies and
reactions. Our major caution in identifying bottom formations is
not to be too precipitous in believing you have one. When you
think you do, you must use other indicators (which we shall discuss
shortly) to confirm that you may in fact have a bottom forming much
more rapidly than is usually the case. Only by doing this can you
verify a rapidly forming bottom pattern.

In any case, it is prudent to use these other indicators as
double-checks whether the pattern for the top or bottom is
compressed or extended in time. Order entry for double-bottoms and
inverse head-and-shoulder formations is handled the same way, as
for market tops, only in reverse. Thus, for a double bottom, you
would place a resting buy order just above the highest point of the
rally that preceeded the second bottom, and place your initial protective stops just below the lower of the two lows. Similarly,
with an inverse head-and-shoulders or triple bottom, your resting
buy order would be just above the higher of the two rallies.

In both cases it is important to calculate your risk in
dollars between your entry point and your stop-loss point. If the
dollar risk is greater than you are willing to assume, you can take
the chance of moving your stop point up higher to a level you can
live with even though you are increasing your risk of getting
stopped out on a reaction.

The absolutely safest bottom formation to enter is one where
prices have been in the extended trading pattern we discussed
earlier and seen in Figure 31, either horizontal or trending
slightly up or down. In this case you draw two horizontal lines,

136

one just above the trading range (even if it is at a slight angle)
and one just below it. You place your resting buy orders just
above the upper horizontal line, and your initial protective stops
just below the lower horizontal line, and again calculating the
amount of dollar risk involved should the market reverse itself.
Often if you look at this horizontal or near-horizontal pattern
very carefully, you can detect a double-bottom or head-and-
shoulders formation which is almost hidden in the length of horizontal movement and the narrowness of vertical price movement.

Many writers have supposedly identified other top and bottom
formations, but all of these are merely minor variations of the
ones we have described. When you see what appears to be a V-bottom
formation, it is best to act with extreme caution because even
though one hears a great deal about this formation, it appears much
less frequently than many writers would have you believe. Unlike
its bull counterpart where the move is sudden and without any
corrections, when a V-bottom occurs there is also in most cases a
tiny double bottom which is often overlooked because it occurs over
a period of two to three weeks. When your other indicators are
calling for a bottom to be formed, and it appears to be a V-bottom,
it is often wisest to watch for and trade it as a compressed double
bottom formation.

There is one little-known method of picking tops and bottoms
that often works with an uncanny degree of accuracy. It does take
a bit of practice to get the feel for it, but the time spent is
well worth it. We call this rule our 65% Method, and simply
stated it is this: when a market that has been moving in one
direction for a significant period of time (in a zig-zag fashion)
moves in the opposite direction 65% of its last move in the original direction, then the trend has reversed itself.

An example will make this clear and can be seen in Figure 37.
Let's say corn has been in a bull market for the past 5 months,
first moving up, then having a reaction, then moving up again, etc.

On the last reaction, it bottomed at $3.87, and then continued up to $4.18, a 31¢ move. At this point it started down again. The question is, was the downmove another in a long series of reactions as the market continued on its bull course toward ever-new highs, or was this latest reaction not a reaction at all but a reversal, sudden and without any head-and-shoulder formation or double-top formation?

What we do is take 65% of the 31¢ last upmove and come up with 20¢. We place a resting sell order there at $3.98, as our rule states that if that point is hit (that is, if the market retraces 65% of its last upmove) then the trend has reversed completely.

Sound too good to be true? Well, the example we used was for the May, 1981 corn contract, and this is exactly what happened before the big collapse of early December. Traders who had a resting sell order in at $3.98 were able to realize a profit of over $1,400 in just 6 trading days! Obviously, this technique will not work in sideways trending markets, but we have our horizontal-lines method for those.

The 65% method does require a sawtooth or zig-zag, clearly trending market in order to work, but it is one of the two best ways to pick up V tops and V bottoms. The only skill that has to be developed is in picking the points from which to make your measurements, but that is not too difficult to do as long as you are using the type of market we described. A good rule of thumb is to make certain that the low point from which you make your first measurement is 3 to 4 weeks distant from the high point. This seems to fit the majority of the situations we have encountered.

We mentioned that the 65% Method is one of the two best ways to pick V tops and V bottoms. We would now like to detail the other method for these situations. It is similar to the 65% Method in that it does take some practice to develop a feel for doing it correctly. But, when used in conjunction with the 65%

138

Method, it provides a double check for picking a V top or bottom. For this second method, we use Weekly Charts instead of daily bar charts.

Weekly charts show the high, low and close for the most nearby contract month, so if the contract month you are interested in is a more distant month, as it probably will be, you must interpolate the figures from the nearby month to the month you are interested in trading. As the bull or bear move progresses over time, you begin drawing trendlines in on your weekly chart, connecting the bottoms of reactions for a bull market and the tops of rallies for a bear market. If the market turn is going to be of the V type, then the trendlines you are drawing will usually become steeper and steeper angles as the weeks go by. When this trendline is broken, IF it is going to be a V top or V bottom, you have picked your entry point by having a resting buy or sell order each week at a tick just below or above the trendline, with your stop placed just above the high (or low in a bear market) of the move.

If the formation turns out not to be a V top or V bottom, but instead turns into a double top or bottom or a head and shoulders pattern, you generally will be safe by having your stop just beyond the contract high in a bull market, or below the low in a bear market. In the case of March, 1981 corn that we used in the previous example, such a trendline on the weekly charts would have called for an entry point of $4.08, instead of the $3.98 called for by the 65% Method. What we have found is that the real professionals who use these methods in conjunction, do so in one of two ways. If the professional is of a conservative bent, he would have used the lower of these two figures even though he had to place his initial protective stop further away, because the lower figure ($3.98) provides stronger verification of a trend reversal than does the higher figure. The more aggressive trader, on the other hand, would have used the higher of the two figures ($4.08) to try to capture more profits. Many professionals, however, combine the two methods if they are trading multiple contracts, and most professionals do. So in this case, if our professional trader were trading in 15 contract lots, he would have sold 5 or 7 of them at the higher level of $4.08 and the balance at the $3.98 level.

Used in conjunction with the other methods of detecting tops and bottoms that we have already discussed, there is only one other really good charting method of picking tops and bottoms, and that is what we call the TRIAD method.

The TRIAD method often will pick up tops and bottoms when other methods fail to do so, and frequently acts as a confirmation and validation of the other methods. When two or more methods all indicate that a top or bottom has been or is being formed, this is an extremely powerful signal; and if a trader is limited in his available capital, and must choose between several possble candidates, he is well-advised to trade the commodity that is showing multiple signals of a top or bottom formation. See Figure 38.

Visually the TRIAD resembles a double top that has been skewed in the direction opposite to the major trend. In a bull market for example, the market forms a peak and retreats from it (but not as much as 65%) and doesn't break the weekly trendline in the process. It starts down in a reaction, stops and goes up again. However, the key difference here between the TRIAD and the double top is that it doesn't rise extremely close to the former peak before it starts another reaction. To use the TRIAD method, you would have a resting sell order just a bit below the low of the last reaction. As an example, March 1981 Soybean Meal rose from about $190 a ton to $300 in a sustained bull move that covered 4 months. After it hit $300, it had a reaction back to about $274, then started back up again, only to stall at $294, which on the charts did not look high enough to be a double top formation.

140

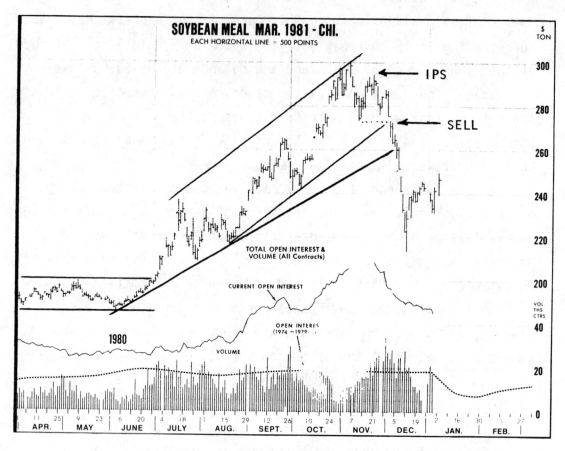

Figure 38

The trader using the TRIAD method would have placed a resting sell order in the vicinity of $272 and waited to see if it was filled. It was, as the market crashed through it and went down, almost straight down to $214, a profit of $5,800 in 9 trading days.

While at times this method can appear to overlap with the double top or double bottom formation, it is actually somewhat different, in that the moves are not sufficiently close to the last top in a bull market or the last bottom in a bear market to really be a double top or double bottom, and therefore they are overlooked by the vast majority of traders. Another advantage of using the TRIAD method when applicable is in the reduction of initial risk. With a double top or double bottom, you normally place your stop

just beyond the contract high or low. With a TRIAD, you can place
your stop, in a bull market, just above the second, or lower peak.

In the preceding example where Soybean Meal topped at $300 and
then on its second move up stalled at $294, your stop could have
been placed at $295, just above the second, lower peak. If you
use weekly instead of daily charts to look for this formation, it
will be much clearer, and the percentage of correct trend reversals will be even greater than if you use daily charts. Again,
if you do use the weekly charts, you must interpolate the figures
from the nearby month (which these charts are constructed from) to
the more distant month that you wish to trade in.

Besides recognizing the chart patterns that indicate tops and
bottoms, a trader must also realize that all of these patterns may
sometimes prove to be traps, in that they do not always accurately
indicate a true top or bottom. How then can the trader find a way
to improve the accuracy of these patterns? Fortunately there is a
way to help validate these potential top and bottom formations,
and that is by the use of Bullish Consensus.

Bullish Consensus states that when 80% or more of the advisory
services are bullish on a commodity, then the bull market is due to
reverse itself, and when 30% or less of the services are bullish on
a commodity, then the bear market is about to reverse itself and
start up again. Traders who use this method almost exclusively in
their trading refer to themselves as "contrarians" and frequently
sell any commodity when its Bullish Consensus rises above 80% and
buy any commodity when its bullish consensus drops to 30% or less.
At times this method works very well by itself, but generally it
does not. Bullish Consensus can be extremely helpful when certain
conditions are placed on its use in validating top and bottom formations.

A good basic rule is to look at any potential top or bottom
formation with a jaundiced eye if the Bullish Consensus is less
than 80% for a potential top and greater than 30% for a potential

bottom. The closer the Bullish Consensus moves to 100%, the greater the likelihood of a top being formed; and conversely, the closer the Bullish Consensus moves to 0%, the greater the chance that a bottom is forming. Another good rule to follow when using Bullish Consensus to validate a potential top or bottom formation is to have a large Open Interest figure. The greater the Open Interest, the more accurate are the predictive qualities of the Bullish Consensus figure; and if possible use Contrary Opinion figures only when Open Interest exceeds 10,000 contracts for the commodity in question.

Another guideline when utilizing Bullish Consensus to validate your formations is to question the Bullish Consensus figures if Open Interest is increasing steadily. Once the Open Interest stabilizes somewhat or is increasing only slightly, then the Bullish Consensus figures become more meaningful. As long as the Open Interest is increasing for a given commodity, new traders are entering that market and the price trend is likely to continue.

The last rule for seeing whether or not Bullish Consensus figures can be used in identifying tops and bottoms is a bit more subjective, but it can be useful at times as a final validation; and that is to watch the news on the commodity in question, preferably in the Wall Street Journal. When you see news that is favorable to the way the market is moving, and the market fails to respond to it by making at least a moderate move in the main trend direction, then the Bullish Consensus figures are confirmed as being indicative of a top or bottom formation taking place.

To tie this all together, let's say you have what may be a double top formation starting to take place in a commodity. The complete validation that it actually is a double top, and not just a consolidation of prices, would be that the Bullish Consensus is 80% or more, and preferably increasing steadily but leveling off; and a press report of a bullish news event doesn't really move the market up to any significant degree. If you have all or most of these pieces in place, the odds are extremely high that you've got a top. The converse is true, of course, for a bottom formation; except that Bullish Consensus must be less than 30%, and the news report would be bearish.

Since we have just mentioned utilizing news reports about the commodity you are following, we would like to state that while this at times is difficult to do unless you have access to sources of up-to-date news on your particular commodity, the importance of this technique should not be minimized. Many professional traders trade only on the news and make an excellent living doing that. Of course, they have developed sources for obtaining the latest news information on as many commodities as possible.

Whenever a bearish piece of news appears about a commodity and the market doesn't respond by moving lower, these traders start buying; and generally they end up with a profitable position, although not necessarily a bottom. Often it is a substantial rally, and they keep their stops close or close their positions out when a target price they feel is reasonable is hit. We mention all of this to emphasize that using news stories and rumors can be a useful adjunct to your other methods of accurately forecasting tops and bottoms.

We mentioned earlier that we have found key reversal days not to be of much use by themselves. One has only to look at a collection of charts to find how many key reversal days occur but do not signal a reversal in trend. One published study found that there was about a 50-50 chance after a key reversal day that the market would continue in its original direction. Of course what we have just said about bull markets applies in reverse to bear markets, where on a key reversal day prices will open significantly lower than the previous day's close, set new lows during the day, end up closing at or near their highs for the day, and close above the previous day's close.

Why then have so many writers emphasized the importance of trading key reversal days as an indication of change in trend,

when there is no better than an even chance that they are such an
indication? We believe the reason is that very often when a
market does top or bottom there is a key reversal day when the top
or bottom is formed, and therefore the assumption is made that all
key reversal days should be traded as if they were touchstones to
picking tops and bottoms. This is hardly true, since there will
be many key reversal days throughout the duration of the main
trend.

Is there any way then that the professional trader can use
key reversal days in this search for predicting tops and bottoms?
There certainly is; and that is by using these key reversal days
only in conjunction with the other methods we have described in
this chapter, as one more piece of data to validate his other
conclusions. If a potential double or triple top starts with a
key reversal day, that adds powerful confirmation to the
formation's really being a top. If seasonally the market is due
to peak or bottom at this particular time and you get a key reversal day, that too is a strong indicator that the market is in fact
topping or bottoming.

If your weekly trendline is broken after a key reversal day,
the violation of the trendline takes on even more meaning. And if
the key reversal day takes place when Contrary Opinion is calling
for a top or bottom, this is just one more sign that you really
have isolated a top or bottom and should start placing your orders.
So key reversal days are not totally useless; it is just that they
cannot be used by themselves unless you are trying to trade short-
term rallies and reactions. Used in conjunction with the other top
and bottom indicators we have discussed, they can mean a great deal
in confirming the other signals.

We now come to the last of our validation indicators, a pair
that many technically oriented analysts use by themselves in an
attempt to predict tops and bottoms, but which by themselves,
while useful, are often incorrect unless combined with the other

methods we have been discussing. This pair of indicators is
Volume and Open Interest. The first rule in using Volume and Open
Interest when attempting to locate a top or bottom formation is to
ignore them completely if they are relatively low. Looking at
your charts you can see from the price action of the preceding
months whether or not volume has dried up. We mean by this not
merely low levels of volume, but _very_ low levels - almost
nonexistent volume - which you will rarely see among the major
commodities; but we mention this as a warning. The same is true
of Open Interest, and this cautionary note would normally apply
only if the current Open Interest is below the curve of the
average Open Interest for the preceding five years.

In our research, we have found volume (unless it dries up
completely) to be of far less use in determining tops and bottoms
than Open Interest, which has significant validation powers. In a
top formation Open Interest will have increased for months, making
normal dips along the way as reactions occur. As the top is
formed there will usually be a decrease in the rate of increase of
Open Interest - a decrease in its acceleration. When open
interest starts leveling off, it is highly indicative that a top
is being formed.

As a rule you cannot wait until Open Interest starts declining
for a confirmation of the top, because that will be too late to get
into the market. You use your other signals and watch for a
stalling in the rise of Open Interest figures. In a bear market
Open Interest will have decreased over a period of months. But in
a bottoming formation, Open Interest will often tip you off to the
bottom before prices have broken out on the upside. Often, but not
always. What you need to look for is a change in the pattern of
open interest, from its declining or staying relatively flat at low
levels to a sudden spurt upwards. Sometimes the increase isn't
dramatic or violent, but comes more gradually as the commercials
begin covering their short positions in the belief that the fun-

146

damentals are about to become bullish. This works especially well in extended trading range bottoms, but it is usually good in the other types of bottoms too.

As we mentioned before, many analysts use Open Interest (and sometimes some sophisticated techniques utilizing Volume) as their sole tool for picking tops and bottoms. We do not recommend doing this, because so often the conclusive change in Open Interest, and in Volume too if it is being used, comes too late to be useful. It is only the use of Open Interest (in particular) in conjunction with your other tools that has true predictive value.

We have now covered all the tools that the professional trader finds most useful in recognizing and predicting tops and bottoms. When they are put together in one package, their reliability is astonishingly high. To summarize: watch your charts for bear or bull moves of long duration. These moves are best for top and bottom picking if they are approaching levels of historical support or resistance, although this is not a necessity. In bull markets, draw your weekly trendlines to catch V tops, and calculate the 65% reaction trend-change points. Look at the seasonal tendencies of the commodity in question to see if tops and bottoms tend to form approximately in the time period where you are now. Examine the Contrary Opinion figures, following the rules for using them that we have outlined above. Look for key reversal days as a potential validation of your other signals. Become familiar with the different top and bottom patterns that we have discussed so that you may recognize them as they begin to form. Watch the Open Interest figures and look for every scrap of news that is available on the commodity in question.

It is rare that you will find every one of these indicators in agreement about a top or bottom, but the more that do indicate a top or bottom, the better your probabilities of finding one and the more heavily you should invest in your position. When you do find a position where the majority of our indicators are in agreement, the chances are you will have an investment from which you can make large sums of money.

CHAPTER 7

PYRAMIDING

Pyramiding is one of the most exciting concepts of commodity speculation, in that it can be the fastest way to creating huge fortunes for the successful pyramider. It is also one of the most nerve-wracking approaches to commodity trading due to the fact that so very little has been written on the best ways to pyramid, and what has been written is often confusing and contradictory.

As with many areas of commodity trading, pyramiding is a subject that could cover an entire volume, but in most books on commodity trading, seldom is there more than a paragraph or at best a page or two devoted to the subject. We believe this is due not to a lack of interest in the subject, but rather to the fact that those individuals who have discovered how to successfully pyramid are reluctant to share their secrets with the general trading public.

Some years ago, I knew an individual who was an author of a number of books on casino gambling. While I had never read any of them myself, I understood that they were quite popular among casino gamblers, and offered a number of "systems" that were semi-successful. He told me that he frequently had to disguise himself when going to casinos, or send accomplices in his place to bet, as the income from his publications was not great enough to support the style of living to which he was accustomed.

When asked how he was so successful that many of the casinos had banned him from their establishments, and yet he was publishing books that theoretically would have caused the casinos likewise to

147

ban all of the readers of them who chose to practice the systems he recommended, his answer was simple: He said that while the information he had in his various books was genuinely informative and worthwhile, he had discovered what he felt was the <u>ultimate</u> way to beat the house at Blackjack, or "21", and that the possibilities of his publishing <u>that</u> for the general public were two: slim and none.

He said that if he did so, the casinos would either change their rules so his two methods would no longer work, or that if enough people started using those methods, the casinos would simply drop the games. How true these possibilities were, I have no way of knowing, but I do know <u>he</u> believed them; and since he was hugely successful in his gaming, he evidently had hit on methods that worked. But despite the fact that he might have been able to sell these systems for tens of thousands of dollars, he chose to keep them confidential, in his own private domain.

I suspect that much the same is true with the successful pyramid traders. Those who have written anything at all about the subject have provided tantalizing bits and pieces about it, giving some general guidelines, a few specific approaches, without putting them all together in a usable fashion. These individuals are the ones who have made millions of dollars by pyramiding, and to divulge to the general public their exact methods and total system for so doing might destroy their own future pyramiding possibilities; or at least they probably believe it would.

Since many traders, especially beginning ones, and sometimes even veteran traders, if they have not actively sought out information on pyramiding, do not really know what pyramiding itself is, it may be useful for us to go over briefly what pyramiding really is and what it really is not. Pyramiding refers to adding additional contracts to a position after the initial position has been established. Pyramiding in the strict sense makes no reference to how many contracts are taken initially, how many are added on subsequently, and whether the additional contracts are added on as the move progresses in the <u>favor</u> of the trader, or on <u>retracements</u> back toward the original entry point.

These factors, and many others, make up the fine points of the different methods of pyramiding. So, pyramiding just means that after you have taken a position in a commodity with "x" number of contracts, at some point in the future, you add either "1/2x" or "2x" or whatever number of additional contracts you like, according to some predetermined method. We say "predetermined method" cautiously, because many traders who do pyramid have <u>no</u> method in mind, and add contracts without a previously established plan of action. Usually, but not always, this is a disastrous approach. The reason not having a predetermined plan ever works depends wholly on chance, because the key to being successful in using pyramids is to have a sound plan, one that fits your personality, can be handled by the amount of capital you have, and is followed precisely yet flexibly.

Flexibility means that while the plan is, on the surface, a very exact one, it can be adapted and modified as circumstances dictate. This flexibility does not mean "flying by the seat of your pants" and changing your rules as time passes, but rather having a set of alternative actions planned well in advance to take care of unexpected occurrences in the marketplace; and if these things turn up, then an alternate route is already part of your plan. If this sounds a bit confusing now, the information that follows will clarify it. The important point here is to realize that pyramiding simply means adding to your original position after it is established.

The pros who pyramid successfully are generally big-money traders, although not many of them began that way. They disco- vered at some point the best ways to pyramid, and over the years have built their original equity up into small or large for- tunes. Unfortunately, from the average trader's viewpoint, these people are little known, and they prefer to keep a low profile. We have spoken with some of them over the years, and without exception, none of them has published any of their ideas or approaches to pyramiding.

Those authors who have published information about pyramiding, by and large, are not those individuals who use pyramiding as their main trading method. All of the pros we spoke with did so on the condition that we not identify them, and even then, they were somewhat nebulous about their exact methodology. Only by taking the bits of information each one revealed, and by piecing them together with what the others said, were we able to come up with a congruent picture of the experts' methods of pyramiding; and even so, some pieces may be missing. Even if the data we have compiled is not totally complete, it is comprehensive enough to enable us to correlate it and come up with a pretty accurate picture of how the pros pyramid so successfully.

The fact that the subject of pyramiding is of so much interest to the general commodity trader may also account for the reluctance of the very successful pyramiding traders to go into too much detail. In conversations with individual traders who either do not pyramid or who have been unable to pyramid success- fully, it has become obvious how much interest they have in the subject. Whenever the topic of pyramiding comes up, it seems that the trader's energy level increases dramatically, probably because he has a "gut-level" feeling that there is a lot of money to be made this way, if only he knew how.

This belies the statement made in one of the most popular books on commodity trading in recent years that the author of this book believes pyramiding is for "squares", and that he himself never, but never pyramids. There is an element of truth in these statements, in that it is very "square" to pyramid unless one really knows what he is doing, because certain types of pyramiding can be some of the fastest ways for a trader to go bankrupt.

In essence then, the people who pyramid successfully, year after year, are truly big-money traders' and for very sound reasons, they prefer not to be known to the general public or to have their methodology become common knowledge. Now that we have seen who it is that pyramids successfully, and why the whole area of pyramiding is so shrouded in secrecy, we will examine just how very profitable pyramiding can be, and how the trader with only a small amount of capital to begin with can utilize this approach.

The concept of pyramiding investment monies is nothing new, nor is it unique to the commodity markets. While race track players didn't originate it, they seem to be the group of people most familiar with the different methods of pyramiding and are also the group to use pyramiding most frequently. A goal of many horse players is to be able to get 19 winners in a row that pay even-money each. For those of you who are not familiar with racetrack terminology, an even-money payoff is one that returns a 100% profit for each dollar bet. Hence, a $2 bet results in a $4 payoff, in an even-money play: the original $2 is returned along with $2 profit. Since even-money horses win with great frequency, percentage-wise, many horse players devote their lives to determining the common factors among those even-money horses that do win; because if one starts with a $2 bet and wins, then bets the $4 back and wins, and continues to do so for a total of 19 consecutive wins, he has converted his original $2 into one million, forty-eight thousand, five hundred and seventy-six dollars; and after the first wager, he has nothing to lose of his own money except his original $2. All the rest he is risking along the way is the "track's" money, or other people's money.

To get back to commodities to give an example, we will use a simple type of pyramid, rounding off the figures slightly. Let's say that a trader, using whatever method he prefers to make his selections, decides that T-Bills, which are currently selling at 87.00, have a good probability to increase over time to 91.00.

152

Accordingly, he buys one contract, risking some portion of his original margin of $2,500, and sits and waits.

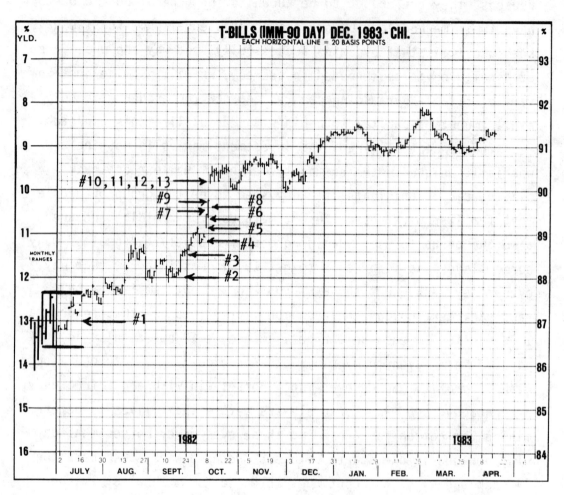

Figure 39

As the weeks or months go by, he is amply rewarded, as the price of T-Bills for this contract month does increase, despite reactions here and there. He hangs on, and when T-Bills hit his estimated figure of 91%, he sells out. Now, on the move of 4%, he has a tidy profit of $10,000; which isn't bad, even for a trade that has taken 6 months to come to fruition.

Now, another trader, who is either a big-money trader or who has learned how to pyramid successfully and knows how to handle the psychological stresses inherent in pyramiding, starts out the same way with a long position at 87.00. Of course, a real pyramider would probably have 5 or 10 contracts to begin with; but to keep this example similar to our first trader, we will assume that our pyramiding trader also starts out with one contract.

At any rate, our pyramider goes long one contract of T-Bills at 87.00. As the days pass, the price increases to 88.00, at which point he has a profit of 1% per contract, and with T-Bills being worth $2,500 for every 1% move, our pyramider has a paper profit of $2,500, which is exactly the amount of original margin required to purchase another contract of T-Bills.

This is just what our pyramiding trader does; he uses the $2,500 paper profits to purchase another contract, this time at 88.00. Notice that he now owns 2 contracts and still is only risking whatever his original risk was. He has doubled his holdings and has not increased his risk at all. When T-Bills reach 88.50, he now has enough paper profits on his first two contracts to buy another contract, so that he now has 3 contracts, again with no more risk than he originally incurred.

As T-Bills advance, his paper profits increase; and each time he has enough paper profits to add another contract, he does so, since he is constantly increasing the number of contracts he owns, it takes less and less of an increase in the price of T-Bills to produce an additional $2,500 worth of paper profits to add another contract.

In fact, it takes only a 0.33 increase from 88.50 to 88.83, to enable him to add his fourth contract. He continues to add contracts as T-Bills increase in price to 89.08, 89.28, 89.45, 89.60, 89.73, 90.20, 90.20, 90.20, and 90.20. His last contracts were purchased with only a 80.47 increase in price due to the gap. He now decides to stop adding contracts, because his target price of 91.00 is starting to get close. He has a total of 13 contracts, and never did he risk more than his original $2,500, which was the amount also risked by our first trader. When our pyramider cashes his contracts in at the 91.00 level, he has profits of almost $57,000 as compared to our other trader who netted profits of only $10,000.

In other words, the trader who pyramided, and risked no more than the first trader, ended up with almost 600% additional profit, all by using paper profits and pyramiding with them. As mentioned before, a real-life pyramider would have used a different method of pyramiding rather than this simplified one, and would have ended up with profits of more than $100,000 on this one trade. Some authors would argue that the trader could achieve the same results by taking an initial position of 6 contracts instead of his single contract, and that by so doing he would have saved himself a lot of trouble calculating the fine points of when and how to run the pyramid.

The latter argument is true; it _does_ take some time to manage a pyramid; but the financial rewards more than justify it. What these authors overlook, however, is that if the first trader had bought 6 contracts of T-Bills, he would have needed 6 times as much as the pyramiding trader, $15,000 as compared to $2,500. If one has the capital to begin with it is far better to start a pyramid with 6 contracts, because the paper profits accumulate much more rapidly, and the pyramider can add additional contracts faster.

By starting with 6 contracts, the pyramider would be able to add his next contract at 87.17 instead of having to wait until prices had increased to 88.00 as he did when he began with only one contract. From this discussion, you can see how extremely profitable pyramiding can be when compared with ordinary trading, especially when you consider that there is no additional risk involved.

Now that we have established how very profitable it is to pyramid, the question becomes "When to pyramid?" Clearly, with between 30 and 40 markets being traded on the exchanges, not all of them at any one time _lend_ themselves to pyramiding. How then

do you select those markets that are the very best opportunities
for pyramiding? Since most pyramids are long-range trades, and
only a few fall into the short-range category, it is obvious that
if you want to run a pyramid, you must identify a trade that has
long-range possibilities and the potential for a sustained and
significant move. There is an instance when short-term pyramids
can be done, and that will be discussed later.

The basic methods for identifying long-term trades are
discussed in another chapter. So, we will forego discussing how
to select long-range trading opportunities here, other than to say
that this type of trade is the most likely to produce gargantuan
profits when pyramiding. If you have your own methods of identifying long-range trading opportunities, you will find that these
methods will work well with our system of pyramiding procedure. We
will mention, however, that there are some basic clues to identifying these long-range trades. When looking for an opportunity
to institute a pyramid of a long-range nature, you must identify a
bottom formation from which prices can be expected either to rise
gradually or to explode upward.

The most useful ways of selecting these opportunities are to
look for those markets that have been in an extended trading range
for a period of at least a couple of months. The narrower the
trading range formation, the better the opportunity for a long-
range pyramid. Let's say Wheat has been trading between $2.75 and
$2.85 for three months, and that this has occurred at the end of a
long downmove. This is an excellent candidate for a long-range
bull pyramid. On the other hand, if Orange Juice has been in an
extended trading range of several months, bouncing back and forth
between 80¢ and $1.00, this is a poorer candidate, generally, because
of the breadth of the trading range.

The absolutely best long-range bull pyramids come from
those commodities that have been oscillating back and forth in a
relatively narrow price range for a significant period of time,

and historically are at a low level of prices. If in addition
this price range was established after a bear move, then this is a
commodity you will want to seriously consider pyramiding with. In
the example of wheat just given, let's say that several weeks or a
month before the trading range began, the price of Wheat for that
contract month was $4.00 per bushel, then came crashing down to
$2.75, and afterwards for weeks bounced around between $2.85 and
$2.75. This is a good possibility for a pyramid. On the other
hand, if wheat had been $5.00 per bushel, crashed down and found
support at $3.50, then moved between $3.50 and $3.60, it may not
be so good a candidate, if the seasonal probabilities are that
Wheat should still be going down for the next several months,
and if the significant chart support for Wheat is in the vicinity
of say $2.80 a bushel, then the trading range between $3.50 and
$3.60 offers limited opportunities of success to pyramid. It
might work, but with these negative factors weighing against it,
it is better to look elsewhere for better pyramiding opportunities.

Another factor that must be considered when identifying good
pyramiding possibilities is the commodity itself. A good candidate
for pyramiding should be a commodity that has a large Open
Interest, which means it is being traded rather heavily. When a
commodity is in an extended trading range, Open Interest, or the
number of outstanding contracts, will fall off due to lack of
investor interest because so little is happening with the price
action. However, among the more popular commodities, Open Interest
will always be high compared to the less popular commodities.
everything else being equal, an investor would prefer to institute
a pyramid in Wheat or Soybeans rather than in Oats or Orange Juice.
And a pyramider would almost never want to start a pyramid in
Broilers, Eggs, Potatoes, or Commercial Paper. The reason for this
is that the data on old charts may make all commodities look like
equally promising candidates for starting a pyramid, but in actual

157

practice, those with insufficient Open Interest or low Volume of trading or both, make it very difficult to run a pyramid successfully. Price action is much more erratic in these less popular commodities; it is often impossible to get decent fills, which are very important to the profitability of a pyramid; limit price action occurs much more frequently in these thinly traded commodities; and besides that, they often are difficult to exit when one wants to get out, especially if the pyramid has built to a significant number of contracts.

Most commodities can be successfully pyramided, and all commodities can _sometimes_ be successfully pyramided; but all in all, it is best to stay with the more popular commodities in order to avoid potential difficulties. Another important consideration in choosing commodities to pyramid is the selection of the contract month to use. Many traders believe the best way to handle pyramids is to initiate them in far distant contract months, since they are aware that if their pyramid is successful, it may run many months before it reaches completion. The difficulty with using this approach is that the most distant contract months of any commodity, even the most popular ones, are lightly traded.

In fact, sometimes the distant months of the most popular commodities are more lightly traded than the closest months of Broilers and Eggs. So by instituting a pyramid in these very distant months, the trader is running the risk of getting poor fills as he begins to add contracts to his pyramid. Since most successful pyramids take 6 months or less to complete, the best approach in selecting the contract month to enter, is to pick the open contract month that is the closest to a maximum of 6 months away. If, for some reason, this particular pyramid takes longer to develop than normally, the trader can roll-over to the next contract month as his contract month approaches its first notice day.

Generally, this will allow successful completion of the pyramid and put the trader in a position of being able to close his positions out at any point he wishes with relative ease, because when he decides to do so, the contract month he is "in" will be heavily traded. An alternative approach is to institute the pyramid position in the nearby month, and roll-over to other months as time passes. There is one instance where we recommend this approach, and that is when it appears that most of the additional positions will have been established in the nearby contract month selected before first notice day is given. If this is done, then rolling over to a contract month, say 4 to 6 months in the future, is a good approach.

Otherwise, if you establish your positions in the nearby month, roll over into the next contract month, and keep rolling over into the next and the next because the pyramid is taking longer than expected, you are accumulating large commission charges due to the number of contracts involved and the fact that you are paying a commission to sell each contract in the month you are rolling over from as well as paying a commission to buy each contract in the month you are rolling over to.

We now want to examine some of the different types of pyramiding that are available to use, remembering that the number of types of different pyramids is limited only by your imagination and ingenuity. The earlier example we used where the trader bought additional contracts each time his paper profits built up enough to do so, would be called a "Fully-Margined Pyramid". In actual practice, this type of pyramid is seldom used by pyramiding professionals because of the risk involved. In this case, the trader would advise his broker to keep adding positions as his profits increased, to keep him fully margined. The danger here is that minor reactions in the market might easily result in requests for putting up additional margin monies, something the professionals will do only rarely, if ever. In actual practice, a pyramider normally instructs his broker to add contracts to keep him 80% or 85%

or 90% of being fully margined. This always allows some cushion
in the pyramider's account to take care of these minor dips, and
prevent calls for additional margin.

A unique method that we have never seen discussed in print,
can be utilized whenever a trader has sufficient capital to initiate 3 positions, or some multiple of 3 positions, in the commodity he wishes to pyramid. In the example previously given,
where T-Bills were in a trading range, between 86.40 and 87.50
for an extended period of time, the procedure would be as follows:
You place a Good Till Cancelled order with your broker to buy 1
contract (or one-third of the total number of contracts you can
afford to invest in) at, say 87.51 STOP. Then, when T-Bills start
their move up, normally it will not be straight up, but rather a
gradual move with some backing and filling. Once it has moved
through 87.51, it may advance to 87.80 or so, and then drop back
down a bit. When it starts back down, you instruct your broker to
buy another contract, or one-third of your total, at the first
entry point, and when the move upward is doubly-confirmed by moving
to say 88.00 then add your last contracts).

We see little difference between buying 1 or 2 contracts at
the first point as opposed to buying 1 at the first point and
adding the second on a pullback to the first point; but the traders
we know who use this approach wait for the pullback to add the
second contract, and they would give no explanation for why they do
it this way. These figures, of course, apply only to this example,
and can be varied even within this example to suit the temperment
of the trader. While one pyramider might use these entry points,
another in the same situation might wait for the 87.60 level for
the first entry point and the 87.70 level for the last entry point.
There are no hard and fast rules for a case like this. Hard and
fast rules seem to apply only when a pyramider is keeping Fully
Margined, or 80 to 90% Margined, in which case the entry points for
adding more contracts are determined in advance.

You must place protective stops with a pyramid as judiciously as with any other position. In the case of starting a bull pyramid, given the previously mentioned conditions, the ideal place to place your initial protective stops is just below the low of the trading range. In this case, with the trading range moving between 86.40 and 87.50, an initial protective stop of at least 86.39 is called for, and possibly a bit lower if the trader is willing to take the slight additional risk. With most trades, we believe that initial protective stops should, whenever possible, be placed so as to risk no more than 50% of the Original Margin requirement; but because of the huge profit possibilities with pyramids, we believe the pyramider should consider increasing the initial protective stop to a maximum of 120% of Original Margin requirements.

In the case of T-Bills just discussed, if the original entry point were at 87.51, the pyramider could have his original protective stop at 86.39, or 1.12% away from the entry point, which would be 112% of Original Margin Requirements. In this example, this would not be necessary unless the trader were convinced that his projected price run-up was worthwhile, and he wanted to protect himself from an unforeseen sell-off that might go through the bottom of the trading range. Please note that the discussion to this point has dealt only with instituting <u>bull</u> pyramids.

In the last example the trader is using mainly his own capital to initiate the pyramid, and not utilizing paper profits. Large traders very often start their pyramids this way, and then use paper profits from there on to add additional contracts for as long as they feel it is worthwhile to do so. Unfortunately, pyramiding is as much an art as it is a science. The pyramiding trader must know thoroughly all the different ways to pyramid, and then, based on his own capital and abilities, choose which type of pyramid might work most profitably in any given situation.

The best way to develop this skill, and it is a skill that must be learned, is to accumulate a number of old daily charts and look for those times when a commodity bottomed, went into a trading range for a period of time, and then went into a sustained bull trend. Using these charts, the trader can examine different possibilities for entry points, initial stop-loss points, points at which additional contracts might have been added, whether they should have been added with paper profits or with the trader's own equity, and so forth. What the student should gain from this exercise is not a set of rules that can be used in the future, because each market has its own unique qualities, but rather a feel for all of the different possibilities, and in doing that, he will probably discover the methods he feels most comfortable using.

Another method of pyramiding that is popular among many sophisticated traders involves the addition of an equal number of contracts at various price levels, whether it be a bear or a bull move. In the T-Bill example just given, the pyramider might instruct his broker to buy the first contract at 88.01, and then add one more contract for every 20 points move upward in price, until a total of 10 contracts had been accumulated. So, contracts would be bought at 88.01, 88.21, 88.41, etc. up to and including 90.01. This approach is normally more successful in the hands of sophisticated traders because they have examined the situation carefully enough that each 20 point move serves as a confirmation to them that a sustained bull move is in progress. This method often requires more capital than the small trader can afford to put up, and often the small trader does not have the expertise to be certain that every 20 point move upward is another confirmation of a bull move, instead of a rally that is part of a continuing bear move.

While the simplest method of pyramiding is not the most profitable, we believe it is the best one for all but the most experienced trader to use. And that is the one mentioned before which involves using other people's money, or more specifically, the market's money. This method is slower, and requires more

162

patience on the part of the trader, but sometimes a conservative
approach in a high-risk venture like pyramiding is the best.

We would therefore, strongly recommend to all but the most
sophisticated traders, that they adopt the approach of using paper
profits to add additional contracts. It is true that somewhat
less profit will be realized this way, but the overall profit
potential in pyramiding is so great to begin with that we believe
the difference doesn't matter that much. We also believe that
staying 90% margined is the best route to go when using this
method, because even though keeping fully-margined will add more
contracts along the way, the risk of receiving additional margin
calls outweighs the advantage of having a few more contracts.

We have discussed initial stop-loss placement, and now we
would like to consider moving stops up as the pyramid progresses.
There are a multitude of ways to do this, but rather than examine
all the possibilities, we would like to offer you the method that
appears to be most satisfactory to us. If you want to examine
other possible methods to determine if they are more to your
liking, you will want to study another chapter on Stop Placement,
which examines all the methods of stop-loss placement in great
detail.

The initial protective stop should if the initial dollar risk
is not too great (which it would be in our T-Bill example) be
placed below the bottom of the extended trading range, usually
about 2% lower than the figure that constitutes the bottom of the
trading range. More aggressive traders may wish to place their
stops even lower, but in no case do we recommend risking more than
120% of Original Margin Requirements. Okay, you have your initial
pyramid order in place and it gets filled. What do you do now with
your initial protective stop? Nothing. You wait until your second
contract point is filled, bought with paper profits, and at that
time you move your protective stop up to the break-even point, or
the point at which you bought your first contract.

Here you have absolutely nothing to lose, and everything to gain, for if your second entry point is hit, <u>which</u> point has been determined by paper profits, the likelihood is very great that you are onto a sustained bull move. Now that you have eliminated any risk from your position, what do you do with your stops from this point on? For pyramiding, we have found that the experts generally use one of two methods. We will present them both in detail, telling you which we personally prefer, and leave the final decision up to you.

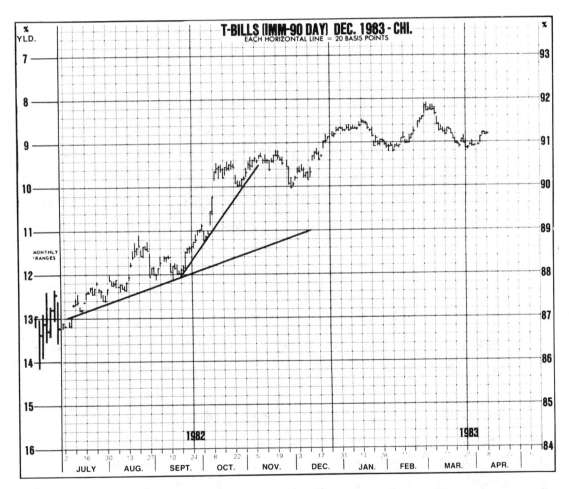

Figure 40

The first method, and the one that we prefer, is to place pyramiding stops a bit below the lowest low of the past four

164

weeks. In the case of T-Bills in Figure 39 and 40, let's say we have reached the first week of September. The low of this week, assuming this week is just over, was about 87.85 and the low of the previous week was 88.39, and the third and fourth week's back had lows of 88.18 and 87.60. We would recommend placing our stops at about 87.59 or 87.49. Statistically, in rapidly moving bull markets, the low of the current or preceeding week if _often_ touched or broken, but _not_ the low of the past four weeks, unless the market has run its course. Admittedly, this means keeping one's stops back a bit further, and if the market has reversed itself, also taking some of the profit out of the pyramid. But, in the long run, we have found this method to be the most successful in keeping a pyramiding position viable as long as possible.

The other method most frequently used by professional pyramiders is to use weekly charts, and draw trendlines between the weekly low or dip points, and then to place the stop a bit below where that trendline will be for the coming week. We prefer the former method because our studies have indicated to us that these trendlines are violated a bit more frequently than the stops as determined by the first method. Whichever method you use, stick with it until you are stopped out or until your Target Point is hit. There are many methods for determining Target Points, so we will not cover that subject here. A detailed discussion of how to pick tops is found in another chapter in this book, and when pyramiding, you want to exit as close to the top as possible. Having determined where the top should be, let's say in the case of T-Bills, 91.00, we suggest selling one-third of your total position when the Target is hit and moving your protective stops at that point up to the Target level once it is past, and then holding on to the balance and positioning your stops by using a tightly drawn trend line in case, as often happens, there is a dramatic upside blow-off at the top.

Bear pyramids are a different case, and virtually no one except the real professionals establishes pyramids on the down-

side. These often are the short-term pyramids in which fortunes
are made in a couple of weeks. There are a number of facets that
are different in getting into a bear pyramid, and we want to cover
all of them. First, when selecting a commodity in which to
establish a bear pyramid, very seldom will you have the advantage
of being able to use an established trading range from which to
start. Bear pyramids develop quickly, sometimes _very_ quickly.

There are basically two types of chart situations that lend
themselves to bear pyramids, and either of them can "trap" the
potential pyramider much more easily than a bull pyramid can. It
is worthwhile going after these bear pyramids, however, since the
profits can often be just as great or greater than in bull pyramids;
and while it takes months to bring a bull pyramid to completion,
often it takes only a few weeks to complete a bear pyramid.

The first way to identify a potential bear pyramid is to
locate a market that has been going up very quickly, setting new
contract highs. It may, in fact be a market in which you have
established a _bull_ pyramid.

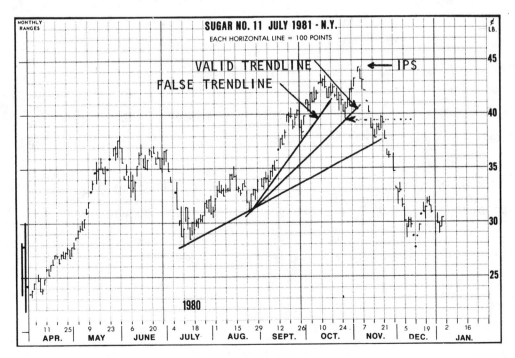

Figure 41

Once you have located a market like this, draw the major ascending trendline along the weekly lows or dips. As the market progresses with its rise, you will notice that in most cases the trendlines start becoming asymptotic. That is, they become steeper and steeper as though they will end by going straight up. Each week as you draw your newest and probably steepest trendline, place your order to sell the first contract in your bear pyramid a bit below the ascending trendline. If the market continues up the next week, cancel the first order and establish a new order based upon the newer trendline. At some point the market will reverse itself and slice through the trendline, usually violently. At this point you establish your initial protective stop just a bit above the high of the bull move.

Prior to establishing this protective stop, however, you must have already placed with your broker the orders for your subsequent contracts. Each weekend, when you draw your newest trendline and fix your new initial entry point, you must at that time compute where your other entry points will be. In the case of Sugar, let's say this weekend you've determined that if the $4.00 level is broken on the downside, then you wish to place your first short order at that point. You must subsequently then place a second order to sell another contract, and then determine where you want your third, fourth, and subsequent contract entry points. These orders, the initial order as well as all the subsequent orders, <u>must</u> be placed with your broker before the opening of the market on Monday morning.

When a market tops and reverses itself, it often does so with extraordinary speed, All of your pyramid orders on the downside must be computed and in place before each week starts. It is actually a good idea to do that with bull pyramids too, but most bull pyramids allow the trader time enough to work day by day without having to have all these orders placed in advance. The true professional pyramiders that we have talked with, do

have all of their orders computed and placed on Monday mornings
before the opening of the markets, regardless of whether it is a
bull or a bear pyramid that they are establishing.

The other type of bear pyramid comes from identifying a
double-top formation, which often slices through the trendline
you've drawn and gets you in what at first appears to be a pyramid
trap once prices start advancing back toward the contract high
while forming the other side of the double top. It is true that
sometimes the first top will not hold, as in Figure 41, but
generally the thrust up will fall short of the first top, just
above which your protective stop rests.

More conservative pyramid traders prefer to trade the
double top formations. This is a "six of one, half a dozen of the
other" situation in that even if a trader gets his initial stop
hit by using the trendline method, he can sit by and wait for the
next chance to get his bear pyramid started. When he does get in
on his bear pyramid, his overall profits will be far greater than
those made by the more conservative trader who waits for the
double-top formation. The trader who waits for the double-top formation will suffer fewer losses on his initial entry, but his
overall profits will be less because of missed trades.

To utilize the double top approach, the trader waits until a
contract high has been established and a reaction takes place. As
the reaction fizzles out and a new upmove begins, he places his
initial entry point just below the low point of the reaction in the
case of Sugar in Figure 41, this would be about 39.40, shown by the
dotted line. If the market is not forming a double top and goes on
to set even higher contract highs, the trader simply cancels his
order and waits for another double-top possibility. It should be
noted that when using the double-top approach, the trader here too
must place his orders simultaneously for selling contracts number
2, 3, 4, etc., because prices often collapse just as quickly from a
double top formation as they do from a top that does not form a
double top.

168

The methods for handling stop-loss placement in a bear market pyramid are the same as in a bull market pyramid, with these exceptions. When entering a bear pyramid using the broken trendline method, the protective stop is <u>not</u> moved down to the break-even point when the second contract is added. The trader should wait until the <u>third</u> contract has been added before moving his stop-loss down to the break-even. This is to prevent the entire position from being wiped out by the formation of a double top that might close the position out on the rally back up which forms the double top.

When using the double top method of bear pyramiding, the initial protective stop should be placed just above the second top, which normally is a bit lower than the first top. After the break-even point is reached, that is, when the second contract is entered into, wait a bit; then shortly thereafter, when prices have moved just a bit lower, the protective stop should be moved to the point at which the first order was executed, the break-even point. Subsequent stop-loss movement, whether it is a broken trendline bear pyramid or a double-top bear pyramid, should be handled in either of the two ways described for moving stops in a bull pyramid.

There are two other points to consider when establishing pyramids that should be discussed as final check points in order to enable you to decide whether the opportunity is a good one or not. The first is Bullish Consensus. Since Bullish Consensus states that when 70% or 80%, depending upon the theorist you choose to believe, of the advisors are bullish, then the market is due to reverse itself. If the Bullish Consensus is higher, say 85% or 90%, then the chances for a significant reversal are just that much greater. We will not go into why this theory works here, but only state that it does work, and is very effective in determining when a potential pyramid situation exists, as long as the other factors previously mentioned are also present. In other words, if you have an increasingly steep weekly trendline situation; contract highs, or a double top formation taking place; and if 70 or 80 or 90 percent of the market "experts" are still bullish, watch out! You have a perfect situation for a bear pyramid, and chances are it may very well be one that is short-term, from the standpoint of the speed with which it occurs.

Conversely, if all the conditions are present for a bull pyramid, that is, a relatively low price that has been in a trading range for an extended period of time after crashing down from a significant high; and seasonal factors do not indicate a great probability of the market going lower at this time of year; then, if the Bullish Consensus figures shows that only 30 or 20% of the "experts" are bullish (which means that 70 or 80% of them are in reality bearish) you have the opposite situation, and you are sitting on a great potential bull pyramid.

Even though we are not discussing why this method works, we would like to say something briefly about it. Basically, year in and year out, the market players, by and large, are wrong. This does not mean the big traders as reflected in the Commitments of Traders, but rather the advisory services and brokerage houses. When a great majority of them are convinced the market is going to continue going in a certain direction, it happens invariably that they are wrong, and that the market by then is tremendously oversold or overbought because of all the individual traders who are following the advice of these sages. So, after you have identified potential pyramiding opportunities by the methods already discussed, one of your two final last checks is to look at the Bullish Consensus figures. They are not always right, but they are right such a great percentage of the time, that it is a good idea to limit one's pyramids to those that are verified by this method too.

The final check, which like Bullish Consensus, is so often ignored by amateur pyramiders, is that of Volume and Open

Interest. Those writers who have commented on the importance of these two figures usually emphasize using both of them. We have found however, that for the purpose of establishing pyramids, only Open Interest figures need to be examined. Once we have identified our ideal candidates for pyramiding, and checked them out with all the previous conditions, including Bullish Consensus, we need to look at the Current Open Interest chart, which is printed by most major chart services.

Figure 42

If you have identified a potential bull pyramid, go ahead and get your orders placed and start watching the Open Interest graph. If Open Interest is <u>declining</u> as with Cotton in Figure 42, it is that much more of a confirmation that you are onto a genuine bull pyramid opportunity. If Open Interest shows a sudden decline over a few days, it means that the big-money traders who have short positions are suddenly covering their positions because they anticipate a rise in the market. When you see this, it is the time to consider increasing the number of contracts you start your pyramid out with. One pyramiding professional we know, in fact, determines how many contracts he will start his pyramid with, by how far and how quickly Open Interest is moving down.

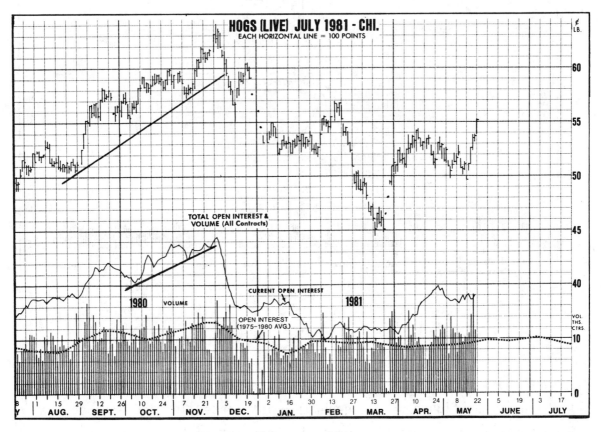

Figure 43

172

The converse is true for establishing bear pyramids as shown in Figure 43, in that the greater the increase in Open Interest, the greater the chance for a raging bull to come crashing down, and the crash usually follows a sudden and dramatic spurt <u>up</u> in Open Interest.

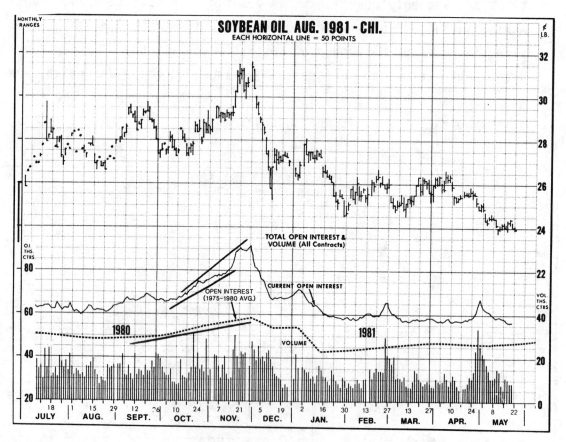

Figure 44

Many chart services show a graph for the Current Open Interest, which is the figure we are generally interested in, and also show a composite average graph of what the Open Interest has been, on the average, say over the past 5 years. Using this graph requires a bit more artistry than just following the Current Open Interest Graph, but it can be another point of validation. Taking Soybean

Oil, Figure 44, for an example: If the Open Interest graph for the average of the past five years usually starts up in October, rising very gradually, at say, a 30 degree angle of incline, and if this year the angle of increase is much greater, say 45 degrees, then that difference in rate of incline is significant in indicating that the market will soon be running out of steam. If this year the rate of incline is also around 30 degrees, as in the past 5 years, then the rise in Open Interest, is by itself, not conclusive. What we would be looking for here is a sudden rise, over a few days or a week, that sharply increases the angle of ascent. This is the confirming key which, when combined with all of the other factors previously discussed, indicates that if you want to establish a bear pyramid, you had better get ready to do so before the opportunity passes you by.

We would like to mention one other method of identifying potential bull and bear pyramids, and that is by using fundamental information. Usually, by the time government or industry reports are made public, it is too late to get a pyramid set up, because if the report contains information that the trade was not expecting, then the market moves too fast to get positions calculated, entered, and filled. There is however, one way to overcome this difficulty.

Let's say a market, perhaps Orange Juice, is at either a low price level or a high price level. That is the only requirement; that the market has to be near historical support or resistance levels, regardless of the commodity in question. So let's say Orange Juice has been trading around 80¢ for a period of time, and an important government report of stocks-on-hand or estimated production is due to be released soon. Now, this does not occur very often, but when a surprise report does come out, it more than repays your having entered, and cancelled, many potential pyramids. In this case let's say Bullish Consensus is of no use, showing a 50% figure. Let's also say that Open Interest is of no use, just moving along sideways like it does every year at this time. So there are no reasons to identify this market as a potential pyramiding candidate other than it has been in a trading range. However, you know from the calendar which is published monthly in Commodities Magazine and in other news sources, that this Government Report is due out.

Evidently no one expects it to contain anything of interest, or the market would be tipping its hand, either in price action, changes in Open Interest, or in Bullish Consensus Figures. You know that the market is probably right, but since it is sometimes wrong, you place an order to buy one contract at 85¢ and another one every 2¢ above that until you have "x" number of contracts. The chances are the report will come out, with nothing dramatic in it, as expected, and you will have to cancel all of your pyramiding orders. But, that one time in 10 when the report does contain the unexpected, and states, perhaps, that a revised estimate of stocks-on-hand shows there to be 25% less frozen concentrate on hand than previously estimated, the market is going to accelerate with a boom; and assuming you don't get caught in limit moves, and can get your orders filled, you have yourself a pyramid going that no one except you and the experts are in.

For practical purposes, a commodity other than Orange Juice would be preferable due to its tendency to have so many limit days in a row. The foregoing technique seems to be the one most closely guarded by the pyramiding professionals, who are willing to calculate and place potential pyramids 10 or 20 times in a row, having to cancel almost all of them, in order to sneak in on a big one almost no one else anticipates.

The one last aspect of pyramiding we want to deal with is the psychology of pyramiding. Psychology can easily be seen in Bullish Consensus when almost the entire trading public believes together that a market is going to continue in one direction indefinitely. But how about the trader who pyramids? What must his psychology be, and to what stresses is he subjected that the ordinary trader does not face? In terms of the stresses he faces, consider this case: You have started out with a two-contract pyramid in Wheat, risking perhaps $1,500 between your entry point and stop-loss point. Prices rise, gradually at first, then more rapidly, and all the while you are adding more contracts with paper profits. All of a sudden you calculate that your initial investment of $3,000 has now grown to $45,000. Forty-five thousand dollars! Why this would get that luxurious swimming pool you've wanted for some time and maybe a little sports car too. Should you cash your chips in now even though you feel the market will go higher, much higher? Sleeping becomes difficult at night. On days when the market is down, you're a bear to be around. Your family is nervous around you. Your head starts to hurt and your stomach churns more and more frequently.

The stress has built up to the point where you start taking some tranquilizers or having a couple of extra martinis. Now you're up to $60,000 in profits and a walking wreck. Has it all been worth it? Yes, it can be, _if_ you prepare yourself for these big successes which are bound to come once you start pyramiding. The best way to handle this is to establish your ground rules in advance, in writing, and then to follow them no matter what. Do not deviate from your strategy of moving stops or when to take profits no matter how the market acts, at least not if tension affects you this way.

Secondly, take some of those paper profits, not by actually taking them out of the market, but by spending a small portion of them wisely in locating and seeing the best therapist you can find. It should be obvious by now, if stress affects you that way, that you have some psychological issues that are unresolved. There is nothing to be ashamed of about this. Virtually everyone does have some psychological "unfinished business". In any case, a small investment in therapy can bring big benefits in peace of mind. If you do not know how to obtain the name of a fully competent thera-

176

pist, you can write or call Taurus in complete confidence as we maintain a list of excellent therapists that covers the entire country, Alaska, Hawaii, Mexico and Canada.

The other psychological aspect is the need to force yourself to be patient in waiting for these pyramiding opportunities to come along. They normally occur at least once in most markets once a year. They did this year. They did last year. They will next year. Be patient and follow the guidelines in this chapter, and by all means, do not try to force a pyramid when one does not exist, or when the signals are mixed or inconclusive. You may miss some of them, but there will always be more next week or next month to latch onto. Be patient.

CHAPTER 8

LONG-RANGE TRADING I

Long-range trading seems to be one of the least well-
understood areas of commodity trading. In fact, it was not until we
examined eight books in our research library before we found long-
range trading discussed at all. Therefore, virtually all of the
material in this chapter is original.

Beginning commodity traders, as well as many seasoned
veterans, really misunderstand long-range commodity trading. The
concept of taking a trade and holding it for many weeks, or even
many months, seems to be a very slow way of making money in the
markets, while in reality, just the opposite is true. Most speculators get into the commodity markets in the first place because
it appears to them to be the fastest way of making a fortune due
to the low initial amounts of money required for margin, the tremendous leverage provided by the commodity markets, and the rapidity with which the markets move.

Certainly commodities offer a much more rapid way of making,
and losing, money than the stock market, trading options, real
estate, bonds, or virtually any other investment other than
outright gambling. It is true, of course, that money changes hands
even more rapidly at the gaming tables in casinos and at the ticket
windows of race tracks, but commodity speculation carries the aura
of being a legitimate investment since it is regulated by the
government to some degree and in fact exists in the first place as
a legitimate method for producers and consumers to hedge with. A
famous trader once likened commodity trader for the speculator as
nothing more than a crap-shoot with slightly better odds than dice.

178

Considering the enormous turn-over of small speculators in the marketplace each year, commodity trading sounds from that standpoint as though it is not much better than a more acceptable, legitimate form of gambling. The novice trader understands the enormous profit potential in commodities but tends to push into his subconscious the enormous risks also involved. Once attracted to this very rapid way to make his fortune, the average trader is looking to speed the process up even further. There is a thirst for action on the part of most traders, especially those who end up losing their money. It has been estimated that 9 out of every 10 commodity traders lose all of their commodity trading funds within 12 months of entering the markets.

So, then, we have our average beginning commodity trader in a real hurry to make his fortune. Typically, after opening his account, he will take a number of different positions, generally using all or most of his total account money for margin. Whether he is following the advice of his broker, using his own methodology, or relying upon advisory services, he gets into and out of trades with great rapidity. He will buy Corn one day at $3.00 a bushel, and if the move goes in his direction, sell it two days later for a nickel or dime profit.

More likely than not, if the market starts down, he has his stops placed too closely to his entry point and is stopped out with a nickel or dime loss. Ultimately, this Corn market may move all the way to $4.00 a bushel, or a $5,000 profit on his original small investment, IF the trader had had the patience to ride with the market. But, instead, typically he is out of Corn one day, into Hogs the next, out of Hogs and into something else in several more days, constantly craving the action and the excitement that goes with it.

What novices really seem to fail to understand is that the great fortunes in commodity speculation are made in big market moves, not by trading the little blips or day-trading. Patience is required in enormous amounts if a commodity trader really wants to make huge amounts of money. Unfortunately, no one generally has told the beginning trader this, but rather that commodities are the fastest game in town, and they are.

Many, if not most, advisory services realize the thirst for action that most traders have and make more recommendations than they really should in order to satisfy their subscribers. Most brokers, since they live on their commissions, don't want their clients to sit on trades and either consciously or subconsciously encourage their clients to over-trade. Even though many beginning traders have a subconscious desire to end up losing their money, those traders too who really want to make money are constantly being bombarded by the news media, advisory services, and in many cases by their brokers to: TRADE, TRADE, TRADE.

Long-range trading is just the opposite of this approach, and probably most of the 10% of the traders who make money year after year in the commodity markets use a long-range trading approach at least part of the time, or at worst, an intermediate range approach. For the purposes of this chapter, we will arbitrarily define an intermediate-range trade as any trade lasting over a couple of weeks, and a long-range trade as one lasting over a month.

March, 1981 T-Bonds are as good an example as any of our definition of a long range trade as can be seen in Figure 45. Numerous sell-signals were given technically and fundamentally toward the end of June, 1980. Traders who sold during that period of time at around 80% were all virtually assured of a profit. However, most of the novice or short-term traders either were stopped out with a small loss when the market rallied in a couple of weeks back through 81% or chose to take their profits at say 78%. Intermediate-range traders probably had their stops hit on a brief rally back up through 76%.

180

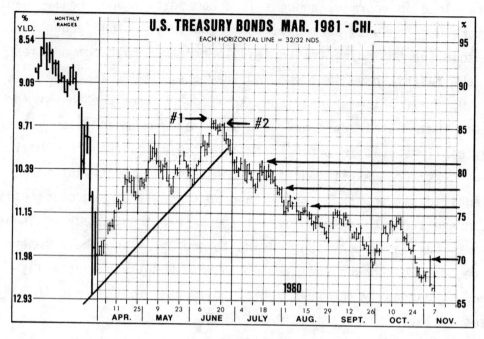

Figure 45

The long-range traders, though, those who really made a killing in this market as interest rates increased to record levels, sold at 80% and may have had their stops hit at 70% during the week before Christmas, 1980. They had held their positions nearly 6 months and instead of losing a percentage point or making just a couple percent, instead made 10% on the move or, in terms of their pro-fits, probably 500% more than the short-term traders.

Now, the short-term traders may very well have made money, albeit a relatively small amount, on this trade, but due to the nature of their trading, were almost bound to end up losing on their next short-term trade. The surest, and in reality the quickest way to make a million in commodity trading is by using the long-range approach. For every short-term trader who does make a fortune by being lucky enough to hit a run of successful short-term trades, there are literally dozens who fall by the wayside trying to use this approach.

Trading on a long-range basis involves two aspects: the first is purely technical from the standpoint of how to do it, and the second is psychological or how to learn to live with this style of trading. Having one without the other will bring the average trader to financial ruin just as surely, though not as rapidly, as the short-term trader. The rationale behind this is quite simple in that if you develop the technical ability to make long-range trades, yet lack the ability to handle the unique psychological stresses that accompany long-range trading, you either will end up reverting back to self-destructive short-term trading, or develop any one of a host of physical problems from the stress. If you are able to handle the stresses of long-range trading and do not have the skills to pick, enter, and trail stops in long-range trades, you will end up losing your money over a longer period of time.

While many traders, and so-called experts assert that large amounts of money can be made trading on reactions or rallies against the trend, it is impossible to consistently do this in a profitable manner. The successful tycoons who use long-range trading shun publicity and are heard about little, as a rule, in the press. They have found their own, sure way of making fortunes, year after year, and they are not desirous of sharing their approach with anyone else. One of the few long-range traders we found who was willing to discuss his methods openly with us frankly admitted that this approach was the key to his averaging profits in excess of a quarter of a million dollars every three months.

From our discussion to this point, it probably sounds like all a trader has to do is to decide to use long-range trades and then set back and wait for his money. Unfortunately, like most good things, long-range trading is just as difficult to master as any other skill requiring great degrees of expertise. The remainder of this chapter will be devoted to those two areas previously mentioned: how to do it, and how to enjoy, or at least, tolerate, doing it. We hope by now we have convinced the reader of the desirability of long-range trading.

182

Due to its very nature, long-range trading opportunities do not arise as often as do short or intermediate-range trades, which is just as well in that it gives the long-range trader more time generally to prepare his program for these trades. If you pick up a set of charts for the current year or any past year, you will notice that some commodities made large, sustained moves at some point during the year, and other commodities, while perhaps ending up the year at a higher or lower point than that from which they began the year did not make a sustained move since, not all commodities in any given year move in either direction a sufficient amount to make huge returns on them.

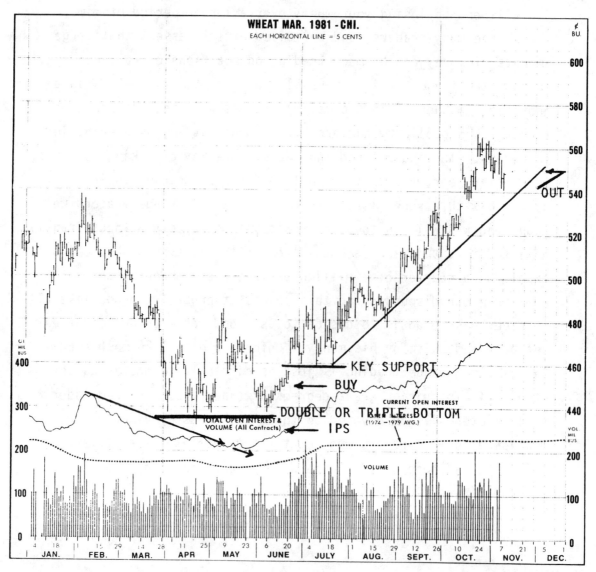

Figure 46

To us, for a long-range trade to be genuinely successful, due to the length of time most of them must be held, the return must be in the neighborhood of 300% of original margin or more. Wheat was a perfect example in 1980, in that the trader who successfully analyzed the double bottom being formed by the lows made in April and June, and here we will be using March, 1981 Wheat as shown in Figure 46, that trader could very easily have bought at $4.50 a bushel, placing his stops just below the double lows, at say $4.30, making his risk 20¢ per contract or 67% of original margin, $1,000. Once the market tested the four-sixty level again in late July and was unable to close below it, the signals were all there for a sustained move upward. We will get into the "whys" later, but for now, let's just look at the profits accumulated by our long-range trader. Based upon the methodology we will be discussing, he would not have been stopped out until around the $5.50 per bushel level, or a profit of 100¢ during the move which would have seen him enter in June or July and exit in November, a four or five month trade. This 100¢ however, represents a profit of $5,000 on an original risk of $1,000, or a 333% return on original margin.

If our trader got that return, starting with only $1,500 original capital, by the end of 4 similarly successful trades, he would net nearly two million dollars, taking somewhere between one and two years total time to do that. If he had started with four contracts of Wheat in this example, it would take him only three similarly successful trades to net over a million and a quarter dollars, possibly within a twelve-month span, assuming he reinvested all of his profits each time into the next position.

When March 1981 Wheat broke through the $5.40 per bushel level, all the signals were there for another long-range trade on the short side which while intentioned to be a long-range trade, may have only lasted a little over a month, with profits on only slightly over 100% of original margin requirements. We mention this here, the second or short sale trade to demonstrate that not

184

all potential long-range trades succeed in netting over 300%
returns on original margin requirements.

Some surprise us with 100% or 200% returns, and occasionally,
but often enough to make it extremely worthwhile, the long-range
trader will get a return of 500% or 600% on his trade. A trader
only needs to make a very limited number of such trades a year in
order to make his fortune. Even if the double-bottom in Wheat had
not held, our trader was only risking $1,000 per contract, and
would have been more than able to make up that loss on his next,
successful trade.

There are a number of factors that must be considered in
order to isolate the best potential long-range trades, and we will
now discuss all of them. It is rare that a trader can find ALL of
these factors poised in his favor, but even if he only has a
majority of them confirming the existence of a long-range trade,
it is well worth entering the trade. The first factor to consider
is the actual price movement on the charts themselves. We have
found two patterns to be the most reliable in initially isolating
our long-range trade candidates.

The first pattern, in which we would consider a long-range
long position is to look for a commodity that has been in an
extended trading pattern at relatively low levels. Soybean Meal as
shown in Figure 47 during the period from March through June of
1980 appeared to be an excellent candidate as prices for the March,
1981 contract were $185 and $200 per ton, a relatively constricted
trading range, at a relatively low price level. Prices had been
falling since the December-January period and then went into a
sideways pattern. So far, this appears to be an excellent candidate for a long-range bull move. The pattern shows up even
better on weekly long-range charts, those which each bar line
represents the high, low and close for a whole week. Sometimes it
is visually easier to see these tight trading patterns forming on
weekly charts. Other times they show up better on the daily charts

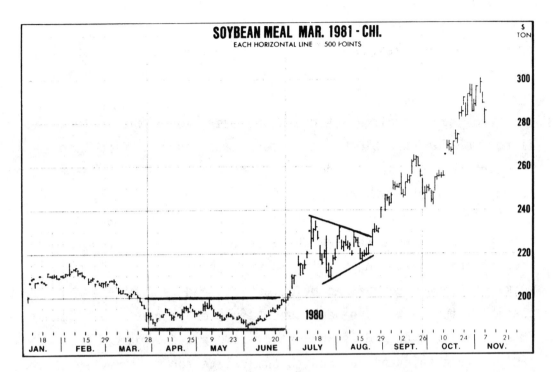

Figure 47

The key determinant in recognizing them seems to be the scale on which the charts are drawn. Different chart services often use different scales for their charts, so a serious long-range trader will want to consider the slight extra expense of subscribing to at least three of the major chart services. Taurus, for its advisory service, subscribes to virtually all of the major chart services, and will be happy to make a recommendation to readers as to which three might be best for long-range trading programs if they will drop us a letter requesting this information.

As an example, looking through old charts from different services, and comparing their daily, weekly, and when available monthly charts, for Soybean Meal as an example, we notice scales for prices ranging anywhere from $1.00 per ton to $10.00 per ton, and in many cases the actual relationship between the sizes of the blocks used on the graphs and the scale, change drastically the visual image the charts present. The chart we earlier referred to of March Soybean Meal was on a scale of every block representing $5 per ton, and the tight trading range was very evident on this chart.

Looking at a different chart, however, where the scale was $1 per ton for each block, it is much, much more difficult to see the tightness of the trading range, and instead, the market appears to be in more of a whipsaw pattern. So, if one is really serious about picking long-range trades, it is well worth the additional cost to subscribe to several chart services. As a last note when picking these bottoming trading ranges, we prefer a <u>minimum</u> of 5 weeks of tightly compressed price action, and even more if possible, though we have seen successful long-range trade signals from as brief a period as 3 weeks of compressed prices, IF other factors were favorable enough to compensate for the brevity of the trading range formation.

While there are other methods for instituting long-range bull positions, this one method we have just discussed is the one that we have found to possess the greatest degree of reliability over the years. If a trader has found some other pattern that he feels sufficiently comfortable using to institute long-range bull trades, we suggest that he check out its reliability when combining it with the other factors we will be discussing before he uses it.

The chart pattern we have found to be most successful for long-range trades on the short side is quite different than that for instituting long positions. However, when comparing the two methods, we have found a slightly higher degree of overall reliability for our bull selection method as compared to our bear selection method, but not enough of a difference to either be statistically significant or to affect the overall results to any great degree.

When prices have gone through an extended bull move, they always at some point run out of steam and start back down. Seldom do they behave as prices at the end of a bear market when they stay in either a whipsaw pattern or trading range for a long period of time. Prices at the end of bull markets have a habit of collapsing quickly, and without much warning except to those who are prepared by watching all of the relevant indicators. The best way to pick up on when a bull market has topped, at least the best initial method, using charts and without using any other indicators to validate the chart action, is to draw trendlines along the bottoms of the WEEKLY lows whenever a double-top or an attempt to form a double-top formation takes place.

The most successful method of accomplishing this occurs after a bull move has been in force for at least 3 months. The longer it is, the more reliable this method will be. Whenever what appears to be a weekly low has been formed, draw the LEAST steep trendline possible between that low and the next low point before that which will, as we said, result in the least steep trendline, or the one with the smallest rate of incline. Since you have drawn a trendline from that week's low, regard it as valid as prices start to increase back up toward the high established earlier in the week or in the week before. If prices break through the old high in a relatively easy fashion, the trendline you have drawn is still valid, but the chances of it being penetrated soon are greatly diminished.

What we are really looking for is a trendline like we just described, from which prices advance toward the former contract high, and either are unable to penetrate it, or penetrate it only slightly and then start dropping again. When this occurs, and a top is confirmed by the other methods we will be discussing, you have a beautiful opportunity to establish a long-range trade on the bear side as soon as prices penetrate the trendline. An even more valid confirmation of a trend reversal is when prices, after having broken the trendline, pass through the price level at which the highest point of the trendline was drawn through.

For example, let's say in Soy Meal as shown in Figure 48 that you have a least steep monthly low trendline drawn and the last two points on it are $225 and $263. After prices have started back up from the $263 low toward the last high which was at $288, they appear to stall at $282 and start back down slightly. The least steep trendline is broken at $268 which issues a sell signal.

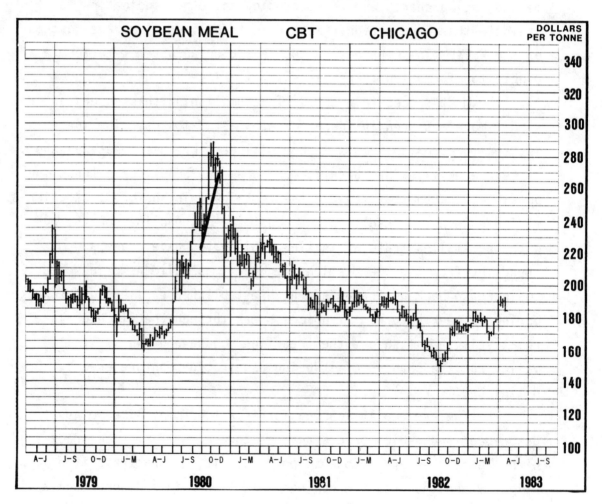

Figure 48

The odds at this point are that approximately 60% of the time, you will by now have a genuine trend reversal. However, once prices drop through the $263 price level, or the highest point on the trendline construction, your odds will improve to approximately 80% that a top has been formed and prices are headed down.

The difficulty with waiting for the second point to be broken through before entering is that very frequently the price move may occur so rapidly that it is either impossible to get into the market at all or the fill is not very good. There really is no hard and fast rule as when to use which method or whether it is best to consistently use one method over the other.

One guideline is to calculate the amount of margin risked by going with each entry point and decide whether or not you are willing to risk the additional monies in order to get a somewhat more valid entry point. Often the additional risk involved in entering the market at the second entry point is so great that a trader will either be forced to enter the market when the trendline is violated or pass the trade altogether. A lot depends here on the degree of confirmation given by other signals to determine whether or not a top has truly been made.

On a long-range bull position, as we discussed earlier, some traders utilize a trendline method for their entry point, but we have found that in tightly packed trading ranges, it is far better to draw a line above and below the trading range, giving a slight space above and below the range for the line's construction, and then use a breakthrough on the upside of the trading range as one's entry point. In the example discussed earlier and shown in Figure 47 for Soybean Meal, where prices were trading for nearly four months between $185 and $200, the lines might best be drawn at the $180 and $205 level, and an open buy order placed to enter the market at $205 STOP, with the order being a G-T-C or Good Till Cancelled type.

Initial stop placement is very important in long-range trading. From a philosophical point, it is often more difficult to realize that since you are going after far bigger profits than

190

the average trader, you MUST be willing to assume greater initial risks than often are otherwise necessary. There are as many rules of thumb for how much initial risk should be assumed as there are writers and theoriticians in the commodity world.

Taurus prefers generally not to risk more than 100% of original margin on a long-range trade, though often we will go as high as 200% or 300% if enough indicators are positive enough to indicate a high degree of profitability for the trade being considered. In the case of Wheat then, we would be willing to risk between $1,500 and $4,500, (assuming the original margin requirements at that time were $1,500) depending upon other factors, which would translate into having our stop between 30 and 90¢ away from our original entry point. Of course, we prefer to have our stops much closer whenever possible.

If, for example, Wheat has been in a trading pattern for some time between $4.40 and $4.60, and our entry point is at $4.70, our stop might be placed at $4.35 or a bit more than 100% of original margin.

If, on the other hand Wheat had been in a range between $4.40 and $4.50, and if all of the other requirements we will be discussing had been met, our entry point might be at $4.55 and our initial protective stops placed at $4.35, which would then involve risking 67% of original margin. If one has to have parameters placed around the amount of risk to assume, we would recommend using the 100 to 300% of original margin requirements.

Now that we have some guidelines as to how much risk it is appropriate to assume on a long-range trade, we need to examine where these initial stop loss points should best be placed in order to determine if the amount being risked is excessive or not. First we will examine initial protective stop-loss placement for long range bull positions. We have discussed drawing two horizontal, parallel lines, just above and just below the trading range, with our entry point just above the upper line. Ideally, the initial stop loss point in this situation will be just below the lower horizontal line.

Unfortunately, we have been unable to find any hard and fast rules as to percentages below the lower line at which the initial protective stop loss should be placed, and we believe that looking at the charts visually, especially after spending many hours looking over old charts at similar situations, will give you the "feel" for how much below the lower horizontal line the stop should be placed. It is a good idea to look at several different points below the line and calculate the risk involved in using the different stop loss points and mentally "factor" the different amounts of risk into your decision.

There should be a distance however, below the lowest point of the trading range between it and your stop loss point as frequently the market will just break the low point of the trading range on a reversal after your entry point has been hit and you already have established positions. That is why we recommend leaving some space above and below the trading range where you draw your horizontal lines to ensure that you do not have your protective stops so close that you are wiped out on a reaction.

Very often prices do not do this, and once they have broken on the outside of a trading range, they frequently never re-enter the price area of the trading range again, at least not during the bull move. However, on long-range trades, where the potential profits can be so enormous, it is best to have an extra margin of safety built in one's original protective stops.

Initial protective stop loss placement is handled somewhat differently in entering a long-range bear position. In the majority of cases, the initial risk to be assumed is higher than in entering a long-range bull position due to the usual volatility of a market as it is topping out. There are two and only two "good places" to place your initial protective stops when entering a long-range bear trade. We have already discussed the two

192

methods of entry points for a long-range bear trade, so since
there are two possibilities for initial stop-loss placement, there
are a total of 4 possible amounts of risk when entering this type
of trade.

It is wise for a trader to calculate all four possibilities in
order to examine the potential risk of each. As we have said,
after prices start back up from the highest "low" on your
trendline, if a reversal is in the making, they will either not be
able to break through the established previous high of the move or
break through it slightly before starting to come back down.
EITHER one of these two high points can be used as a point above
which to place one's initial protective stop.

It has been our experience that, when everything else is
equal, if the run-up in prices stalls BEFORE it breaks the previous
high identified as #1 in Figure 45, the initial protective stop can
generally be safely placed just above this second high #2 in Figure
45, the one that falls short of establishing a new high. However,
when the run-up seriously tests or slightly breaks through the previous high before starting down, it is best to place one's protective stops just above the second high point. So, in either case,
protective stops are best placed just above the second of the two
highs whether or not it breaks through the price of the first high.
However, a slightly greater degree of safety in not getting stopped
out of a long-range bear move results from placing your stops above
the HIGHER of the two highs if this is the first high.

This is where it is necessary to calculate the amount being
risked for all four possibilities; two different entry points and
two different initial stop-loss points. Sometimes the differences
will be so relatively insignificant that it makes little difference
at which point the initial protective stop is placed, in which case
it is strongly recommended that it be placed slightly above the
highest of the two highs.

Since we have just been discussing stop-loss placement for

long-range bear positions, it is appropriate to mention one different type of topping action that has more initial risk involved,
from the standpoint that it is not as frequently a genuine reversal, but when it is, the profits to be made are generally even
more spectacular than with the cases we have already described.

Figure 49

A good example of this occurred in the December, 1980 Copper
contract as shown in Figure 49. Prices soared for over 7 months
from 80¢ per pound to over $1.50 per pound. Then, in the middle of
February, 1980, prices started to nosedive. The tremendous decline

that followed was foreshadowed by many indicators, which we will be discussing shortly. However, once the least steep trendline was penetrated, there really was no significant rally back to the previous high of $1.52; a slight, 3-day rally from $1.27 to $1.36 was the closest move that even approached an attempt back up. Those long-range traders who waited for an assault on contract highs found themselves unable to satisfactorily get into this market, as it plunged from $1.52 a pound to 93¢ a pound in 6 weeks with a number of gaps along the way.

Now, the long-range traders who did not wait for an assault on contract highs and sold when the trendline was broken, managed to get in somewhere around $1.38 a pound, and were able to realize substantial profits of over $10,000 per contract. The danger inherent in this approach however, was that if the trendline, once broken, did not precipitate a trend reversal, then prices may very well have resumed their climb back up and through the $1.52 level, and long-range traders would probably have had their stops at the $1.54 to $1.56 level and gotten stopped out with substantial losses of over $4,000 per contract. Whether or not to utilize the trendline method with stops placed just above contract highs is an individual matter of choice for each trader. However, when this approach is used along with other indicators that signal a top is being formed, the risk of being wrong is significantly reduced.

Once the long-range trade has been entered and initial protective stops placed, then it is necessary to decide on how to move or trail your stops in the best manner to prevent being taken out of the market too soon by a rally or a reaction, and yet to keep your stops close enough to get out of the market once the trend has ended.

In the case of a bull position, where we have entered our positions after the market has broken through on the upside of the trading range, it is important to leave the original protective stops in place until at least one reaction has taken place as the drop back to about 210 in late July for Soy Meal in Figure 47. If the market advances and then starts back down and then starts back up again, the next stop move would be to your entry point or break-even point IF the market dip did not enter back into the trading range zone as bounded by the two horizontal lines. If the dip did enter into the trading range and starts back up again, your initial protective stop should be moved up to a point slightly below the low point of the dip, somewhere in the trading range. This does not yet get your stop up to the break-even point, but it will normally substantially reduce your risk factor. Then on the first reaction back toward the trading zone that stops short of entering the trading zone and prices start advancing again, your stops should be moved up to the break-even point.

In the case of a bear position, if you have entered on a trendline breakthrough instead of waiting for an assault on contract highs to confirm a double-top formation, prices, if your analysis is correct, will be falling in most cases relatively rapidly, and you normally can move your initial protective stop down to the break-even or entry point after 5 to 7 trading days of the penetration of the trendline. Where you have entered a long-range bear position after waiting for an assault on contract highs for a confirmation, the decline in this case is generally more gradual and given more frequently to some rallies during the first few weeks of the move. In this case it is best to wait two or three weeks before moving your stops down to the break-even point unless it becomes evident that the drop in prices is becoming pre-cipitous, in which case, here too you can move your stops down to the break-even point after 5 to 7 trading days.

Once you have your stops to the break-even point, all risk is normally gone, barring a reversal with a number of limit days, which is infrequent. Now, you have the opportunity to take more time in calculating your stop placement. For the first three

196

months of a move, your stops should be placed a bit below the high
or low, of the previous month, Depending upon whether it is a bull
or a bear move. By the time this three-month period is over, you
will have some significant points on which to draw trendlines.
Now, the least steep trendline should be drawn from the weekly
highs or lows of those three months, and your stop should be
trailed weekly just beyond that trendline, whether it is an
ascending or descending one.

There is a good deal of mathematical verification for this
approach in that very often the reactions or rallies of the first
three months of a major move give misleading points from which to
draw trendlines, and without waiting for at least a three month
period of time to pass, a trendline method may end up with
an invalid trendline because it is too steep and will be
penetrated sometime during that three-month period. After three
months have passed, the trendline becomes very valid in most
cases, and some traders prefer to draw tighter and tighter
trendlines after the third month since most moves do not last much
longer than this.

Often it is best not to draw steeper trendlines even then
unless other indicators are pointing to an end to the trend. After
the third or fourth month of a move in either direction, your profits should be very substantial, and now you must make a choice of
whether or not to take your profits or try to squeeze even more out
of the market.

In the case of a bear position, it is somewhat easier because
they are not normally given to sudden turn-arounds, though they do
occasionally happen. In the case of a bull position, since the
reversals are often very sudden, one often finds that he is out of
the market at a point substantially below his stop due to a limit
down move or a big gap. The ideal way would be to be able to
select a target at which to take profits, regardless of the direction of the move.

Unfortunately, every method tested by us has failed to find a consistently accurate way to establish targets, since, more often than not, the target will be hit, profits taken, and then the move will continue for a far greater distance. Overall, we believe the best methods to use to close a position out in a long-range trade are to be taken out by one's stops, regardless of whether it is a bull or a bear position, and by moving the stops in accordance with the guidelines previously given.

Often, in the case of a bull position, this will call for a reversal to a long-range bear position at the same point or close to it at which you are stopped out of your bull position. The opposite is generally not true in that normally you will not be reversing from a long-range bear position to a long-bull position until a protracted trading range has been formed at the bottom of the move. Some optional methods of stop-loss placement are described in another chapter, and the enterprising trader may wish to investigate some of these methods in an attempt to find a more perfect way of moving his protective stops.

One point not yet discussed, but which too, is covered in another chapter, is pyramiding your positions. The long-range trader who masters this technique in addition to the art of long-range trading will end up with profits far in excess of his counterparts who do not pyramid. We suggest that the more aggressive traders examine the concept of pyramiding as it applies to long-term trading as the potential results are well worth the extra effort and slight extra risk involved. When one has correctly identified a long-range trade, scaling in additional orders, or pyramiding, is the quickest way to make money in long-range trading. This should appeal to all traders who are in a hurry to make money but who can develop the patience to trade on a long-range basis.

The confirmation signals we have been alluding to previously that a long-range trader must be aware of and take into account before initiating a long-range position are only a few. These will seldom be all in agreement, but when 3 or more of the 5 we will be discussing are in agreement that the trend is about to reverse, that, along with the chart patterns we have been discussing, should be sufficient confirmation.

While all five indicators are important, there appear to be slight degrees of difference in importance among them. While we have not been able to quantify these differences, we want to state that we believe that they exist in order to make the trader aware of three differences in importance between them. We will discuss the five in order of importance, beginning with the most important.

Bullish Consensus or as it is often called, Market Sentiment or Contrary Opinion appears to us to be the most important. We have found these figures to be true generally ONLY when combined with the charting methods we have discussed earlier in this chapter. Many, many times we have witnessed trading ranges that appeared to be natural candidates for a long-range bull position move through their upper trading range boundary, only to have had the Bullish Consensus figures throughout the period of time prices were in the trading range hanging somewhere around 40 or 50 percent without much real motion, and not change very much once the upper boundary of the trading range had been violated.

When this has occurred, UNLESS some of the other indicators were calling for a bull move, usually prices retreat back to the trading range and stay there for a significant period of time. In other words, the breakout of the trading range was a false one. The converse is true with looking to establish a bear position in a soaring market. If your chart patterns are looking favorable for a top and Bullish Consensus is below 70 or 80 percent, the odds are that the market still has a lot of room on the upside to go before it tops out. Again, this is not an absolute indicator, but must be taken into account with not only the chart patterns but also the other four indicators we will discuss.

To us, the next most important signal to look for is in the Committment of Traders figures for Large Speculators. In an extended trading range preparatory to a long-range bull move, as time passes, you will generally notice a gradual, or sometimes not so gradual, change in the percentage of Large Speculators who are going to establish long positions. These traders are normally the smart-money traders, and if anyone has any inside information it will be them and they will be gradually getting their long positions established. On the other hand, as a market is soaring up, watch the Committments of Large Speculators to see when they are starting to close out their long positions. As they start to do so, they are convinced the market is not far from a top, and while they are not infallible, it is an excellent clue to use as a confirmation of your chart signs.

Some of the most successful long-range traders we know who have the time to do so, keep a graphical representation right on their price charts of both Market Sentiment and Committments of Large Speculators to enable them to pick up more quickly on major impending changes. Unfortunately, we know of no chart service that provides both of these figures in a chart form along with prices, so the serious long-range trader must do this on his own.

Open Interest figures are the next most important indicator, and at times they can be the most important one. Fortunately, these figures are available from all major charting services in graphic form along with the price charts. In looking to establish a long-range bull position, when you see Open Interest decreasing ever so slightly or even more dramatically during the trading range period, it means the large commercial interests are covering their shorts because they just don't believe the market has much potential on the downside as can be seen in Figure 46. When this condition exists, especially when combined with our other indicators, it is an extremely important confirmation of an upcoming major bull market.

Conversely, if Open Interest is increasing ever so slightly during this trading range, the odds are slim that a bull market will ensue. In the other case of looking to establish a long-range bear position, the Open Interest figures will be increasing all the while the preceeding bull market move is taking place. There may be some minor dips indicating a realignment of who is holding all of the open contracts, but this in itself is not too significant. What the long-range trader will want to look for is ever-increasing Open Interest figures, far above the 5-year Average Open Interest graph.

The higher the Open Interest climbs, the more vulnerable the market is to topping out. Unfortunately, there is no absolute way to determine when Open Interest has reached a point at which the top has been reached. In this case, about the only thing a long-range trader can do is to keep watching the Open Interest climb and be aware that the higher it goes, the more likely his chart patterns and other indicators will be valid indicators of a turn-around. The one exception to this rule is when occasionally, especially when the other indicators are pointing toward a top, Open Interest really shoots up over a week or two. That is especially predictive of a market reversal, though it does not happen too frequently.

The fourth and fifth indicators are judged by us to be less important than the three just discussed, but often they alone will be the only signals to confirm the chart patterns as they take place. The fourth indicator is watching the Seasonal Pattern for each commodity, where they exist. Most commodities have seasonal tendencies that depend upon harvest, slaughtering, home-building starts, the automotive industry, etc. If, in the case of a grain as in Figure 50, the seasonal tendency is for it to bottom during a certain time frame, and if for this year it has followed its normal Seasonal Pattern of topping during the approximate time frame it normally hits its highs in, then if the trading range formation is taking place during the normal seasonal low, a breakthrough of the trading range upper boundary is a very important confirmation of the beginning of a bull market.

Seasonal Pattern: CORN

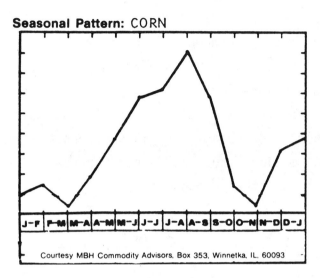

Courtesy MBH Commodity Advisors, Box 353, Winnetka, IL, 60093

Figure 50

Conversely, if this market is in its trading range and the seasonal factors are not calling for it to make a bull move, this must be taken into serious consideration and a bull move must be being called for by the other indicators before a position should be taken. The opposite is true when looking to establish a long-range bear position, wherein if the seasonals indicate the market generally reaches its yearly highs during the time period you are then in, this is another confirmation that your long-range bear position will be a valid one if your entry point is hit.

The fifth indicator is Moving Averages, and there are a multitude of ways to utilize them, which decreases their effectiveness unless one picks one way of doing it and stays with that method. To use too short a time-frame moving average will whipsaw the trader with false signals. To use too long a moving average causes the trader to get into trades too late to take maximum profits out of them. We have found either a 25-day moving average OR a composite moving average of 10, 20 and 40 days to be the best ones to us. Fortunately, they are available from different chart services to save the average trader the time involved in calculating them.

When the daily closing price of a commodity passes through either of these two moving averages as in Figure 51, it often is a valid signal of a trend change WHEN confirmed by the other signals we have been talking about and when the appropriate chart patterns exist. Some traders believe that using such a moving average cross-over through the daily closing price graph is sufficient to indicate a major price change, but it has been our experience that while this is sometimes true, it is <u>not</u> the case often enough unless confirmed by other methods too.

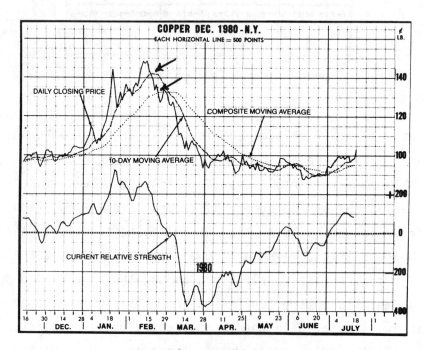

Figure 51

There are many, many more different type of technical indicators and some few fundamental ones that can also be used to validate the key chart patterns we have described, but it has been our experience that, with one exception, they are not worth the additional time and trouble to keep track of. The one exception that we would add to the five indicators if we were going to add one more would be a Relative Strength curve or Momentum Oscillator,

both of which are available in different forms from various
charting services.

Picking the correct contract months sometimes appears to be a
problem to the beginning long-range trader, but it need not be.
The beginning trader is often afraid that he will not be able to
control his entry point precisely enough unless he uses a nearby
contract month. When he does this and initiates a successful
trade, then he is forced to roll-over into subsequent months as
time goes by and the contract month he is into reaches first
notice day. There is not too much wrong with this approach,
except for the additional work of deciding when to roll-over,
which month then to pick, keeping charts for multiple months, etc.

When initiating a long-range bull trade, select a contract
month 6 to 8 months from the present time. Normally, unless the
commodity is a thinly traded commodity, your fill should be relatively close, and if the commodity is a thinly-traded one, you may
want to give second thoughts as to whether you want to get in the
position at all. By the time this contract month reaches first
notice day, you will normally be out of your long-range bull trade.

But if you are not, and the signs are increasing that a top
may be near, all you have to do is to roll-over, that is close out
your position in the month you are in as the first notice day
approaches and simultaneously take another long position in the
next contract month, which normally will be more than adequate to
handle the trade to its conclusion. The same basic 6 to 8 month in
advance rule applies to most long-range bear positions, but since
they often end more quickly, 4 to 6 months lead time may be substi-
tuted instead.

We are often asked whether using point and figure charts are
better when doing long-range trading, and the answer quite simply
is that sometimes they show better results and sometimes they do
not. We have been able to find no common denominator as to when
to choose using point and figure charts over bar charts. For

204

those traders who prefer point and figure charts over the conventional bar charts, there are some general guidelines that we have
found to be useful.

The first thing we would insist on when using point and
figure charts is to use optimized ones for the daily charts, and
to also use weekly and monthly point and figure charts in conjunction with them. We have not been able to find any advantages for
using optimized weekly and monthly point and figure charts. After
this, all of the preceeding information in this chapter applies,
from the standpoint of trading patterns, trend lines, Bullish
Consensus, Committments of Large Speculators, Open Interest, Moving
Averages, and Seasonals. The only time we would recommend to a
long-range trader to use Point and Figure charts is when it has
been his preference all along to use this type of charting.

Another point that is very important in Long Range trading is
the selection of one's broker, and while this subject is covered
in much, much more detail in another chapter, we will touch on it
briefly here due to its importance when using the long-range
trading approach. Brokers quite frankly live or die on the commissions generated by their clients. Most brokers, either
consciously or subconsciously, want their clients to trade a lot in
order to generate more commissions and to keep the broker's income
at an adequate level. Not too many brokers are interested in
clients who take positions and hold them for from 3 to 8 months,
regardless of how great the profits are that are accumulating for
the client, the broker is only making the same commission.

Therefore, unless the long-range trader can learn to ignore
most of his broker's comments and suggestions or find a more compatable broker, the additional pressure can very easily destroy the
best laid long-range trading plan. A constant tatoo from one's
broker suggesting that a position should be closed out because the
market is getting ready to change its direction, even though your
indicators are not picking a change up, or suggesting better opportunities in other markets can have a very debilitating effect on

the trader unless he has the ability to ignore these comments.

We believe it is far better to come to an understanding with one's broker that you want absolutely no information or suggestions from him unless you ask for them. And then only ask for information that you cannot get elsewhere or which is delayed in coming to you because of the Postal Service. Never, but never, ask him for his personal opinion, because no matter how well-meaning he might be, there is the subconscious desire on his part to get you to trade more. If you cannot reach an understanding with your present broker, it is then time to find another one, and upon written request, we at Taurus will recommend such a broker from our list of recommended brokers whom we have checked out to the best of our ability.

The last major area we wish to touch on in our discussion of long-range trading is the one we began our discussion with: that is, how difficult it is for most traders to acclimate themselves psychologically to a patient, long-range approach. It seems to almost be a sociological phenomenon in the United States to want to get rich quickly and to believe that in this land of so-called golden opportunity that it can be done. We believe that it can be done, but the key point is what one means by "quickly".

To us it seems relatively quick to be able to take a small amount of money and turn it into a million dollars or more in two years. To the average trader this seems like forever. This is, in psychological jargon, a contamination, which quite simply means a holding of misinformation as being true. Normally in thereapy, a contamination can be cleared up by providing the correct information and proving it to the satisfaction of the client. We hope that throughout this chapter we have been able to correct most of the misinformation that exists on getting rich quick by demonstrating that, while one can get rich in a relatively short period of time, it very, very rarely happens in a few months or few weeks. We do not know of any "sure-fire" "get rich quick" methods

206

that do not require at least a year or two and also require enormous amounts of patience.

The patience is as important an ingredient as almost anything else, as if a trader has a potential long-range bull trade in the offing and prices simply refuse to move out of the trading range and the other indicators may or may not be indicating an upward move, it is so very, very easy at times to want to go ahead and get into the market before it moves out of the trading range or before more of the indicators confirm such a move. We have seen traders initiate such positions on occasion, but normally they only succeed when and only when 4 or even all 5 of the previously mentioned indicators are pointing for a bull move. And even then, patience should be exercised for the market to move out of its trading range first as the final confirmation of the bull move.

To act in haste and prematurely becomes a pattern with traders, especially if it is occasionally successful, as it will be just by chance alone, and will destroy what would otherwise have been a successful long-range trading program. If a trader finds that he is frequently doing this and seems unable to control his lack of patience, we suggest reading the chapter on "How Your Mind Affects Your Trading" and then if he still seems to have difficulty in following the program he has outlined for himself, to seriously consider getting some therapy. Seeking therapy no longer has the onus in our society that it once did and the costs in seeing a therapist for either a few times for a few months is far better than losing all of one's trading capital.

We do believe that the individual long-range trader, as he gains experience, will discover improvements on the methodology discussed in this cassette, and even if he does not find technical improvements, as time goes by, by hard work his skill will increase in being able to automatically recognize the signs that tip-off long-range trading opportunities.

CHAPTER 9

LONG-RANGE TRADING II

Long-Range trading will not suit every trader, either from
the standpoint of his personality being suited to it or from the
standpoint of Long-Range trading being appropriate to his investment requirements. The psychological aspects of Long-Range
trading will be covered later in this chapter, so for the time
being, we will look at the investment appropriateness of
Long-Range trading for you. First, while Long-Range Trading is
safer from a risk standpoint than commodity trading in general,
due to its higher reliability, greater percentage of winning trades, and lower risk/reward factor, Long-Range trading is not
suitable for many investors.

These investors fall into two basic categories: First there
are those who need to expand their equity quickly, or "get rich
fast". Typically investors approaching the marketplace from that
perspective are psychologically setting themselves up to lose. But
for a moment, let's assume that this trader, who needs to make a
lot of money rapidly, is psychologically healthy. For him,
Long-Range Trading is not what he needs, since typically many
months are needed first for a trade to fill and secondly for the
trade to come to completion. These traders are far better off
trading short-term or even day trading with the best possible techniques they can find.

The second type of trader that Long-Range trading is not
appropriate for is the trader who is seriously undercapitalized.

207

While it is possible to begin Long-Range trading with only sufficient margin in one's account to initiate <u>one</u> Long-Range trade,
it is far better to have sufficient capital to embark on at least
several Long-Range trades in different commodity complexes, thereby
minimizing the risk of failure by diversification.

   We will assume for the purposes of this chapter that the
investor who is going to participate in a sound Long-Range trading
program, has at least $10,000 risk capital - capital he can afford
to lose without significantly altering his life or life style.
This amount will provide him with the opportunity to, on the
average, initiate 5 Long-Range trades simultaneously, and lose all
5 of them - a highly unlikely occurrence - before being unable to
trade further. Incidentally, no one should probably be trading
commodities to any degree without at this very minimum this amount
of risk capital.

   To be simplistic, commodity prices, or the prices of anything
else for that matter, can only go three ways: up, down, or
sideways. While this rather trite statement may sound out of
place in a chapter on Long-Range trading, it is at the heart of our
entire approach to Long-Range trading. Obviously, we do not want
prices to go sideways for us in our Long-Range trades, but we do
want them to go up or down. The ABSOLUTE KEY to selecting
Long-Range trades is to pick a commodity that is selling at
historically low levels or historically high levels, or somewhere
approximately half-way between historic high and low levels.

   What do we mean by historic high and low levels? Well, for
example, as we write this, Sugar prices are now trading around 8¢
a pound. In the past 10 years, which by the way is the time frame
we will use for our judging historical price levels, Sugar has
NEVER traded below 5¢ a pound. It has traded as high though as
66¢ a pound. So, obviously, Sugar at this time, at 8¢ is almost
as low as it has ever been. Historically it is at a very low
price level.

On the other hand, Pork Bellies are trading at this time at about 85¢ a pound, and over the past 10 years, they have ranged as high as slightly over a dollar to as low as 26¢. So, Bellies, while not as high as they have ever been, are at historically high price levels. Incidentally, it will be rare for the Long-Range trader to frequently find potential Long-Range trades where prices are AT their absolute high or low price levels for the past decade.

The third potential Long-Range trading situation is when prices are about the midpoint of their hi/low range for the past 10 years. At this time Wheat is a good example of this case, since it is trading at about $3.50 a bushel, and its range for the past 10 years has been from about $6.40 to $1.40 a bushel. Not perfectly in the middle of the range, but near enough for Wheat to qualify as a potential Long-Range trade.

In order to understand the importance of identifying these three situations, it is necessary to consider our objectives. We want to find a commodity that has the potential for a very substantial price move, and generally the first two cases, when prices at historically high or low levels, means that the market has the most ROOM to move, hence the most profit potential. Thus, Sugar is a far better candidate for initiating a Long-Range trade on the long side when trading at 6¢ a pound than it does when it is trading at 20¢ a pound.

The third case, or the midpoint of the historic range, is a special candidate for a long-range trade, since whichever direction it does move, the potential for profit has already been greatly reduced by the fact that it has started from a HALF-WAY point. The only reason we consider this situation at all, is that when prices are at this point, and certain other qualifications are met - which we will discuss later in this chapter - the reliability, or probability of the trade being successful - is increased tremendously.

True, the potential profit is reduced, but statistically the chances of the trade being successful are so high that we believe

210

this third case should be included in a Long-Range trading program,
and also because some years it is very difficult to find any commodities, or few at best, trading at historically high or low price
levels.

Figure 52

The beginning Long-Range trader might ask how he can determine if a commodity is trading at historically high, low or mid-
point levels. The best way is to look at monthly price charts for
each individual commodity as illustrated in Figure 52, such as
those published by Commodity Research Bureau. Spending just a
brief bit of time scanning these charts will immediately tell you
which commodities initially qualify for consideration as potential
Long-Range trades.

Very often, you will find that virtually every commodity,
when looking at the monthly charts, qualifies as a potential
Long-Range trade, because virtually all of them are at histori-

cally high or low levels or in the mid-range of the past ten
year's prices. At this point, some narrowing of the field of candidates become necessary. It is best to eliminate from consideration those commodities that are lightly traded, such as
Oats, Feeder Cattle, those on the Winnipeg exchange, OJ, Plywood,
Leaded Gas, Eurodollar, Palladium, and sometimes Coffee. In
general, any commodity that is showing less than 10,000 contracts
of Open Interest and/or an average daily trading volume of less
than 5,000 contracts is a questionable candidate for Long-Range
trading.

These markets are referred to as being thinly traded, and as
such they lend themselves to manipulation by holders of large positions and often it is difficult to enter and exit them at consistently favorable prices. Of course, there are always exceptions
to rules such as this one, but everything else being equal, it
makes sense, IF there are other commodities that fulfill the
requirements for a Long-Range trade, to not enter into positions
in these lightly-traded commodities.

Unless a trader is sufficiently capitalized to initiate a
number of positions simultaneously, and absorb losing them if his
analysis is incorrect, the best approach is to diversify, and
select one position from different complexes, such as one Grain,
one Meat, one Foreign Currency, etc.

Earlier studies by us indicated that it was best in
Long-Range trading to generally select a contract month that was
6-8 months distant from the time of entry, and stay with the
contract month throughout the duration of the trade, based on the
assumption that the majority of Long-Range trades will be
completed by the time 6 to 8 months has passed. Subsequent
research by us has confirmed that as a rule, this is still the
best approach to use. Keep in mind though to change the contract
month as time passes if you do not get your position filled within
a reasonable period of time.

212

For example, let's say it is now January, and you see a good candidate for a Long-Range trade in Corn. Six to 8 months into the future would place you in following the July contract of Corn. You place your order to enter the market at a set point for July corn and wait. Two months go by, and now it is March, or getting close to March and your order to enter has not yet filled. What you should do at this point is to cancel your order for July Corn and re-issue it at the appropriate, but different, entry point for the next contract month, in this case September. This way you can ensure that whenever it is you do get your order filled, you will still be in a contract month 6 to 8 months into the future.

At this point, you have identified the likely candidates for Long-Range trades from your monthly charts at historically high, low, or mid-point levels, and you have decided how many of them your finances will permit you to trade, and you have identified the contract months you will perform your technical analysis on, and you will have eliminated from consideration thinly traded commodities, unless for some reason you have a special interest in one of them or a high degree of expertise in one of those thinly-traded commodities due to your profession or background. Where do you go from here?

What you need now are CONFIRMATION or SCREENING techniques which we touched on briefly in the last chapter and will cover in more detail now. These techniques, when applied intelligently and correctly, will enable you to identify with an extraordinarily high degree of accuracy, those commodities which have the highest probability of success for a Long-Range trade. For example, let's say you have identified Sugar as a good potential candidate for a Long-Range buy position. It is a relatively heavy-traded commodity, it's at historically low price levels, and you've identified the contract month to position yourself in. That's all there is to it . . . right?

Wrong. If you know from these CONFIRMATION or SCREENING factors that Sugar is under the influence of Long-Range cycles that

are not calling for a turn up in prices, or that the next 6 months
are SEASONALLY a time when sugar prices fall, or if there is
overwhelming fundamental information - and, in the case of fundamentals the information had better be OVERWHELMING - that calls
against an up move in prices, then any of these factors should put
Sugar out of consideration as a Long-Range trade candidate.

In order words, the mere fact that prices are at historically
high, low or mid-point levels, is not enough in itself to justify
a Long-Range trade. However, without prices falling into one of
these three categories, we will not even be considering that commodity as a potential Long-Range trade in the first place.

These confirmation factors are most important when prices are
historically low or mid-range, because when prices are historically high, markets, as a rule, do not stay at that level for very
long, but typically "blow off" upward and reverse themselves just
as quickly and crash regardless of cycles, seasonals, and fundamentals. This is not to minimize the importance of cycles,
seasonals, and fundamentals in any way but typically either these
considerations are already in favor of a crashing market or the
tremendously overbought situation brought about by a blowing-off
market is just overridden by supply/demand considerations. In any
case, we will want to examine cycles, seasonals, and fundamentals
for all potential Long-Range trades, whether at a high, low, or
mid-point price level.

It is our belief that once a potential Long-Range trade is
identified, the next most important factor to consider is that of
Cycles. The type of cycles that are most critical to us here are
those of a long-range nature, as measured in years, and not months
and weeks. The shorter cycles ARE important, but they all tend to
top and bottom with the Longer-Range Cycles anyway, so we will
concentrate our efforts of the Long-Range Cycles. You can quite
easily identify, in most cases, these long-range cycles by taking
a pencil and marking the monthly high peaks and low points on your
monthly price chart.

Much of this work has already been done by a number of analysts specializing in cyclical analysis, such as Jake Bernstein of MBH Commodity Advisors and Walt Bressert of HAL Commodity Cycles. If you choose not to do this cyclical analysis on your own, or if you want a confirmation of your own analysis, it is an excellent idea to get confirmatory cyclical data from outside sources who specialize in it.

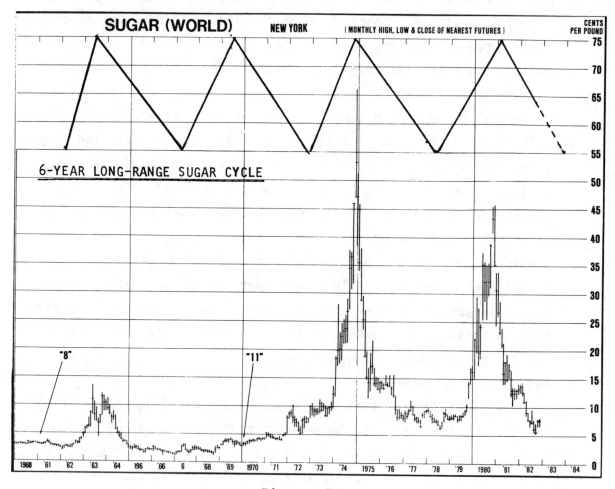

Figure 53

In the case of Sugar, cyclical analysts have identified an approximate Long-Range cycle of 6 years from top to top and bottom to bottom as seen in Figure 53. Hence, if Sugar IS about to make a major move up, one in which we want to position ourselves for a Long-Range trade, the Long-Range Sugar cycle should be somewhere about 6 years from its last significant bottom. We say approximate, but cycles, like most areas of commodity analysis, are not EXACT, but are subject to distortions due to a number of outside factors. But cycles ARE exact enough to merit our serious consideration when it comes to selecting our Long-Range trades.

On our monthly charts we can see that Sugar had its last significant low points back in 1977 and 1978. This would indicate that from a Long-Range cycle standpoint that the next major low in prices SHOULD occur sometime in 1983 or 1984. If the long-range cycles are "OFF" in their timing, they are probably not off from the standpoint of being early since prices are at historic low levels right now. Even if prices still have lower to move before the bottom is reached, nothing is lost by having a "RESTING" buy order, at an appropriate point above the market. So, by looking at the long-range 6-year cycle, we are able to confirm that there is a high probability of prices not only being at historic lows, but also, and more importantly, they are DUE to be bottoming sometime soon.

While it is possible that at some time we may miss a Long-Range trade because the cycles are off so much, due to unusual fundamental considerations or for some other reason, by looking at only those long-range trading candidates that fulfill our cyclical criteria, we will at least restrict ourselves to those trades with the most likelihood of success. For example, Sugar in mid 1981 dropped down to 10¢, which while not the lowest price in the last 10 years, was definitely near the low part of the price range for the past decade.

Without taking the long-range cycles into consideration, a Long-Range trade may have been initiated solely on the price level, and while there was a rally during late 1981 and early 1982 up from the 10¢ price level, it was a relatively brief bear-market rally,

216

and not the type of move we are looking for in our Long-Range
trading. What we are attempting to do by incorporating the
Long-Range cyclical analysis into our trading program is to enhance
the probabilities of our success. In other words, we are
attempting to get as many factors in our favor as possible in order
to maximize the chances for each Long-Range trade being successful.

So, then, Long-Range Cyclical examination is the first test
we apply to our potential Long-Range trades. The second criteria
we look for are the Seasonal Patterns that exist for every commodity. Every commodity has some type of seasonal pattern, or
yearly cycle if you will, that runs each year. Some of these
seasonal patterns are highly reliable, that is, they occur with a
high degree of regularity, generally due to supply/demand factors,
or harvesting, or weather or general economic patterns. Seasonal
Probabilities are typically given in chart or graphical form by
the analysts we've already mentioned and are also available from
other sources. What we want to look for here, in these seasonal
probabilities is the overall pattern of them. That is, how do
prices tend to behave each year THROUGHOUT THE ENTIRE YEAR, not
just on a month-to-month basis.

Many traders, and some analysts, are so used to using seasonal probabilities on a short or intermediate-term basis that they
become very concerned about the reliability, or percentage of time
such a move occurs, from any one given month to the next. This is
not our concern in Long-Range trading.

For example, if we are considering a Long-Range trade in
Gold, and it is now early in the year, it should not be our concern that Gold only has a 33% reliability of increasing in price
from May to June. Rather, we need to look at the overall pattern
for Gold for the entire year as shown in Figure 54, which shows
that seasonally Gold tends to rise in price from September through
March, and then decline from April thru August. Obviously, Gold
does not increase in price EVERY year from September thru March,

nor does it increase in price EVERY MONTH from September thru March
in those years during which prices are rising GENERALLY from
September thru March.

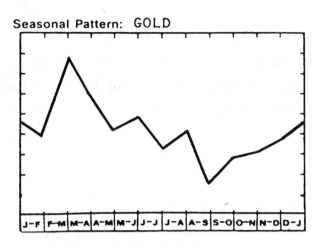

Seasonal Pattern: GOLD

Figure 54

    Seasonals are important to our analysis, but not as important
as the Long-Range Cycles. The Long-Range cycles can easily
override the seasonal probabilities, but typically the seasonal
probabilities will not override the Long-Range Cycles. Seasonals
may DISTORT the long-range cycles somewhat, but here we would have
one factor acting in opposition to another, and not creating our
desired effect of having everything point in one direction.

    So, while we will not necessarily eliminate a potential
trading candidate just because the seasonal probabilities are not
in the direction in which we want the move to take place, if we do
have the seasonal factors pointing in the desired direction, we
achieve two things: first, the odds of the major Long-Range move
taking place at all are increased, and secondly, the extent of the
move, hence our profit potential, is greatly enhanced.

    There is no hard and fast rule concerning when to institute a
Long-Range trade when you will be going against the seasonal probabilities for the next six months, but our inclincation is to go
against them when the long-term cycles are overdue to bottom or top

218

- as the case may be - AND when Bullish Consensus AND open interest both indicate a move is coming. We will now discuss using these two factors, Bullish Consensus and Open Interest as additional ways of confirming whether or not we should be entering into a Long-Range trade.

These two criteria are primarily used by us for entry timing, that is, to determine when it is time to initiate a Long-Range trade. While that is true, we want to emphasize that if the Seasonal Pattern is against the direction of the trade for the next six months or so, we will NOT initiate a long range trade unless the long-term cycles, Open Interest and Bullish Consensus are in our favor.

We will not go into the details of WHY Open Interest and Bullish Consensus affect market turning points, but instead we will touch on their causative factors briefly, since for our purposes the WHY is a lot less important than knowing HOW TO USE these two indicators.

First, regarding Open Interest. You will be able to obtain these figures from virtually any of the chart services you choose to use. Open Interest, quite simply, is the total number of contracts, for all contract months combined, that are held. When Open Interest is increasing, the total number of contracts that are in existence, and have not been "cancelled out" is increasing, and vice versa. We will almost never institute long-range positions from the long side if open interest is flat - going sideways - or increasing. We will want to initiate Long positions if Open Interest is decreasing even a little bit as shown in Figure 55.

Conversely, when prices are near the highs of their historical ranges and we are considering issuing long-range short positions, we will prefer to have open interest increasing, most preferably a sharp increase.

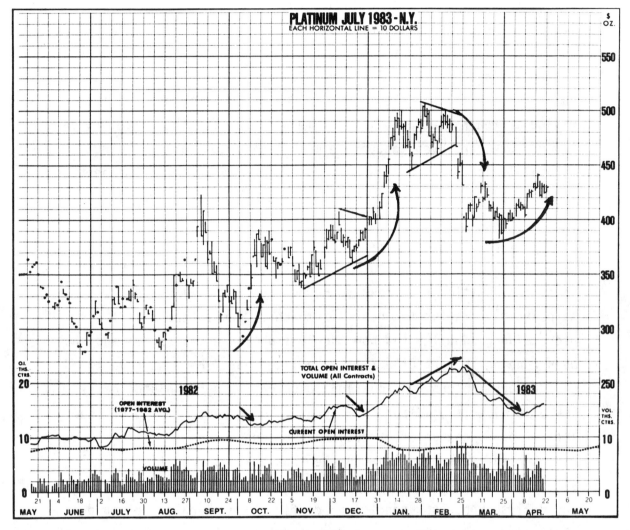

Figure 55

We will never use Open Interest by itself, but rather as
another confirmation that prices will be reversing out of their
historically high or low levels. There are too many instances in
the charts over the years when prices have reversed without this
confirmation by Open Interest to allow us to use it all by itself.
One good way to approach using Open Interest for Long-Range
trading is to not place as much emphasis on it when the other factors, that is, the Long-Range cycles, the Seasonal Patterns, and

the historic price levels are all in agreement that a price turn
is coming. It IS nice to get more confirmation from the Open
Interest figures, and often they can help our timing by permitting
to place our order entry point a bit closer than we had originally
intended - a subject we will cover later in this chapter.

If the Bullish Consensus is 70-80% or greater, and has been
rising to reach that point, the time has come for the market to go
lower. However, even though the market will generally GO LOWER,
it will typically be only a correction in prices before the next
leg of the upmove commences UNLESS the other factors are all
calling for prices to go lower also.

To take our earlier example of Sugar, let's say the long-
range cycles are calling for higher prices, that is, a bottoming
in prices sometime this next year, but the Seasonal Pattern
is pointing down for the next six months, Open Interest is
decreasing gradually, and now the Bullish Consensus is 40% and has
been running in sort of a flat line like that. Here we have two
of our four factors (in addition to prices being at historically
low price levels) indicating a turn up in prices, and two of them
indicating no change of direction in prices.

Our analysis of this would be that this is an "iffy"
situation, but that despite the Seasonal Pattern being against us
and Bullish Consensus sending no confirmation signals, we would
still place a "resting" buy order, substantially above the current
market price, just in case the move occurs against the Seasonals
and the Bullish Consensus. What would we do in this case if now
the Bullish Consensus had dropped, either gradually or precipi-
tously to 15%. Here, with 3 of our 4 factors - especially the
second most important one, Long-Range cycles, second in importance
only to the historic price levels - being in our favor, we would
place our resting buy orders considerably closer to the current
market price levels. How much closer? We'll look at that in a
moment.

To summarize our basic approach to selecting commodities for
Long-Range trading positions: first it is necessary to isolate
those commodities that are trading at historically high or low or
mid-range price levels, then it is extremely important to see if
long-range cycles are at turning points, and if not, where they
are, and then to see if we can get a confirmation of a major price
move from the Seasonal Patterns, Open interest changes, and
Bullish Consensus. These latter three factors, Seasonal Probabilities, Open Interest and Bullish Consensus CAN all be ignored if
the historical price levels and long-range cycles are pointing
strongly enough for a major price direction change.

Unfortunately there are no "hard and fast" rules as to what
percentage, say, of importance to place on all of these factors.
It IS nice when they are all in agreement, but since this does not
always happen, the best a long-range trader can do is to have a
good feel for the relative importance of each factor, and then
trust his intuition and act accordingly.

We now come to the actual entering of the Long-Range trades.
At what point do we place our orders at which to enter the market?
If we place them too closely to the current prices, and if our
analysis is incorrect, we may very well take a substantial loss.
It is better to sacrifice, in most cases, part of the move, by
placing initial entry points a bit further from the current market
prices. The further our entry points are from the current market
prices, the more of a confirmation we have of a long-range move
once our entry points are hit.

Of course, some reason must be applied to this approach, and
the entry points must be at a reasonable distance from the current
price levels, not too far and not too close. We will want to move
them closer if, all of a sudden, the Open Interest and/or Bullish
Consensus factors move in such a way as to indicate a major change
in price is imminent.

222

While there are many techniques for determining one's initial entry points for a long range trade, we believe the best are the ones we will now discuss, and, of course, individual traders may alter them somewhat, or combine them in different ways. Probably any combination of these methods will work relatively well.

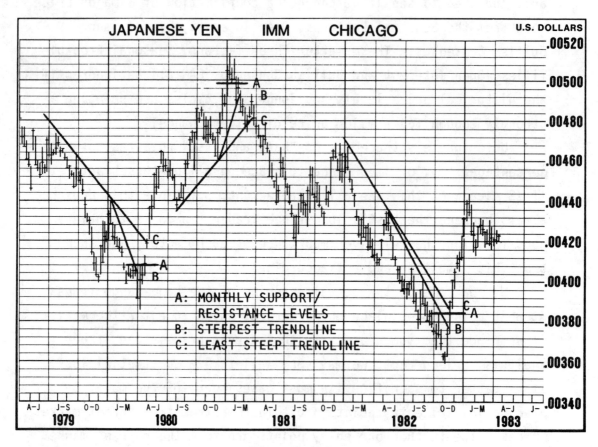

Figure 56

The first is to draw long-range trendlines connecting the weekly highs or lows on your weekly chart, and placing your order to enter just beyond the trendline, of course, adjusting it weekly as the trendline inclines or declines. Often you will be able to draw more than one trendline, some more steep than others, connecting the weekly peaks or valleys. In this case, the most conservative approach is to place one's entry points just beyond the

LEAST STEEP trendline, which, of course, if your other analysis is correct, sacrifices a lot of potential profits. See Figure 56. The more aggressive approach is to take a violation of the STEEPEST trendline as an entry signal. We believe that this approach can be used quite safely when as prices approach the steepest trendline we get a confirmation from Open Interest and Bullish Consensus.

We are, of course, assuming that prices meet their historic qualifications already, and that a thorough analysis of the cyclical and seasonal considerations have already been made. A variation of this approach, which is quite conservative, is to use a breaking through by prices of a previous monthly peak or valley, which are considered as price resistance or support levels, as a point at which to enter. This approach involves typically giving up some of the potential profits, but does have an even greater degree of reliability for a successful trade, and when the other factors under consideration are all in agreement, the most conservative of long-range traders may wish to use this violation of monthly support or resistance levels not only as an entry point but as a final confirmation.

While determining the entry point IS important, it is not nearly as important about being right about the Long-Range trade in the first place. IF your analysis is correct about prices being historically high, low or mid-range, and your cyclical and seasonal analysis is correct, then the Long-Range trade IS probably going to come, and your entry point is immaterial EXCEPT for trying to maximize your profits and for serving as a FINAL CONFIRMATION that prices are in fact going to move in the direction you wish them to.

In the case of Sugar, trading in the nearest contract at 7¢ a pound, say the month we're looking at 6 months away prices are at 8¢, and with historical price support at 5¢ a pound, you COULD buy at the market, RIGHT NOW, given you are correct about the seasonal and cyclical factors, but to do so might tie your capital up in that trade for months, possibly even years if the cycles have expanded for some reason.

The hitting of your entry point placed at a distance from where the market is currently trading, in this case say at 9¢, may cost you a couple of cents in profit, or over $2,000 in the case of Sugar, BUT in addition to this price being hit providing an additional confirmation of the Long-Range moving actually taking place, it keeps your funds from being tied up for a long time before the move actually develops.

After that example, this is an appropriate place to mention one other confirmator factor: POSITIVITY versus NEGATIVITY, or as is often called by other analysts: bullish and bearish divergence. Positivity simply means that the more distant you go into the future among contact months, the higher prices are for those months. Negativity means just the opposite, that is, prices are lower in the more distant contract months than they are in the more nearby months.

While this, like all other indicators, is not an ABSOLUTE indicator, it is better for the long-range trader who is planning on going long to have POSITIVITY on his side. As this is being written, with nearby Sugar selling for 7¢ a pound, and six-months away sugar for 8¢ a pound, the most distant contracts, those slightly over a year away are selling for almost 11¢ a pound. This is a far degree of positivity, and since the bulk of trading in the distant contract months is done by commercial interests who have available to them frequently a lot of information which is not known by the public and the press at large, these commercial interests at least believe prices are going to be increasing in the months to come.

While this factor of Positivity or Negativity cannot successfully be used by itself, at least not consistently, for Long-range or any other type of trading, this can provide one more piece of data to confirm your other analysis. If your other analysis is, so to speak, "on the fence", and about evenly divided between instituting a long-range trade or passing it by, you can use POSITIVITY and NEGATIVITY to break the deadlock.

Your initial protective stops, and they should ALWAYS be used, define exactly at what point you will terminate a trade that goes against you. And they should be placed with your broker at the time you make the initial order or as soon as your Long-Range trading order is filled. As with entry points, there are different techniques you can use to place your initial protective stops. But unlike entry points, in which case if your analysis is correct of the market's direction, it is not always crucial where you get positioned at, with your stops it is very important where they are placed, for two reasons.

First, if you are incorrect in your analysis of the direction of prices, even if for reasons beyond your or the market's control, such as tremendous unforeseen fundamental changes, and the market goes against you, your initial protective stop determines how great a loss you will suffer. But, at the same time, you do not want to risk any larger amount of your money than is absolutely necessary to do, and therefore want to keep your initial protective stops as close to your original entry point as possible.

The best way, of course, is to place your stops a bit BEYOND the lowest price level, in the case of positioning yourself on the Long side, and above the highest price level in the case of initiating a short position. By highest and lowest, we mean the high or low point for that contract month as you see it on your chart. Frequently, however, that point is so far away from your entry that an inordinate amount of dollar risk is involved. If that is the case, then other procedures can be used individually or in combination.

Since in most cases you will not have a trendline to work from initially, at least not from your weekly charts, two alternate procedures are to either place your stops a bit above the highest price reached during the past 4 weeks of trading or, if possible, to draw the least steep trendline possible on your daily price chart and place your initial protective stop a bit above it.

Another excellent procedure for initial stop placement is to calculate the point which is 65% from your entry point to the contract high or low and place your stops at that point, and if your other analysis is correct, and nothing unexpected occurs in the fundamentals of that particular market, prices will rarely retrace themselves 65% from an entry point determined by any of the methods we've described back to the contract high or low. When to use which of these methods can be determined from calculating the amount of risk for each stop placement point, and then, depending upon your financial situation and psychological taste, use the method that fits best for you.

Trailing stop placement is another matter entirely. Moving one's initial protective stops as the Long-Range move is taking place must be done with great care in order to stay in the move as long as possible to get the maximum amount of profit and yet to protect as much of your accrued profits as possible should the move reverse itself on you, for whatever reason. As with initial protective stops, trailing stops can be "SET" in different ways, some conservative, some aggressive, and none of them infallible.

Throughout the initial months of a Long-Range trade, we prefer to use one of two methods, or a combination of them. The first method involves drawing the least steep trendline possible from your daily price chart and placing your stops a bit beyond that. Generally that is a "safe" method, but since it is used by so many traders, frequently it is better to place your trailing stops at a distance of 65% from current prices to the lowest price - in the case of a rising market - of the past 4 weeks, if that price is a bit further away from the current price than where you would place your stop based upon the least steep trendline method.

As prices reach a TARGET AREA, which we will discuss shortly, you should begin moving stops in much closer, generally by drawing steeper trendlines and placing the stops just beyond them whether you plan to take profits at a target area or not, in order to lock in as much of your profits as possible. Also, if you find that the Bullish Consensus has quickly moved into a dangerous range, say above 80% for your long position or below 30 or 20% for your short position, AND if Open Interest is calling for a price turn, it generally is best to move stops in tight with a steep trendline, because while a reversal in prices _may_ only be temporary, if you already have substantial profits and these two indicators are calling for a change in direction, then the change may NOT be only temporary, but may signal a significant price reversal, and to not move your stops in close would be to jeopardize much of your open profits.

We've waited until now to discuss that situation where prices are somewhere near their historical mid-point plus or minus 5% for the last decade as shown in Figure 57. People often ask why near the mid-point? Why not 30% or 70% within the last 10-year's range? Our studies have indicated to us that the most profitable long-range moves come from prices being near their historic high or low levels, OR from the mid-point range, and not from 30 or 70% levels. We're uncertain why this is the case other than they have more potential, but statistically it HAS been the case for the last 20 years.

There are three ways to approach these mid-point situations: to enter a resting BUY order, a resting SELL order, or to do both with an OCO (One-order-being-filled-Cancels-the-Other) type order. The first two cases, those of going long or going short are handled in EXACTLY the same way we have been describing for approaching markets that are at historic high or low levels, that is, examining the Long-Range Cycles, the Seasonal probabilities, Open Interest, Bullish Consensus, and Positivity and Negativity.

228

The same considerations also apply for determining initial entry point, initial protective stop points, and trailing stop placements.

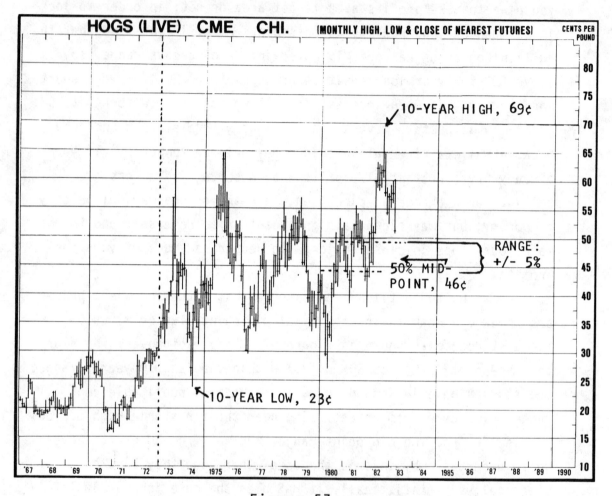

Figure 57

For this last case, that of placing an OCO order, when prices are at the mid-point of the range, and the other indicators are unclear or contradictory, from a statistical standpoint whichever way the market breaks first, there is an extremely high probability that prices will then continue to the area of historic highs or lows - a move substantial enough to produce significant profits and therefore justify entering a Long Range trade.

You determine your entry points for both sides of your OCO order individually, as well as your initial protective stops, just as you would if you were only considering going with one position, that is, either going just long or just short the commodity. Whichever order fills first, the second is either automatically cancelled by your broker or you cancel it yourself - even if you are depending upon your broker to cancel the other side of your OCO, it is a good idea to check to make certain it has been done! After you have gotten a fill on either side, you trail your stops as you would normally. The one nice thing about this type of trade is that since it typically carries to historically high or low levels, it immediately upon completion presents you with another possible long-range trade in the opposite direction, assuming, of course, that there are enough other factors to confirm that prices are about to change direction.

Target Selection, or the point at which to close out a trade and take one's profits is as difficult an area in commodity analysis as any. There is always the temptation, and the very real possibility, that prices will continue on, if not forever, at least a lot further than you or anyone else thought possible, and to take one's profits too early always can end up in losing substantial profits as the move continues on, and on, and on.

There are, at our last count, at least 27 published methods for establishing when to take profits. We have at one time or another examined them all, played with them, tried altering them, combining them, etc. in order to increase their reliability, but so far to no avail. Unfortunately, it has been our conclusion, that at least at this time, there is no ONE method or combination of methods - YET - with which to determine when to take one's profits.

We believe therefore that the best approach is to generally let positions be terminated by ever-increasing the "tightness" of trailing stops as APPROXIMATE target zones are approached. By

230

doing this, if there is still more "steam" left in the market, you
at least stand a reasonable chance of being on board to acquire
additional profits, and frequently the one last upside or downside
blowoff carries quite far, thereby increasing profit potential tremendously.

At this point, it is important to look at the short and
intermediate-term cycles, those lasting about a month and a year
and to either compute them yourself or obtain them from one of the
sources we mentioned earlier. If prices are near their historic
highs, OR if from a psychological standpoint you have all of the
profits you need, want or CAN STAND, OR if the Bullish Consensus is
in dangerous ground, OR if Open Interest is changing significantly,
then we believe it is best to get your stops in close to lock profits in.

Connecting weekly lows with a trendline and placing your
stops just beyond that point is AS GOOD a method as any at this
time. An optional method is to sell at the market anytime prices
close lower (in the case of a long position) or higher - in the
case of a short position - than the PRECEEDING TWO days closes.
But, the only time to use either of these tight stop placement
methods is when you have substantial profits and it is beginning
to look like there is a very real danger of the market topping or
bottoming out.

Some people prefer to use stop placement techniques based on
moving averages, relative strength indicators, etc., and any of
these methods that gets your stops in close to the current price
level will be satisfactory to achieve your goal of locking profits
in place. The choice of method is not critical, BUT USING SOME
method IS critical.

The reader by this point may wonder why virtually nothing
has been written in this chapter about using fundamentals. We will
discuss them briefly here, but with the understanding that it is
our firm belief that 99% of the time, the markets have already

taken into consideration the fundamentals and are showing them in their price movement. While many fundamentalists would disagree with us, and most probably have statistics to back themselves up, we believe that you can be very successful in long-range trading with only a minimal concern for the fundamental aspects of any market you might trade.

That 1% of the time that you need to be concerned about fundamentals is when there appears to you to be SOMETHING, ANYTHING that might suddenly affect the market, and which is not commonplace knowledge to the trading public. You might well ask, "If it's not common knowledge to the trading public, how in the world would I know about it?" And most times you will be correct. IF your profession involves some commodity or complex of commodities, you MAY be aware of some potential occurrence that has not yet received public notice. Chances are slim, but they still exist that this can occur. In such a case where you are placing a long-range buy order, and you become aware of a potential situation that may drastically affect the market negatively in a month or two, most probably after you have gotten a fill on your long-range order, you may well decide not to place the order at all. After all, there are always other candidates for long-range trades without entering a position prone to reversing itself with limit days.

The other instance that can occur is when an important government report, such as a crop report, an export report, unemployment, housing, car production, etc., any report which may affect the markets, is due to be released. At these times it is best to withdraw any resting Long-Range, orders that you have in place that may be affected by these reports. Often otherwise you may find yourself filled, say on the long side, in the brief fluster of enthusiasm after the release of the report, only to find yourself stopped out the next week as the implications of the report are thoroughly realized.

232

If, after such a report, the market has moved thru your original entry point and NOT retraced back thru it, you can then decide
whether to buy at the market or on a reaction, with your stops
either placed as original protective stops or computed then as a
trailing stop. The amount of dollar risk will generally be the
determinant of whether to then get in the market at all and which
type of stop placement to use. If after such a report prices move
through your original entry point and then retrace back through it,
and all of the other factors are still favorable toward your original long-range analysis, go ahead and re-institute your original
order and original protective stop and wait to see if you get
filled.

Incidentally, we receive a lot of questions about the effects
of inflation or the lack thereof on the markets, and the effect
of government deficits, news stories, international bankruptcy,
etc. Our position is that all of these things have typically only
short-term effects that are consequential. The long-term effects
of these occurrences, and there ARE long-term effects, are
reflected in the markets just as are the other fundamentals.

Hence, just because inflation appears to be under control, we
do not see ANY reason for not initiating long positions in commodities affected by inflation. For the long-range trader, the
markets by their price movement, will reflect whatever significance
there may be of national and global financial considerations.

The last technical aspect we want to cover in this chapter is
that of Pyramiding, or adding to your original position as the
move continues in your favor. We are of the belief that it is best
for Long-Range Trading to build a pyramid from the base, that is,
to BEGIN with multiple contracts if you are into pyramiding and
then add additional contracts in lesser quantities as the move
progresses. Or, at worst, to begin with a single contract, BUT to
add the additional contracts as rapidly as possible.

Probably the best way to do this is to have your entry points
just above the previous week's high, and trail your stops using one

of the methods other than the one you are using for your original position. We believe the Long-range trader is best served by building his pyramid quickly, as we've just suggested, and by trailing his stops slightly differently, at least up until the time it appears the market is getting ready to reverse its major trend.

Our financial research indicates to us that a trader who is doing long-range pyramiding should have as a rule approximately three times the capital required than if he was not pyramiding at all. Pyramiding can be a wonderful way to increase one's profits when a really good long-range trade is hit, but it does require additional working capital, additional time for analysis, and generally more patience.

One commonly overlooked area especially in Long-Range trading, is the selection of one's broker. While such selection is important for any type of commodity trading, it is VITALLY IMPORTANT for the Long-Range trader. Why? Because brokers exist on the commissions their accounts generate, and the less you trade, the less income your broker makes, or so it seems to many brokers. A few, more dedicated and intelligent brokers approach the long-range trader from the standpoint that they will retain him as a client for a long time, perhaps indefinitely, since long-range traders are normally successful ones, and the broker will not have to find another client in a month or a year to replace an unsuccessful client who loses his money and drops out of the markets.

To use a broker who does not have this approach to his clients is to endanger oneself from a psychological level. If you have a broker who is only interested in HOW MANY trades you make, not how successful you are, he will consciously or subconsciously be sabotaging you by suggesting you enter additional positions, that you move your stops in closer, etc. Even if you are of a mind to resist such pressure, it does not make for a pleasant relationship with your broker.

It is far better to have an up-front understanding with your broker, whoever he is, that you do not want suggestions, comments or whatever from him unless you solicit them, and generally it is best <u>not</u> to ask for his comments. If you have any difficulty locating a broker who is willing to use this approach with your account, just contact our offices and we will refer you to one that we know is compatable to having his clients use a long-range approach.

The only area we've not yet mentioned is the psychological aspect of long-range trading. The majority of commodity traders do not like long-range trading because, regardless of its higher profitability, it is not exciting enough for them. Of course, the majority of commodity traders lose all of their money in the first 12 months of trading and drop out of the markets. If you feel that long-range trading is not for you, and yet consciously you want to make money in the markets, we respectfully suggest you look, inside yourself to see if you REALLY do want to make money in the marketplace.

The chances are that subconsciously you do not and for whatever reasons are afraid of success. We suggest if this feels "right" to you, that you read our book <u>Games Investors Play</u>, and the book <u>Overcoming the Fear of Success</u> by Dr. Martha Friedman. If you still, after reading these books carefully, have an uncomfortable sensation when you envision yourself as being very wealthy, we suggest you see a competent therapist to resolve whatever subconscious issues there are that prevent you from succeeding. We maintain a directory of excellent therapists nationwide and will be happy to refer you to one of them in complete confidence.

The material in this chapter may sound rather elemental at first reading, and possibly not as "advanced" as you might have expected. We don't believe that is the case, as frequently the simplest approaches to anything ARE the MOST advanced, and that is the case with Long-Range trading. It really is quite easy as far as the basic principles are concerned, once one knows WHAT those principles are, and they are those factors we have dicussed in this chapter.

The skill of blending these different factors and approaches together can only be acquired by practice, as it is a skill that must be developed to some degree. Not that it is difficult to acquire this "feel" for long-range trading. It isn't. It just requires understanding the basic principles, having the right market information, and some practice. We suggest you acquire from some of the chart services old charts, or just use monthly charts, to practice those concepts we have developed in this chapter. With a little bit of practice, you will be absolutely amazed at how much you can accomplish with long-range trading.

CHAPTER 10

PLACING YOUR ORDERS

There seems to many traders nothing so mundane as a
discussion of how and when to use the different types of orders
when instituting or closing out a trade. This is truly unfortunate since the correct selection of the order type is not only a
most useful tool but one that can add significantly to a trader's
profits at the end of the year. Many traders believe that as long
as they are adept at following trends, picking tops and bottoms,
and using their own technical and fundamental information, then
they know everything that is required to be successful in commodity trading. Unfortunately, nothing could be further from the
truth. They are no better off than a pysician who knows how to
diagnose an illness and which medication to prescribe, but who has
never learned how to administer or inject the medicine. So it is
with many commodity traders. This chapter on how professionals in
commodity speculation place their orders to maximize their profits
and keep themselves out of losing trades, will explore the subject
in great detail.

Placing orders is both an art and a science. The professional trader must be knowledgeable about all of the types of
orders available to him, and when to use each type of order; and
he must also have a broker who is willing to work with him when it
is necessary to place the less-frequently used orders. The latter
is especially true when he needs to use a type of order that is
not accepted by a particular exchange. In that case, since the
order cannot be placed as he wishes directly with the exchange, he
must have a broker who will watch the market for him and get him

236

in where he wants. We will have more to say about this later. It is not enough for him just to call his broker and tell him he wants to buy 5 contracts of Cotton. Even if he is correct about the trend of the market, he may suffer far lower profits by such sloppy trading; and in fact even if his judgment of the market direction is right, he may end up losing money. We may seem to be nit-picking in our emphasis on the importance of correct order usage and placement, but it is intentional because we want to emphasize (to the reader) how very important this subject is if he is to succeed to the fullest extent in his commodity trading program. In fact, no matter how skilled and astute a trader has become in paper trading, we would exhort him to refrain entirely from actual trading until he not only has a grasp of trading techniques, but also has a thorough working knowledge of which orders to use and when. The remainder of this chapter will cover these twin subjects.

First we will describe the different types of orders that are at every trader's disposal, and then we will explain the proper use of each of them for the best results. One of the most commonly used orders is a <u>Market Order</u>. This is an order which is to be executed at the best possible price the moment the order reaches the floor. Prices are constantly changing on the floor of every exchange as bidding goes back and forth between buyers and sellers. The phraseology the trader would give his broker would be" "Buy 1 May Cotton Market". You will notice that we did not have to specify a particular exchange since Cotton is traded on the New York Cotton exchange. Many commodities are traded in mini-contracts on the Mid-American Exchange, and if the trader wants to place his order there, he must so specify to his broker. This is also the case with other commodities such as Gold and Silver which are traded on more than one principal exchange, in which case the trader must specify whether he is talking about IMM Gold or COMEX Gold. Normally in such cases where a commodity is

238

traded on more than one major exchange, an astute broker will ask
the trader which exchange he is talking about; but since brokers
work under tremendous pressure it is best not to take a chance,
and to specify what you want in order to avoid any possible misunderstandings later on.

An important point needs to be made here, and that is with
the placement of grain orders. Grain orders are phrased only in
multiples of five, so that if you wish to buy or sell a single
contract of say, wheat, you would say "Buy 5 July Wheat" instead
of "Buy 1 July Wheat". If you are dealing in single contracts,
your broker will pick this up and change it to read 5 July Wheat.
However, if you are unaware of this distinction and really want to
buy a total of 5 contracts of July Wheat and tell your broker "Buy
5 July Wheat," he will end up purchasing a single contract for
you; whereas if you had told him to "Buy 25 July Wheat", you would
have ended up with the correct amount of a total of 5 contracts.
Many a trader has gotten himself over his head by getting the
grains confused with other commodities and telling his broker to
"Buy 5 March Coffee", which at the present time would cost him
$40,000 original margin, instead of "Buy 1 March Coffee", which is
what he really wants. So care must be used when giving the quantity of contracts you really wish to buy or sell.

Market orders to sell are just the reverse of market orders
to buy, and are executed or sold at the prevailing price the
moment they reach the floor of the exchange. Such an order might
be given to the broker as" "Sell 1 May Cotton market." Another
type of order is a Limit Order, either to Buy or Sell. Here the
price at which the order is to be executed is specified, and if
the price on the exchange floor does not reach that point, then
the order will not be filled. In this case the trader wishes to
get into a market at a specific point and is unwilling to
establish a position unless his order can be filled at that point.
An example would be: "Buy 1 May Cotton 91.10". This means that

unless and until May Cotton is trading at 91.10, the order will
not be filled under any condition.

Here we would like to point out an important fact about
orders. All commodity orders are considered to be Day Orders
unless specified otherwise. A Day Order means that the order is
good only for that day, and if it is not filled on that day it
will automatically be cancelled. Unless you tell your broker
otherwise, he will assume that you are giving him a Day Order. We
are pointing this out because very often you should not use Day
Orders, and virtually all of the Taurus' newsletter Recommendations are given as not being Day Orders. The way to do this is
to use a Good Through or Good 'Til Cancelled order, which is often
abbreviated as G-T-C. In our example about cotton, if you want
the order to remain in place longer than the day you place it,
your instructions to your broker would be: "Buy 1 May Cotton
91.10 stop G-T-C." In this case, the order will remain effective
either until it is executed or until it is cancelled by the trader
at a later date. By using this type of order, the trader does not
have to follow the market minute-by-minute or even day-by-day. If
he believes Cotton will continue to rise if it hits 91.10, he can
place his order G-T-C, and, while we do not ever recommend not
following markets that you have positions in or open orders for, a
trader with a G-T-C order can afford to ignore the market to a
degree, or at least, not to follow it as closely as he might
otherwise have to.

One of the more infrequently used orders is the Fill or Kill
order, which is abbreviated as F-O-K. In this case, a price is
specified, and if the order cannot be filled at the specified
price when it reaches the floor, it is immediately cancelled, or
"killed". This order would be given to your broker as "Buy 1 May
Cotton 91.10 F-O-K". With a multiple contract order, such as "Buy
5 May Cotton 91.10 F-O-K", if 2 of the contracts filled at 91.10
and the market then moved up, the remaining 3 would not be filled

240

even if the market retreated back down later to the 91.10 level. Often this type of order is used by commercials or large traders to test the market to see what, if anything, it will do when the order hits the floor of the exchange.

An order that is finding increasing popularity among large professional traders is the <u>Scale Order</u>, in which positions are scaled in as the market moves, either way. Scale orders require that the initial order be for a minimum of 2 contracts, and that it specify the points at which additional contracts and their quantity, are to be bought or sold. Scale Orders may be used with Stop Limits or with Market Orders. An example of the former might be "Buy 4 May Cotton 91.10 stop and 4 more each 20 points down, total 28 day". In this case the floor trader will buy the trader 4 contracts of May Cotton at 91.10, an additional 4 at 89.90, 4 more at 89.50, etc. as long as prices reach those levels. If the original order was "At the Market" then the 20 points down at each level would be computed from the initial entry point.

One of the orders that Taurus uses most frequently is the OCO order, and unfortunately it seems to be one of the most difficult for the average trader to understand. Later in this chapter we'll explain its applications thoroughly, but here we will describe what an OCO order is. The OCO stands for <u>One Cancels Other</u> - O-C-O, and it means that two orders are placed simultaneously, and whichever is filled first, the other is immediately cancelled. An OCO order can be used for two different commodities, such as "Buy 1 May Cotton 91.10 stop OCO Buy 1 March Cocoa 1980 stop". The use of an OCO order this way is infrequent, but is sometimes done when a trader lacks sufficient capital to enter both trades and wishes to be certain of getting into the one that hits his entry point first. The more usual way of using an OCO order is within the same commodity, such as "Buy 1 May Cotton 91.10 stop OCO Sell 1 May Cotton 85.90 stop". This means that Cotton will be trading somewhere between the two points, and if it rises and hits

91.10 first, you will be long 1 contract of May Cotton and your sell order will be automatically cancelled. The reverse would be true if Cotton headed down and touched your sell order first, in which case the long end of the OCO order would be immediately cancelled. Since many if not most exchanges will not accept OCO orders, it is up to you or your broker to cancel the second order after the first one fills.

Another popular type of order is the Stop Order, which is sometimes referred to as a Stop-Loss Order. A Stop Order is an order to buy or sell at the market when the market reaches a certain price. A Stop Order to buy, such as "Buy 1 May Cotton at 91.10 stop", means the market is currently trading below 91.10 and when it reaches that figure, the trader's order is triggered and becomes a Market Order. Just the opposite occurs with a Sell Stop Order, in that the market will be trading above the stop price when the order is placed. In actively moving markets, the order is frequently filled at a price quite different from the stop price. In the case of the "Buy 1 May Cotton at 91.10 stop", the order may end up getting filled at 92.10 in a rapidly moving market. Buy Stop and Sell Stop Orders are also used for protective stops. Most brokers will understand when you place your original order, say "Buy 1 May Cotton at 91.10 stop with initial protective stops at 89.90", that you want to go long Cotton at 91.10 if the market reaches that point, and simultaneously you want to sell 1 contract of Cotton at 89.90 to close your position out if you are filled at 91.10 and the market then starts down. Generally as a market moves in your direction, and you move your stops, it is sufficient to tell your broker to "move my stops up to 92.30" or whatever, and he will enter a sell order for you at that point to close your long position out should the market start back down. Technically, however, you would give him the order as though it were a separate Sell Stop Order; but if you have an experienced broker (which you should) you do not have to go into that detail to place your protective stops.

Another useful order is the Stop Limit order which combines the features of both the Stop Order and the Limit Order. In this case, whether it is a Stop Limit Order to Buy or a Stop Limit Order to Sell, the order is not triggered until the price reaches the stop point and then is executed only if it can be done at the limit price. An example would be: "Buy 1 May Cotton 91.10 stop, stop limit 92.00". This tells the floor broker that the order is triggered at 91.10 and he is to fill it before it reaches 92.00. The limit provides some protection in a rapidly moving market where the trader wants to define his risk more closely. If prices are moving rapidly upward and the floor broker cannot fill the order before the 92.00 level is hit, he must wait then until prices come back down below 92.00, if they do, before he can fill the order. There is one variation of this type of order which is called a Stop-and-Limit Order, and in this case the stop and the limit are one and the same. In the previous example, the order would be given as: "Buy 1 May Cotton 91.10 stop limit". This means the order is not triggered until the 91.10 point is hit, and can be filled only at the limit price or lower. As with all limit orders, the floor broker stops trading on that order when the price moves outside the specified limit.

An order that is very useful when you are attempting to buy into a bull market on a reaction or sell into a bear market on a rally is the M-I-T Order, which stands for Market If Touched. It differs from a Stop Order in that in a bull market, a Stop Order is placed above the point at which the market is trading, and in a bear market a Stop Order is placed below where the market is trading. In a bull market, an MIT order is placed below where the market is trading, if the order is to buy; and in a bear market, an MIT order is placed above where the market is trading, if the order is to sell. For example, if our May cotton is trading around 93¢ and we want to buy it on a dip to 91.10, our instructions to our broker would be: "Buy 1 May Cotton 91.10 MIT". If the market dips to 91.10, then the order is activated to buy at the market. If we wish to sell cotton at 91.10 and the market is trading around 89¢, then the instructions to the broker would be: "Sell 1 May Cotton 91.10 MIT". This type of order is a very useful one, but unfortunately it is not used nearly as often as it is called for.

Two other types of useful orders are Opening and Closing Orders. These instruct the floor broker to buy or sell at the open or close of the market. They can be given with or without a limit. Examples of instructions to your broker might be: "Buy 1 May Cotton Opening Only" which would instruct the floor broker to place your order as a Market Order when the market opens for trading. An example of a Closing Order would be "Buy 1 May Cotton MOC", the MOC standing for Market on Close, which means your order will be filled at the closing price of the market and treated as an "At the Market" order. Variations of these close orders would be used for placing stops, so that your protective stop would be activated only if the market closed at (or below, in the case of a long position) your close-only stop.

There are a number of more exotic types of orders that are used mainly by commercial interests, or are types that we have found to be of little if any, use to the speculator. We would include spread or straddle orders in this category, as we do not believe they are the types from which substantial profits can be made. Some of these other orders that we will not discuss include: Market Basis Orders, Sell When Tendered and Redeliver Orders, Switch Orders, and Contingent Orders.

One cautionary note should be sounded here. As we mentioned earlier, not all exchanges accept all types of orders. For example, at the time this chapter is being written, the Chicago Board of Trade does not accept MIT orders. Since exchanges change their rules from time to time, when you are in doubt about whether or not an order will be acceptable to an exchange, it is best to

244

check with your broker. Let's say that Wheat has started an uptrend and you are not yet long. Your calculations show you that Wheat probably will be having a reaction back to the $4.00 level and is now trading at $4.25 per bushel. Since the Chicago Board of Trade won't accept an order that reads "Buy 5 July Wheat 4.00 MIT", if you feel you need to use this type of order to maximize your profits and/or minimize your risks, you must have a broker who is able and willing to work closely with you. If he understands what you want him to do, and if he has the time and the disposition for doing it, he will watch the July Wheat market for you, and when July Wheat drops down to the $4.00 level, he will enter your order as a Market Order. Only experience or a recommendation from one of his other clients can assure you that he will do his best for you in the execution of such an order. You really must have a professional broker to handle these special situations, and the subject of locating one is discussed fully in another chapter of this book. In fact, if you do not have a thoroughly experienced and professional broker, virtually any of your orders may be confused or placed incorrectly. For their own protection, many professional traders tape-record their telephone conversations with their brokers so that if there is any misunderstanding or mistake, they have solid documentation to fall back on. No matter how well you choose and word your order, if your broker doesn't understand it, or is inexperienced, the correct placement of your order is in jeopardy.

We have found the most useful entry order to be the Stop Order. Generally when a market changes trend, it has to move in the direction of the new trend to a certain degree before the change in trend is confirmed. For example, let's say that Wheat has been trending down for a period of months and seems to be flattening out, for whatever reasons, and is trading around $3.80 a bushel. As can be seen in Figure 58. Your indicators, whatever they are - including Cycles and Seasonals, Trendlines, Point and

Figure charts, Contrary Opinion, or those indicators that pinpoint a bottom formation - tell you that the market is due to change and start up.

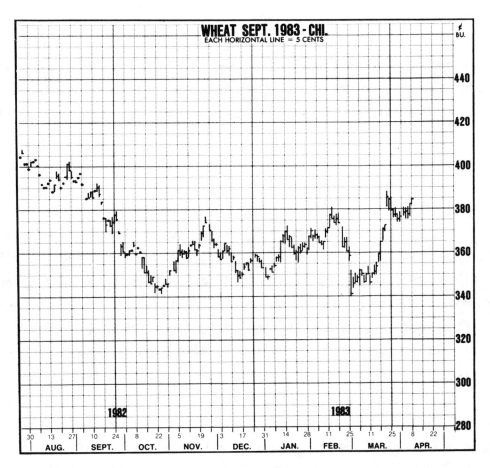

Figure 58

Should you buy immediately? Even though it would mean that you would be entering at a better point, thereby lowering your risk and increasing your potential profits, the answer is no. A market changes trend and moves in the other direction only _after_ the move starts. We realize that sounds simplistic, but scores of hours of research have convinced us that it is unwise as a rule to enter a

246

market until it has moved in the direction of the new trend sufficiently to validate the existence of a genuine change in trend.
So in this case you would not buy Wheat at $3.80; using whatever
technical methods you are familiar with, you would instead enter
your orders to buy at say $3.90 or $4.00 Stop, which means that
unless you are right and the trend really has changed and is now
starting up, your order will never be filled. This will keep you
out of numerous losing trades. An MIT Order has the same function
when you are late getting into a trending market. But neither the
Stop Order nor the MIT Order should be used if the trend has per-
sisted for several months or longer, as you are in danger then of
having the major trend reverse on you completely. In the Wheat
example just given, if you missed getting in at $3.90 or $4.00 and
the market over the next month has moved up to say $4.20 and your
calculations show it is due for a reactionary correction, you might
place an order to buy at $4.10 MIT in order to save 10¢ which you
would lose if you bought at the market. If you are incorrect and a
reaction doesn't come back to the $4.10 level, then you won't be in
the market; but often it is better to miss a position entirely than
to assume unnecessary risks. The markets have been around for a
long, long time, and the probabilities are that they will be around
for many years to come. If you miss a position here and there,
there are always other positions to take, and it is better to
search for them than to risk too much of your capital. Taurus can
look back many times at positions which for one reason or another
we "missed". trader can be eminently successful even if he
misses many of the winning trades in the marketplace, as long as he
gets a fair share of them and does not assume unnecessary risks
along the way.

Over the years, we have found protective stop placement to be
one of the most difficult aspects of commodity trading, due to the
large number of variables that affect their correct selection. One
ideal method is to calculate how much you are willing to risk in

terms of dollars, convert that to points, and see where that would place your stop. If it is below a trendline, in a long position, or below the low point of the last reaction, then you have a fair probability that the stop is well-placed, however unscientific this method is. When we feel we have gotten into a market that has topped or bottomed, we have found it best in most instances, to place our stop (if our capital reserves permit it) just beyond the suspected high or low of the move. In a bull or bear position when the market hasn't been trending for long enough (in months) to put it in danger of running out of steam, we prefer using the 65% Method. For example, if Wheat is trading at $4.50 a bushel, and the last reaction from which it rose to this point was at $4.20, the move up to this point covered 30¢. We take 65% of 30¢, which is 19½¢, and subtract it from the $4.50, which gives us a figure of $4.305. This is where we place our stop. If Wheat continues up to $4.60, then the move from the reaction low of $4.20 is now 40¢, and 65% of 40¢ is 26¢ which we subtract from the current high of $4.60 to get $4.34; and that is the point up to which we move our protective stop. This method is based on the research finding that when a move retraces more than 60%, then the trend generally has reversed itself. The technique requires following the market daily, and changing your protective stops with your broker each time a new high is made, or each time a reaction point is established. The method works equally well in reverse in bear markets. Even though you would probably tell your broker just to change your protective stop, the effect would be of cancelling your former order and instituting a new Stop Order.

OCO orders are extremely useful when prices have been in an extended trading range for a period of time, and when you are attempting to pick either a bottom or a top. For example, let's say December Gold for the past 5 weeks has been bounding back and forth between $430 and $470. As shown in Figure 59.

248

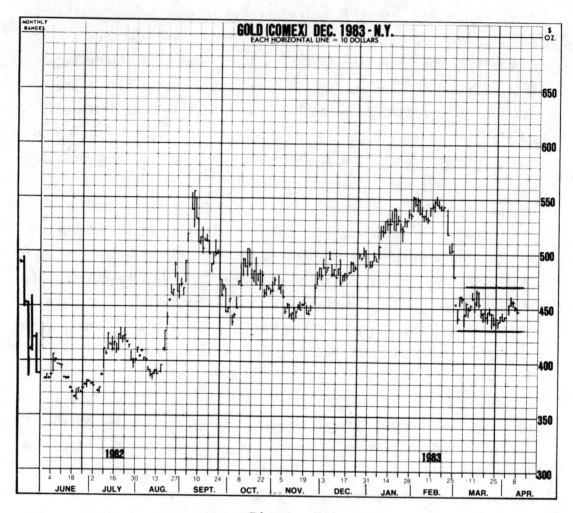

Figure 59

This is a perfect example of a trading range; and we would like to note here that the longer prices remain in such a trading range, and the more compressed vertically it is, (i.e. the less difference there is between the high and low prices), then the greater the probability is that once it moves out of the trading range limits, the move will be substantial. In the given example of Wheat, we would place our order as follows: "Buy 1 December Comex Gold $475 stop with initial protective stops at $425, OCO Sell 1 December

Comex Gold at $425 stop with initial protective stops at $475".
Thus by using an OCO order, you are assured of getting into the
market whichever way it breaks out; and generally the direction of
the breakout holds, and the trend continues in that same direction
for some time.

Taurus rarely recommends using a Stop Limit Order because if a
market is trending at all, a Stop Limit Order is extremely difficult to
get filled and generally the trader finds himself without a position. We believe it is better to use a Stop Order without a limit
restriction on it in order to assure entry into the market even if
some points are lost as a consequence.

We will on occasion recommend taking a position at the
opening of a market, especially if a market seems to be trending
rapidly and we have already missed the point at which we would
have used a Stop Order; or if we do not foresee a reaction with
which we could utilize an MIT Order. We strongly recommend to the
reader that he use orders at the opening of the market exclusively
in these same situations, and the only time that a Market Order
should be used is in a similar situation, where for some reason

you have missed the point at which you would have liked to enter
the market and you do not foresee a reaction coming shortly. If
this is the case, often it is advisable to enter at the market in
order to get a position established. However, it is far better to
be prepared in advance and have resting buy or resting sell orders
already in place so as not to miss out on the market move. As we
said earlier, a resting buy or sell order is simply a Stop Order
placed above the current market price (in the case of a desired
long position) or a Stop Order placed below the current price (in
the case of a desired short position) in order to catch a trend
when it is changing.

Another excellent way to use resting buy and sell orders is
to place, a resting buy order just above the peak of the last
rally in a bull market that has retreated in a reaction. In the

case of Wheat, let's say the market had advanced to $4.50, after having been in a bull phase for at least a few weeks, and then retreated back down. Then a resting buy order is appropriate at $4.51, because if the market comes back up from its reaction, whether it is a 65% reaction or not, the chances are that the bull trend will continue. So in this case you instruct your broker to "Buy 5 September Wheat at $4.51 stop."

Very often Roll-Over Orders are indicated, and there seems to be a good deal of confusion about exactly what rolling over is. Rolling-over is simply closing out your position in one contract month and establishing a similar position in a more distant month. Let's say you are long May Wheat and First-Notice Day is approaching. You feel that Wheat is going to continue its advance, but you know it is time to get out of the month you are in. The procedure to follow in a case like this is to close out your May position and establish another long position in a more distant month, say July. So you instruct your broker to "Sell 5" May Wheat at the open and Buy 5 July Wheat at the open". This effectively closes out your May position and reinstitutes your long position in the July contract. Such a roll-over does not have to be at the market's open; it can be done on a stop basis if you have been following the market closely enough and feel you can pick up some extra points. Using this example, if May Wheat today closed at $4.40 and July Wheat closed at $4.60, and you believe (for either technical or fundamental reasons) that the market is due for a slight correction, you could place the order as: "Sell 5 May Wheat at $4.40 stop and Buy 5 July Wheat at $4.55 stop." The figures may vary of course, according to your calculations; but the point we wish to make is that although rolling-over is simplest to do at the market opening, you may increase your profits, if your analysis is correct, by using Stop Orders instead of Market Opening Orders.

Strange as it may sound at first, psychology affects your choice of order placement, especially your protective stop place-

ment. It is useful to calculate where other traders holding the
same position as yours are keeping their protective stops. Often
this can be roughly established by drawing a trend line. Many
traders will have their stops placed just below the trendline,
usually on a stop basis. When you believe this is the case, it is
beneficial to place your own protective stops on a close-only
basis because often the market during the day will break that
trendline, only to rally and close above the trendline (in the case
of a long position) at the end of the day. By using a Close-Only
Stop Order you have kept yourself in the market while many other
traders have been stopped out. Much the same procedure applies
with resting buy orders and resting sell orders, especially when
prices have been in an extended trading range. In this case a
resting buy or sell order on a close-only basis may save you from
getting into a position that would otherwise turn out to be unprofitable because of the large number of traders who will have
resting buy or sell orders (though not necessarily on an OCO basis)
on either side of the trading range. The important part of using
psychology in order selection is to figure out what the majority of
traders will probably be doing, and then to choose a type of order
that will protect you if they are wrong. One way to do this is to
subscribe to as many advisory services as possible from both private market analysts and brokerage houses. Even though this is
expensive and time consuming, it may be the very best way to place
your stops. If the majority of the services which are long Wheat
have their protective stops at $4.40, it is good psychology to have
yours a bit lower than that or to have them (if $4.40 is the place
you want to put your stops anyway) on a close-only basis. This
will keep you in many positions that otherwise you would be stopped
out of unnecessarily.

The ultimate order to pyramid with is the Scale-In Order,
whether you use it at specified price levels or scale-in on a
point basis. Let's say you believe you have detected a major bot-

tom formation and wish to establish 10 contracts on the long side. You know from our earlier discussion that you want to enter on a stop basis.

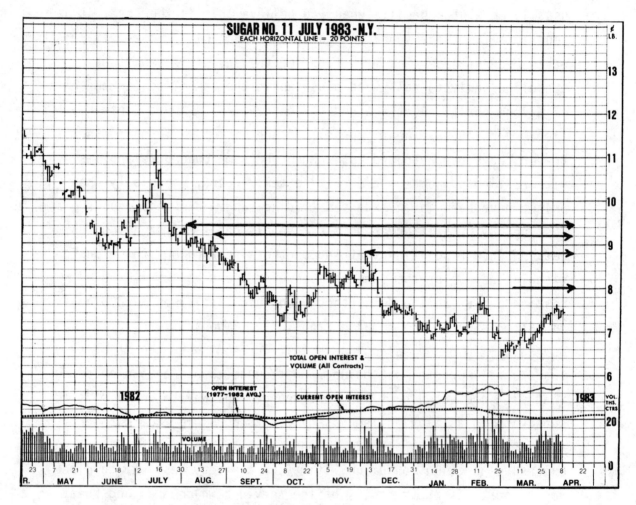

Figure 60

Suppose the market is Sugar, see Figure 60, and you believe it has bottomed in the vicinity of 6½¢. The best way to get your 10 long positions established is to pyramid them by scale-in orders. Strictly speaking, this procedure is not really a scale-in order; but it has the same effect as one. When pyramiding, you want your paper profits to pay for all or part of your additional positions, either to reduce your initial risk or because you do not have enough capital to finance all of the positions at once. Let's say your analysis leads you to believe that Sugar will break the 15¢ level before it tops, so you enter your order with your broker as: "Buy 1 July Sugar at 8.01¢ stop, Buy 1 July Sugar at 8.81¢ stop, buy 2 July Sugar at 9.21¢ stop, and Buy 6 July Sugar at 9.41¢ stop." You have established your pyramid by using a sequence of stop orders at different levels, effectively scaling yourself in. Of course the actual entry points at the different levels will vary, depending upon the amount of capital you have available and how much of the position you want your paper profits to cover. You would, of course, at the same time establish with your broker the positioning of your protective stops for each level (or at least for the initial purchase) and as each new level is hit, you would re-adjust your initial protective stop and establish a protective stop for the new position.

Contract months can affect your order choice, and this is an often overlooked facet of order placement. Normally the nearby months are the most volatile, due to the increased volume of orders taking place in them. As a result, if you wish to get in a market at a specific price and want to use a Limit Order, you will generally find it very difficult to do in the nearby month. However, if you are using a more distant month (anticipating perhaps a long-range trade) a Limit Order has a much better chance of being filled since there is so much less "action" taking place in that month. If you're using a Stop Order, a Market Order, an Open Market order, or an MIT or OCO order, it makes relatively little difference what contract month you choose to enter into. These statements about contract months generally hold true only for the most popular and actively traded commodities. If you are into commodities such as Broilers, Eggs, Barley, Palladium, Commercial Paper, the Mexican Peso, etc, you are best advised to place your orders, no matter what type they are, in the nearby

254

month; because with the lack of volume in these markets your Limit Orders stand a poor chance of being filled in any but the most nearby contract month. When trading these relatively unpopular commodities and using orders other than Limit Orders, you will often get bad fills due to the thinness of these markets; and the more distant the contract month you select, the greater your chances for a poor fill.

There are numerous ways to select targets, or how far a move will go before it falters. There are more than a dozen different methods, and most chartists and technical analysts have their own favorite or favorites. It is our experience that no one method works consistently well by itself, but only in combination with other methods. It is not the purpose of this chapter to discuss how to establish target prices, as Taurus' research on further perfecting target measurement and analysis is still incomplete. In any case, once a trader has selected his target (that is, the point to which he believes the market will advance or decline before either pausing or reversing itself) he needs to decide what type of order to use to close his position out. Our preliminary studies indicate that whatever method is being used to establish a target price, this price should be reduced by 5% for the initial target. Let's say you've established a target of $1.00 for Cotton. If you are trading single contracts and it is a long position, you should instruct your broker to "Sell 1 May Cotton at 95¢ MIT". If you are trading multiple contracts, it is better to use a pyramid-reversal order. For example, if you have 5 contracts long in Cotton, you might instruct your broker to "Sell 1 May Cotton at 95¢ MIT. Sell 1 May Cotton at $1.00 MIT. Sell 1 May Cotton at $1.05 MIT". And you could have him leave the remaining two contracts in place in case a runaway market occurs, or you could instruct him to sell 2 May Cotton at $1.10 MIT. There are infinite variations on this theme, but we believe MIT Orders are the best to use when working with targets. If you use a Stop Limit Order instead, you run the definite risk of not getting out of your position at all; and if your target has been accurately selected, the market may very well reverse on you at that point and leave you forced to liquidate your position at the market price - which may be substantially lower by the time you get your Market Order in. If for some reason you have neglected to place your order to close your position out when your target is hit, or if you have only just arrived at your target computation and find the market is already there, these are really the only times you should close out your positions on a Market Order basis. (Of course you could also do so if your computation clarifies the situation before the markets have opened.)

To summarize everything we have covered in this chapter: First it is important for you to learn what the different types of orders are, how they are given to your broker, and in which situations they are appropriate. Depending upon your style of analysis, there are some types of orders that you may never use, or use only infrequently. It is important to understand their advantages and disadvantages anyway, so that if a situation comes up where one of these atypical orders will work better than the others, you are familiar enough with them to recognize the situation. You must also recognize the influence of fundamentals in your selection of order type. If there is a lot of news breaking about the commodity you are considering taking a position in, you would never use a Stop Limit Order if you definitely want to get into the market, because the news will increase the market's volatility. Conversely, when there is a lot of news about a commodity, and you feel you <u>must</u> clearly define your risk, then a Stop Limit Order is definitely called for even though you may not get filled. Seasonal fundamentals work in the same way in that if a market is seasonally due to bottom or top, then a mere Stop Order will assure your getting in regardless of the volatility of the market; and on the other hand a Stop Limit will define your risk exactly, even though you may not end up with a position in the market.

On targets you have selected yourself, remember to use MIT Orders only; and with multiple contracts having a predetermined target, use a pyramid-reversal type of order. Be sure your broker understands you, and if you must use orders that will not be accepted by the exchange you are trading with, you must make certain that your broker is both willing and able to follow the market closely enough to see that your order is taken care of as well as possible. You must make certain when placing your orders that your broker understands exactly what you want, so don't be reluctant to have him repeat back to you his understanding of what you want. If you have difficulties in getting your orders placed the way you have specified, change brokers. When using Stop Orders, you must be prepared for the fact that your fills will not always be where you would like them to be. If you believe this is your broker's fault, you can always get him to provide you with the Time and Sales data that will clearly indicate whether it is his fault or not; usually it isn't. After the actual selection of the type of order that is best for your trade, your broker is the next most important link in the chain of order execution. Make certain he understands what you want to accomplish. Remember that OCO Orders are extremely useful when dealing with trading range markets, and that they will generally assure you of getting positioned on the correct direction of the next trend. If your technical skills include being able to judge reaction points in bull markets and rally points in bear markets, then by all means use MIT orders to minimize your risks and maximize your profits. If the exchange doesn't accept MIT orders, then find and use a broker who will help you with them as much as possible. Use a series of Stop Orders at whatever levels you deem appropriate when entering a pyramid trade. Use Close-Only Stop Orders when you are trying to outguess the rest of the traders in a market. Try not to use Stop Limit Orders in volatile markets, or in markets about which a lot of news is appearing, unless absolutely necessary to define your risk. Trade the nearby contract month or the next month out whenever possible, using Stop Orders for your entry points.

If we were limited in the types of orders we were allowed to use, Taurus would pick as the two most important the Stop Order and the OCO Order. We have found these over the years to be the easiest to work with in most situations. This is not to discount the importance of the other types of orders, because they all have their applications, even if these situations occur less frequently. The next most important orders we believe are the MIT Order and the Close-Only Stop Order. Buying at the market can bé invaluable in order to catch a very rapidly moving market, and buying at the open is the easiest way to handle roll-overs. We believe that in the majority of cases all orders should be GTC or Good-Til-Cancelled rather than Day Orders. There are some exceptions to this rule, but they are infrequent unless a trader is day trading or trading short term swings.

CHAPTER 11

YOU AND YOUR BROKER

Next to actual trade selection and money management, there is
probably nothing so important as the selection of one's broker.
On the surface of it, this sounds like a pretty extreme statement.
After all, many people would argue, "How important is a broker?
Really?" Knowing this is a common misconception among commodity
traders and other investors was the prime reason for writing this
chapter, because we disagree very strongly with the view that
one's broker is not all that important.

Fortunately, there are a wealth of books, articles, and other
sources of information on trade selection and money management.
Unfortunately, after going through our entire library of general
and specialized books on commodity trading, we found very, very
little in the way of useful, specific advice on the importance of
having a competent broker or how to go about finding one. Hence,
the majority of information contained in this chapter is original
from the standpoint that it has been developed from our own
experience over many years and from conversations and meetings
with traders and brokers in an effort to expand our own experience.

It is indeed unfortunate that brokers are generally only paid
commissions on the trades they execute. It would be far better if
they were paid a flat salary, or even better if they were given
bonuses based on the profits they managed to generate for their
clients. The "commission-only" approach lends itself to many brokers not really caring whether or not their clients make money,
only that their clients continue to trade and trade as often as

258

possible. Few things bring more joy to the average broker than
securing a new client who is interested in day-trading, as this
will generate commissions quickly.

Many traders somehow feel that the commissions they pay on a
trade go directly to their broker, not considering that the broker
works for a brokerage firm and that the brokerage firm has huge
overhead costs. As a result, the individual broker receives only
a portion of the commission charged a trader. A typical case
might be about thirty-eight percent of the total commissions, so
on a trade for a single contract with commission charges of $50,
the broker would only receive $19 for himself. It's pretty easy
to see from this example that, especially in these inflationary
times, brokers _must_ generate a lot of trades, and/or have a lot
of clients, in order to even make a decent living. Using this
example, if a broker places 30 trades a week, he will gross
approximately $30,000 a year. But, if he places 60 such trades a
week, he will gross $60,000 a year! It should come as no surprise
then that many brokers encourage over-trading so much.

This is not to say that most brokers are unethical. This is
just the way the game is played, and if a broker doesn't generate
enough trades, he quite simply does not generate enough income to
survive. It has been our experience that the vast majority of
brokers are very honest and very ethical, but they are faced with
the fact that well over 90% of the accounts they have on January
1st of any year will no longer be with them on December 31st of
that year. Therefore, it is really not in the broker's best
financial interest to develop a lasting relationship with his
clients, since most of them won't be with him that long anyway.
To develop lasting relationships takes time, and if most clients
are short-lived, then it becomes a waste of a broker's valuable
time to do so when he could be using that time soliciting new
clients to replace those who will continually be falling by the
wayside. One broker we know of had 1,000 clients over a 7-year

260

period, and none of them ended up with a profit! This despite the
fact that this particular broker was a very honest man.

The few unethical brokers who are in business are like the
few bad physicians, lawyers, businessmen or any of the few "bad
apples" that exist in any profession. They are the ones we read
and hear about because they are making news. We rarely if ever
hear about the top notch brokers because they not only keep a low
profile but also because they are not newsworthy. The majority of
unethical brokers will make every attempt to secure discretionary
powers from you so they can trade your money themselves and
thereby can "churn" your account and generate as much commission
as possible for themselves in as short a time as possible. This
is not to say that giving your broker discretionary powers is bad.
There are instances where it is very wise to do so, and these will
be covered later in this chapter.

What then is a Super-Competent broker? Well, quite simply, he
is one of those rare creatures who is genuinely interested in his
clients. He is a broker who not only doesn't want to have to replace
90% of his clients every year, but actively tries to keep that
from happening and to keep his clients making money. He is the
broker who would rather have a handful of successful clients
because he knows as their profits and equity increase, they will
be trading a larger number of contracts for each trade, and his
income will grow proportionately.

True, not too many beginning brokers can afford to take this
approach, because like trading itself, it is a long-range
approach, and one can starve to death waiting for the profits or
commissions to become sufficiently great on which to live. If
this is the case, how is it that there are any top notch brokers
out there? Frankly, we're not sure how they became that way or
got to where they are, but we do know they exist. Since our purpose is not to train brokers in this chapter, but to help you, the
trader, we are not going to pursue theories as to how or why some

brokers become the true professionals. Taurus Corporation does maintain
a listing of brokers who have been recommended to us over the
years by our friends and subscribers. Brokers who, as nearly as
we have been able to determine by talking with them, meeting them
whenever possible, and speaking with as many of their clients as
we could, all seem to belong to that exclusive circle of true professionals. Taurus will be happy to refer any of its subscribers to
one of these brokers, and we only ask that if you have such a
request, you write to ask instead of phoning.

By now, after examining the mechanics of the average broker's
income, it should be apparent to you why it is important that you
have a top-flight broker for yourself, just from the standpoint of
guarding your equity. While this is, without saying, extremely
important, there are many, many other reasons why you should have
one of these quality brokers, and we will examine all of them
in this chapter.

Where are these brokers? That is, will you find them concentrated in any one place or area that will simplify your search?
Unfortunately, there are two sides to this question. We used to
believe that it was mandatory to have one's broker in Chicago, the
heart of much of the action. Our second choice used to be New
York. However, we have come to the conclusion now that the true
professionals are not only in New York or Chicago, but also in the
Denver's and Boston's, and even smaller towns. The reason for our
original conclusion, was, we believe, due to the fact that there
are so many more brokers in Chicago and New York that it appeared
to us that this was the only place the pros were. That, and the
fact that up until not too long ago, the only true professionals we
knew were in these two towns. True, it may be easier to find the
broker you want in Chicago, due to the very concentration of brokers there, but we now believe that the pros are everywhere, even
in Podunk; it's just that with so few of them to begin with, proportionately speaking, it seems that the majority are in the big

cities. The one advantage of having a broker in Chicago seems to
be due to the fact that since the vast bulk of trading takes place
in Chicago, <u>sometimes</u> a broker there is more in touch with floor
traders, the CFTC, etc., due to his location.

We have heard stories, pro and con, about the relationship
between brokers and their floor counterparts. Supposedly, there
are instances of floor traders and brokers "scratching each
other's backs" and exchanging favors and courtesies on occasion.
Due to the controversial nature of something like this, it is very
difficult, if not impossible, to verify these theories. It may
well be true that personal relationships between brokers and floor
traders can be advantageous to the broker's clients when problems
arise, but we are uncertain how important this is, especially
since instances when favors may be needed are infrequent. This is
one of those "gray areas" in commodity trading that is perpetuated
mostly by rumors and gossip, and may or may not be of any
significance.

Regardless of where you find your professional broker, he
should be able to straighten out your problems for you, when they
arise, in a prompt, efficient, and courteous manner. Only too
often a trader will find that his broker seems to be the paragon of
friendliness and efficiency, <u>until</u> a bad fill occurs or a problem
arises with his account. There are too many times that even the
best of brokers may make a mistake in understanding the type of
order his client wants executed. When a mistake occurs, for whatever reason, you need a broker who is on your side. He should be
willing to quickly get you time and sales reports if you question
a fill that you get, and if there has been a mistake on the part
of the floor trader, your broker should get the matter into
arbitration and resolved as quickly as possible. Obviously, a
trader has the responsibility in not demanding services frivo-
lously, such as time and sales reports, as doing chores like this
obviously take up your broker's time which, as we've explained, is

a very valuable commodity to him. A measure of reasonableness
should prevail on both sides of the broker-client relationship. It
is frequently the case that a truly top-notch broker can get
better fills for his clients. He does not do this by manipulation, magic, or by doing anything unethical. Instead, he is aware
of what is going on in all of the markets, and if you have given
him some latitude, he takes the time and effort to act in your
best interests. This is especially true in the use of "Or Better"
orders. For example, if you give your broker the order: "Sell 5
July Soybeans at 880 Or Better", this is not like a "stop loss"
order. In this example, Soybeans may be selling at 885 or 890.
This is higher than the price limit put in the order.
Nevertheless, to ensure the sale of the July Soybeans, you are
willing to put in an order below the current market price. This
gives your broker some leeway in the execution of the order, and
the designation "or better" prevents the order from being sent
back from the floor with the question "Do you mean a stop?" This
would be a logical question, since the order comes in to sell at a
price below the market. The designation "or better" prevents the
order from coming back with this question and permits the order to
be executed quickly and efficiently. If your broker has a good
feel for the market action in Soybeans that day, and is willing to
exert the effort, he may very well be able to enhance your profits. Likewise with most other types of orders, a top-notch
broker may be able to get your position established at a more profitable point than specified in your order. As another example,
if your order was to sell the July Soybeans at 880 stop, and if
the market is behaving in a very volatile manner, your broker,
with your consent, may wish to sell at 882 or 885 instead of the
880 because of his perception that the market will probably move
through 880 so rapidly that unless he takes this precautionary
action, you may end up getting filled at 875. An even better
example occurs when you wish to place a type of order that is not

accepted by the exchange on which the commodity is traded. Let's say that the method you or your advisory service is using indicates, in the above example, that a true downmove is in progress, but that the way the market is, you would have to risk too large an amount of money in the placement of your initial protective stop if you entered the market at this point. Since Soybeans are traded on the Chicago Board of Trade, and since as of the time this text is being prepared, the Board of Trade will not accept a Market if Touched, or "M.I.T." order, you obviously cannot give your broker an order to Sell July Soybeans at 890 M.I.T. with beans now trading at 880. However, if you feel you must wait for a reaction to the 890 level before executing your order, in order to reduce your initial risk, your broker can, by constantly watching and monitoring this market, get your order executed when Beans have reacted back up to the 890 level or thereabouts. This takes your broker additional time and care to accomplish, and it is quite understandable for brokers to not want to have to do this, because, again, it takes time for them to do it. But, if your broker is a real professional, and interested enough in your account to want you to succeed, he will, if at all possible, make the extra time to help ensure your making additional profits. As he does this, and your account grows in size, instead of trading single contracts, you'll be trading two or three or more contracts of each trade, and his investment in time will start being rewarded by the additional commissions generated by your success and his work. It is easy to understand why even the best broker in the world at times doesn't really want to have to take such special care of orders, but the really good ones will do so as often as possible, whether they feel like doing it or not.

A question that we are frequently asked, is "How do I know it's time to change brokers?" The obvious answer would be that if it is time for you to find another broker, or begin your search for your own top notch broker, you will just "know" that it's

time. It has been our experience that even the real pros are
not perfect. They have their bad days, they make mistakes, they
come to work after an argument with their spouse; in short, they
are human. So, being human, they will make their share of mistakes, and sometimes not be as helpful and pleasant as you might
like. However, their "share of mistakes" and "unpleasantness",
will be far less frequent than their counterparts. There is no way
to have a scorecard that we know of to keep track of mistakes and
irritability, and to be able to say, "Well, John made two mistakes
this month, and was unpleasant at least once on the phone, so it's
time to change brokers." Would that it were that simple. It is
more, as they say in psychology, a "gut-level feeling", where,
after a lot of thought and consideration, you "feel" that your
broker isn't the professional he once was or that you thought he
was, and that it is time to change brokers. Most brokers certainly
do not want to lose their clients, especially not while they still
have money to trade. Too often the average broker will be pleasant
to his clients whether he really feels that way or not, and will be
extremely self-effacing and obsequious when mistakes occur, so that
it becomes even more difficult at times to decide whether or not he
is or isn't really a pro.

When you begin to experience a feeling of discomfort when
talking with your broker, and it persists, it is then time to
start asking yourself whether or not you are getting your money's
worth in your client-broker relationship. You can begin by going
over in your mind the conversations you have had with him, whether
he has been helpful in getting you information you needed on the
markets, how well he has handled the inevitable problems that have
arisen, and any other question you can think of that might relate
to the feeling of discomfort. After some careful thought, your
subconscious will "tell" you whether or not it is best to stay
with him. The only double-check you should make involves your own
psychology, and is more thoroughly discussed in another chapter.

Some traders, unconsciously, select brokers in much the same way they do spouses, only to undergo divorce after divorce. If you have had a history of changing brokers, it may very well be because you have just not yet found the right one. It may also be for your own psychological needs of having to have someone to criticize, or to feel that you have been persecuted by your broker. This would happen most likely if you have really found a top-notch broker, and subconsciously are feeling uncomfortable with his not playing games on a psychological level with you. A good way to look at this is to ask yourself: "Is my broker helping me to make money, and if he is, why do I feel uncomfortable in my dealings with him?" Some honest soul-searching may reveal that the problem is not with your broker, but is within yourself. If that is the case, by all means, do not change brokers, as this will not solve anything for you. In this case, either reading some good self-help books on psychology, such as Muriel James' Born To Win, or if necessary, seeing a good therapist, may be called for.

Incidentally, throughout this chapter, we have referred to brokers only in the masculine gender, and that has only been for the simplicity of being able to say "he" instead of "he or she". We are aware that some of the professional brokers out there are women, and that if they appear to be in a minority, it is only due to the fact that there are a lot less female brokers to begin with, which is due to sex stereotyping within the brokerage industry over the years, and which fortunately appears to be diminishing as time goes on. There is the question, on a psychological level, of whether it might be best for your broker to be of the same sex or of the opposite sex. Feminists may scream that this is a chauvinistic question, but we do not believe that to be the case. Since, from early childhood, all of us have had definite memories imprinted in the unconscious circuitry of our brains, it is only natural that each of us tends to get along better with one sex or the other. If you are aware that this is

the case with you, it certainly would be counterproductive to pick
a broker of the sex that you traditionally have difficulties with,
unless you are working in therapy on cleaning up those sex-role
linked difficulties. Since this is such a large area in itself, we
will not pursue this in detail beyond the discussion up to this
point. We do feel it is necessary, however, for the trader to be
aware that the sex of his broker may have some bearing on their
client-broker relationship.

A true professional broker has another characteristic that it
is important to be aware of and to consider. He is able to get you
the information, whether of a technical or fundamental nature, when
you need it, and in the format that you have requested it in. He
should have access to as many sources of such information as
possible that are unavailable to you. If you are considering a
position in Copper, and request help from your broker in the form
of fundamental information, it does you little good if he comes
back to you with information like "Inventories of manufacturers and
producers are down right now." Down how much? Compared to when?
Last week or last year? Does it make any difference how low they
are due to the overall figures on the economy, or does it make any
difference because it looks like a predicted upcoming strike will
be averted? When you need data from your broker, it should be fast
and accurate. It does you little good, if you request this information to help you make a decision on taking a position in the
market, and by the time your broker gets back to you, whether it is
measured in hours or days, the market has already moved 20¢ in the
direction you were considering establishing your position.

It is true that many traders do not need this type of information, rarely if ever, and if that is the case for you, it makes
no difference as to the research and data-accumulation capabilities of the firm with which your broker is associated. That is a
question only you can answer for yourself. It might be well to

consider, however, that even if you are presently using an advisory service or your own methodology in selecting positions, that the time may arise when you do need some piece of technical or fundamental data that you cannot acquire on your own. Everything else being equal between two brokers, it would seem to make much more sense to deal with the one who seems most capable of getting you information if you need it. As an interesting experiment, we once had ten of our subscribers call their brokers, and we called ours, to ask about a government report that had just come out that day, specifically a U.S.D.A. report on Livestock Slaughterings. The first question asked was, what were the figures; secondly, how did they compare with the figures that were anticipated to be reported; what significance did these figures have relative to the upcoming direction of the markets; and lastly, what action was recommended by the brokers called. There was no difficulty getting an opinion from the brokers as to the direction of the market or establishment of a position in it. However, some had difficulty even locating the exact figures in the report, and more had difficulty in determining if the figures reported were what had been predicted. Some of the pros recommended instant action in establishing positions, which they evidently quite honestly felt should be taken, but some recommended staying neutral and keeping out of the market. None of the brokers, though, who had difficulty in getting the figures or giving comparative information on them, had any difficulty in suggesting that immediate orders be placed. We found this most interesting in that if they had trouble getting exact data, how in the world could they be in a position to know what to do in the markets? Obviously, not too many successful traders will call their brokers with questions like these and then initiate positions based on the information they get from their broker unless they already are ready to take a position and only need confirming or validating information. The important point here, however, is that if you require information, your broker

should be in a position to provide you with it. With all of the
markets being traded, and the swift pace with which the markets
change and new information on them becomes available, it is
impossible for any one broker to have all the figures and data on
the tip of his tongue. It is possible, however, for the big-
leaguer to have access to whatever it is that you need. Maybe not
100% of the time, but at least a significant portion of the times
you request such information. The research departments within the
brokerage firm he works for must be sufficiently adequate in their
capabilities in order for him to have such access. If he does not
know the information himself, he should be able to get it for you
within a reasonable period of time. Obviously, some traders abuse
this, and are constantly calling their brokers requesting information they have no real intention of acting on, or information
that is available to them elsewhere, such as in The Wall Street
Journal or commidity yearbooks. We strongly suggest that you treat
your broker in this respect the same way you would want to be
treated if the shoe were on the other foot, and only call and ask
him for data when you genuinely need it and cannot get it
elsewhere. To do otherwise is definitely counterproductive in your
relationship with him. If you have two brokers and are considering
just retaining one of them, or are trying to make a final decision
between two different brokers, or simply trying to decide whether
or not to change your broker for a different one, a good way to
approach this question of being able to obtain information is to
call both of them, one right after the other, with several per-
tinent questions about a particular market, ones that probably will
take them at least a little while to answer, and then hang up and
wait for the responses. A little imagination on your part should
enable you to come up with these questions, and they should be ones
that you would normally not be able to answer for yourself. You
can keep a scorecard here, especially if you've told them you need
the information as soon as they can get it, and see how long it

takes each of them to get back to you, how complete the information is, how accurate it appears to be, and what if any interpretation and recommendations they make to you. This is most effective if you ask the questions about a market that you have reason to believe the brokers in question do not specialize in and are not the most active or popular markets. Platinum, Coffee, Potatoes, etc. would be such types. By comparing how fast the responses are, and the content of them, you should have a pretty good idea which broker can be the most helpful to you when you have to have information from him. This will help you determine if either or both of them are really professionals or not.

Another interesting aspect of picking the best broker, and one we touched on briefly already, is the subject of the quality of the fills you get on your orders. Obviously, your broker, whoever he is, cannot control the rapidity with which a market moves. If you've given him an order to sell Soybeans at 880 stop, and the market moves from 885 to 875 in a matter of minutes with only a few trades being executed along the way, he doesn't have any control at which point your order gets filled. We have, however, heard over the years that certain brokers and brokerage houses, due to their relations with the floor brokers, invariably get "better service" on order execution, especially in fast-paced markets. It appears to be impossible to validate this thesis one way or the other, and we mention it only to make you aware of such a possibility. If you and a friend are trading the same markets generally, and you find that one of the two of you is consistently getting somewhat better fills, as we have often heard the case to be, it would seem that the conclusion to be drawn is that one broker or brokerage house, for whatever reason, even if it only be coincidence, is able to get better fills, and all other things being equal, would be the best to deal with. We are implying no improprieties here, simply because we do not know if any exist or not.

One of the most frequently overlooked areas in the search for
a top notch broker is that of using a discount broker. And,
while this is a very easy question for a trader to answer, it is
still a highly individualized one. Once a trader is generating
large numbers of trades, or few trades with a large number of
contracts involved for each trade, the amount of savings that are
involved by using a discount broker can be substantial. There
are, however, some important questions a trader must ask himself
before deciding to go with a discount broker. There is the old
adage of being penny-wise and pound-foolish, and it is easy to see
how, by using a discount broker to save on commissions, it would
be possible to save relatively small amounts of money of commissions, only to be seriously hurt financially in the handling of
trade execution, requesting information, types of orders accepted
by some discount brokers, etc. On the other hand, there is
another "old saw" about saving money wherever possible on the road
to making a fortune. So, clearly, the question appears to be a
complex one. However, in reality, it is not. The first thing you
must ask yourself is "How important to me is the ability to get
any kind of technical or fundamental information from my broker?
Depending upon the advisory service you are using, or whatever
methods you use to make your trade selections, this may or may not
be an important factor. If you determine that you do not need to
get information from your broker, at least almost never, then the
option of using a discount broker becomes a more viable one for
you. However, if on the other hand, you find that at least on
occasion you need this type of information, then a discount brokerage firm may not be for you. The second point to consider is
whether or not the discount brokerage firm you are considering will
accept all of the types of orders you will want to be using. Many
traders find it necessary to use G.T.C. - Good Till Cancelled -
orders, which simply means the order stays in place to buy or sell
at a certain level until the trader cancels it, even if weeks go by
before it gets filled.

Unfortunately, some discount brokerage houses, at the time this is being written at least, will not accept such orders, forcing the trader who feels he must use this type of order to call the broker every day and re-instate the order. There are a number of other types of orders, other than day orders, that the discount brokerage house may or may not accept, such as M.I.T. orders, Or Better orders, etc. So, if you have determined that you do not need any information from your broker, and you either will not be placing specialized orders or using only day orders or "at the market" orders, so far a discount broker may be fine for you. There is just one other point you should consider before going this route, however. Not too long ago there were four bankruptcies or receiverships of brokerage houses within two months. Some were discount brokers and some were not. One of our own subscribers, we learned, was unfortunate enough to have an account with one of these brokerage houses which was placed into receivership and does not know if he will ever get his money back, or if he does when, or what the percentage will be. Needless to say, this is quite a disturbing thing to have happen. None of these firms were what are known as Clearing House Members, and what we are about to say applies as much to any brokerage firm as it does to discount brokers, but since this would be the last check-point to consider before choosing a discount broker, this appears to be an appropriate place to discuss it.

On any day, many transactions in the markets are consummated. These trades have to be "matched up" according to prices and delivery months. To make this easier, all trades are cleared through an organization called a "Clearing House", which is an adjunct of the exchange and therefore works closely with it.

The Clearing House also guarantees performance for each trade that it clears. In other words, it guarantees the trade and the payment for it. Since anyone who buys a seat on an exchange is not forced to become a member of the Clearing House, anyone who conducts business on the exchange who is not a member must have those transactions cleared through a Clearing House member. Rigid financial and many other types of qualifications must be adhered to before one is approved as a Clearing House member. Any member of the exchange who is not a Clearing House member and who is clearing transactions through a member is <u>not</u> responsible to the Clearing House itself, but to the member. Clearing House members have impeccable credentials; however, it is up to them to decide upon the credentials of those members of the exchange who are clearing transactions through them. Clearing house members' accounts and financial information have to be submitted to the exchange daily. Non-clearing members often only have to provide it to the clearing member once a month, opening far greater possibilities for mismanagement or incompetence to go undetected until it is too late. We are not saying that non-clearing house members are dishonest or disreputable in any way. We simply want to point out that there is an increased risk to a trader's money when it is being handled by a non-clearing house member. If the broker you are currently using or plan on using does not belong to a firm that is a Clearing House member, you can minimize or eliminate any risk to yourself by requesting financial information on the brokerage firm itself, depending upon their past reputation, etc. So, this would be one of the last elements to consider when deciding whether or not to go with a discount broker.

Another question to consider when looking for your top notch broker is whether or not it is important to have a broker who is with a firm which specializes in commodities only, and not stocks and bonds. At one time we took the policy of advising subscribers in general to deal with a broker who was assocated with a firm that specialized in commodities only. We did this because at the time it had been our experience that a trader was far likelier to find his super-broker at such a firm due to their specialization in commodities. We would still recommend not dealing with a

274

broker who was handling stocks or bonds or options in addition to commodities themselves, unless the trader knew that this broker was exceptional enough to be able to fulfill the other requirements that the trader had established for his broker.

Many "full-service" brokerage firms that handle stocks and bonds as well as commodities have such excellent research departments, financial standing, and attract so many top-flight brokers these days, that we now feel it is irrelevant whether your broker works for a specialty or a full-service brokerage firm. In some cases, especially where information-getting requirements are important to you, you may get more of what you need from the broker with the full-service house. Note that we say some cases, as this is not universally true. It seems then that the choice between a specialty brokerage house and a full-service brokerage firm is much more dependent upon the broker himself and your requirements for obtaining information than it is upon the nature of the firm.

The ultimate way to determine if the broker you are considering is one of the real professionals is to ask those who have been dealing with him for some time. The easiest way to do this, of course, is if someone you know and trust has referred you to him in the first place. Unfortunately, this is not always a viable possibility, so often you must find another way. Once you have determined that a broker meets all of your other requirements, you can come right out and tell him that while you trust him and like what you hear, you never make a decision to buy anything, (and you are buying something here too), without talking to customers who have used the product before. Normally most brokers will understand this if it is put to them in the proper way and not feel offended. In most cases the broker will tell you that he must check it out with some clients first, to get their permission, and get back to you with their names and phone numbers. Of course, like references on a resume, no broker is going to pick out dissatisfied or disgruntled clients to refer you to. Even so, his willingness to do this, coupled with the information you get from the clients you talk to, will give you a wealth of information. Be specific, though, when you make this request of the broker and ask for only clients who have been with him for longer than 6 months or a year. This enables you to talk with those clients who have been with the broker long enough to have gone through the normal ups and downs of any broker-client relationship. Unfortunately, this is not to say that if a broker refuses to check with his clients and refer some to you that he is not a reputable broker or that he has anything to hide. It does indicate, however, an unwillingness to cooperate with you, take the extra time to check with his clients, and may very well be indicative of his not wanting you to talk to any of his clients, or that he doesn't have any satisfied clients or that he doesn't have any that have been with him that long, none of which are very positive indicators of a true professional.

One of the most potentially dangerous or profitable ways to deal with a broker is by setting up a discretionary account with him, in effect giving him the power of attorney to trade your money in your behalf. Potentially dangerous in the case of a broker who only wants the commissions he can generate by churning and over-trading your account. Even though there are legal remedies available to deal with such a situation, they can be long and costly, and churning can be done in a slow and careful manner to conceal over-trading. However, if you do not have the time to make your own selections and want someone else to do it for you, having a discretionary account can be a very profitable way to go as well as freeing you up from decision-making. In such a case it is most necessary to have not only checked this broker out with a number of his clients, but also to obtain a track record that will indicate how successful he has been over the years. There is no question in our mind that there exist such professional brokers who not only perform all other functions in an expert way but also are able to profitably select trades on a regular basis. It is often useful in such a case to set written parameters around what the broker can and cannot do. We are thinking in particular as to what percentage of your total account he can invest in any one commodity or complex of commodities, what percentage risk of original margin you will permit on any given trade, whether or not you will permit day-trading, and so forth. These different parameters are covered more fully in other chapters in this book. In any case, it is useful to decide upon the guidelines or rules involving a discretionary account and have them spelled out in a written agreement in order to prevent any possible future misunderstandings. If one is unable to find a broker who possesses the ability to consistently pick winning trades, there is another option available for the trader who does not wish to become involved in the decision-making process or the placing of orders, changing of stops, and so forth. That option is to set up a discretionary account, again after checking the broker out thoroughly, and after establishing the guidelines around which your account will be traded, and then having the broker use only the recommendations from a reputable advisory service that you feel is the best you can find. If the broker does not already subscribe to the service, you can merely assign your subscription to him or subscribe for him. Many "Taurus" subscribers do this, as most of the brokers on our "Recommended List" are already subscribers to Taurus and are using the Taurus recommendations. Often a good broker who does not have the knack of making his own selections can look at recommendations made by a service and somehow hunch or figure out those which have the highest likelihood of success. Often this may also be due to the fact that there is normally a time lag between the time an advisory service publishes its recommendations and the time an order would be placed by a subscriber or broker. Often in the interim there has been some

occurence, usually fundamental in nature, that causes the quality
of the recommendation to change and have a poorer chance of success. If the broker so involved is a professional, he will be on
top of the markets enough to know if something has taken place in
the past few days or few hours to raise questions about the recommendation and therefore can often decide not to enter the trade.
Some statistics we have accumulated suggest that among the top
advisory services, well over 80% of the losing recommendations are
due to some fundamental occurrence taking place after the recommendation was made or after the trade was entered that was either
difficult or impossible to foresee. Oftentimes a broker using
such a service has access to last-minute information that can save
his clients many thousands of dollars.

Another subject that must be considered in your search for
your professional is confidentiality. This is a subject which is
almost never written about and almost as infrequently discussed.
It may not seem to be a major point to many, while to others, confidentiality and secrecy reaches an obsession that nears paranoia.
A professional broker will and should give you a clear
understanding that your account and your trades are held in the
strictest of confidence. You should not be faced with the possibility that your broker will bandy about with his other clients that
you have just gone long 20 contracts of Coffee in order to get
them to place their own orders. This tends to become more of a
problem the more successful you are in your trading, because all
brokers like to look good and be able to let their other clients in
"on a good thing". Of course, a broker can do this without mentioning your name. He merely has to say, "one of my biggest
clients" or "one of my most successful accounts" in order to have
his other clients fall all over themselves placing orders the same
as yours. Not only will he look good to these other clients,
assuming it is a winning trade, but he will be generating a lot of
additional income for himself at the same time. And if it turns

278

out to be a losing trade, he doesn't have to take the blame himself, as, after all, it was his mysterious "big client" who made
the mistake, and the broker still ends up with the additional profits from the commissions he has generated. This is particularly
bad for the successful trader, since this type of thing can spread
like wildfire through other brokers in the same brokerage house,
between clients who use different brokers. Many times we have
heard of a trader who has just been phoned by a friend of his who
has this hot tip from his broker about a big trade being entered by
a big trader. It can get to the point where there are so many
orders bunched at a certain spot that they in themselves generate
so much volatility in the marketplace that fills do not merely
become bad, they often become atrocious.

There are a couple of different ways to deal with this
situation. Often, even if you have talked to old clients of the
broker you are considering, they may not be aware of the situation
if it exists. Or they may not think to volunteer the information
you need to determine if this broker is a blabbermouth. One way
to help determine it is to ask the clients you talk to if they
have had much success with the trades suggested to them by this
broker because one of his successful accounts had just placed an
order. This is a relatively innocuous way to question them, and
if they say anything to indicate that the broker has made such
recommendations, successful or not, you know that if he is
following this practice for others among his accounts, you cannot
trust him to keep your trades in confidence. This is probably the
best way to determine whether or not you can trust him in this
respect. In addition to that, we still suggest a clear
understanding with him that if you ever learn of his doing
something like this, you will close your account with him
immediately.

Another option for ensuring or helping to ensure confidentiality which is more cumbersome, but is also effective if you
have the time and resources to do it, is to have accounts with

more than one broker. We know of one individual who is quite successful in the markets, but none of his 6 brokers views him as
being anything but a successful small-fry. That is because if he
wants to buy or sell say 6 contracts of a commodity, he will go to
the trouble to enter one order for one contract with each of his
6 brokers. If he sees 6 different positions he wants to enter
with a single contract for each trade, he simply places one order
with each broker. Admittedly this increases paper-work, record-
keeping, and increases the amount of time a trader must devote to
his account. It is effective however, if one is willing to devote
the time and effort to establishing multiple accounts, and
assuming, of course, that the trader has sufficient capital to
open more than one account. There is still no guarantee, however,
that all of your trading will remain confidential, but these precautions can certainly be taken in order to minimize the risk of
losing this confidentiality. A top-flight broker with a well-
deserved reputation for honesty and integrity is the absolute best
way to avoid difficulties in this area.

Once you have examined all of the preceeding points, you
must ask yourself whether or not you are compatable with the
broker. This subject was touched on briefly before, but this is
important enough to examine more closely. Few things are more
disconcerting in trading than to have a good selection method,
good money management, good trade execution, confidentiality
assured, and all the other requirements of a professional broker,
only to find out that you just plain either don't like your broker
or worse, that you can't stand him. Many readers especially if
they have never had that type of relationship with a broker, may
be asking themselves why this is so important. After all, the
trader doesn't spend that much time in communicating with his
broker, and even if the broker is a pure pain, as long as he gets
the job done, isn't that enough? Well, it may be for some people,
but the majority of traders with whom we have talked who have

experienced situations like this wouldn't agree. So, the last requirement we would add for a truly professional broker is whether or not you find yourself to be compatable with him. This is not necessarily a moral judgment of the broker. He may have several dozen other clients who feel he is the salt of the earth. But, due to your own individual background and personality, he may be obnoxious and objectionable. We are often asked what general personality traits we look for in a broker, given that every trader is an individual and different, and that every broker is human and imperfect. Well, a good relationship between a client and a broker is like a good marriage: unless it is good for both, it is good for neither party. We would not want to expect more of a broker than he can deliver. His foresight will never be as good as your hindsight. A way we suggest to prevent or circumvent personality clashes with a broker, is to establish at the very beginning what your ground rules are. If you want him to give you advice, tell him. If you never want his advice, insist upon that and confront him if he violates your rule. Some traders thrive on hearing from their broker daily, while to others this can be a most irritating experience. Personally, we have never appreciated unsolicited advice, phone calls, criticism, or praise, and have always insisted "up front", at the beginning of a client-broker relationship we were entering, that these were our ground rules. By the same token, we have always insisted on being able to get specific information from him quickly if it was unavailable to us from any other source and to be contacted with any late-breaking news that might affect any positions we were holding or had open orders for.

Some writers have suggested that a broker's background is of paramount importance when selecting a broker. While we wouldn't want a broker with a bad background, it is unlikely that you would find one in the business. Just because a broker is young, or old for that matter, has been with the firm for a year or thirty years, does not seem to us to make much difference as long as he meets all of the requirements that you have decided upon. Obviously, a beginning broker may make more errors occur and may be not as able to get you the information you require, and it may be more difficult to make a long-range check on his references than the older, more established broker, but this by itself is no reason to disqualify him.

To summarize, your checklist for searching for your ultimate broker, or for evaluating your own broker, would include deciding upon whether or not you can use a discount broker, then whether or not you want to give him discretionary powers, whether or not you want or can handle multiple brokers, seeing how able he is to provide you with information, checking his references, determine if he will maintain confidentiality, checking his own firm to assure your peace of mind if they are not a Clearing House Member, determining if his personality will be compatable with yours, and making sure if he is not very experienced yet as a broker, that that will pose no problem for you.

CHAPTER 12

MONEY MANAGEMENT

There are probably few topics in the arena of commodity trading about which there exists such sparse information as about this one, the actual management of money. There are numerous books and articles for the commodity speculator on how to select commodities to trade, and on how the commodity markets work in general; but unfortunately there is little information available to the trader on how to manage his money.

It is a fairly common experience to see people with the ability to select winning commodity trades, who know when to enter the markets as well as when to exist them, who have found a good broker, have no psychological "death wish" to lose their money, and yet who inevitably end up losing either a substantial amount of their equity capital, or all of it. We will examine in this chapter how you, as a commodity trader, can avoid having this happen by judiciously and prudently managing your money. There is no profit in your being able to select winning commodity trades if at the same time you also lose your trading capital.

The first point that must be considered is the nature of your original equity money itself. Commodity trading should never be done with "meat and mortgage" money or with borrowed funds. Regardless of how good either your method of selection or your advisory service is, monies invested in commodity trading must be only those that you can afford to lose without seriously damaging yourself financially, physically, or psychologically.

Any method of selecting commodites, no matter how successful it is in general, has its periods of time, which are usually cycli-

cal, in which the selections are not profitable. And because of
fundamental market forces and changing conditions in the world, a
method that has been successful for the past 100 years until the
present day, has no guarantee that it will work from today on.
There is always the remote possibility that a war, depression,
hyper-inflation, or some other disaster will cause the commodity
exchanges to close. The President of the United States has the
power to do this himself, granted him under the Emergency Powers
Act, simply by declaring a state of emergency; and it is unclear
whether under such circumstances traders would be able to get their
money back, or whether it would be frozen in the brokerage houses,
or exactly what might happen in such a situation.

What then is a recommended amount of money for the beginning
or established trader to have on hand in order to initiate trading
successfully and to be reasonably hopeful of making large amounts
of money from his trades? While an account of $10,000 certainly
stands a better chance of success than one with only $5,000 a
$10,000 account is still not sufficient to significantly enhance
the possibilities of success.

Based upon our observation and research, if there is any such
thing as an "ideal" amount, it would probably be $30,000. Again,
this is not to say that you cannot succeed with a 5 or 10 or 20
thousand dollar account; but a $30,000 account has a number of
advantages. It allows you to trade virtually all of the commodities, again depending upon their original margin requirements;
it permits you to diversify into different commodities and
complexes; allows you to be able to pyramid your positions when
required; and in general gives you a high degree of probable success. Anything over and beyond $30,000 just makes it that much
simpler to trade successfully.

Any method of selecting positions is going to be imperfect and
involve losing trades. Since selection methods tend to be cyclical
in terms of their success-to-failure rate, if you initiate trading

284

by any generally successful method, there is always the possibility
that you will begin trading at the inception of one of these losing
cycles. In that case, the larger the amount of original capital,
the better your chances of weathering the storm of the losing cycle
before successful recommendations start you winning again.

If you are not fortunate enough to have $30,000 in risk capi-
tal available, you must adjust to that reality and be flexible
enough to alter our guidelines to fit your position. $30,000 is
neither a mandatory figure, nor an arbitrary one; but it is an
optimum.

We come now to the question of whether broker selection is an
important area of money management, and if it is, how to handle
it. It is our belief that next to actual trade selection and
money management, your broker is the next most important feature of
your trading program. The specifics of how to select a top-notch,
competent, and compatable broker are covered in another chapter

Another important consideration in the management of your
money is the subject of managed accounts. A managed account is
arranged by placing your funds in the hands of a money manager.
This has the big advantage of freeing you from any decision-making
or tension in the day-to-day handling of selections. But going to
a managed account can also be fraught with difficulties, since you
have little or no say in how your money is being invested; and
often once a person invests in a managed account, the past performance or track record of the account seems to go up in smoke. Here
more than anywhere else, the preservation of your capital depends
on the selection of an honest, competent manager.

Unfortunately, this seems to be even more difficult than the
selection of a broker. The only method that seems to work is for
the manager to be recommended by one of your friends who has used
the service for some time and can verify both the accuracy of the
account's track record of past performance, and the integrity of
the principals. At this point the only danger is that the selec-

tion method used by the managed account may fail; but that risk is inherent in any selection method, whether it is theirs or yours or an advisory service's.

There is one psychological aspect of using a managed account that should also be examined, and that is, if the account succeeds, will you as a trader be satisfied with the profits accrued, insofar as you had little to do with their actual accumulation? In other words, if the account earns money, will your pride in having selected a good managed account be enough for your ego? And, if the managed account loses money, will you feel better because someone other than yourself actually lost it, or will you feel even worse because of wondering if the losses might not have occurred at all if you had handled your money yourself? Seriously, this is an important question to consider before opening a managed account, and it is one that we can only point out to you, because its answer will be entirely an individual matter.

An alternative solution to the whole question of managed accounts versus your own selection making, is to use a discretionary account with the good broker you have located. In simplest terms, this means that you legally give him power to invest for you, giving him whatever limitations or parameters you choose, if any. You can specify for example, that the broker not trade certain commodities, or that he trade no more than a certain number of different commodities at any one time, or that he trade no more than a certain number of contracts per commodity at any one time, or that he not trade more than one commodity per complex.

The key here then becomes the method of trade selection, and that is crucial. If the broker has a good and verifiable track record, then that takes care of the problems, once you are satisfied about his honesty. A different and possibly better way of handling selections is to specify that the broker use a certain method or advisory service as his sole criterion for selecting trades. Some of _Taurus'_ and _Capricorn's_ subscribers use this approach, especially with the brokers on our recommended broker's list who have been subscribers for some time. But **any** good and consistently profitable advisory service can be **utilized for this** approach.

Another area that needs to be considered is the utilization of trading mini-contracts on the Mid-American Exchange. This approach too, has its advantages and disadvantages. The major advantage is the reduced margin requirements, which is especially attractive when you wish to trade commodities that normally are relatively high-margin ones on the major exchanges. This advantage permits the trader to diversify far more, especially if his account is somewhat limited in nature.

Selective diversification isn't much of a problem for a trader with an account of at least $20,000, and definitely isn't a problem for a trader with the $30,000 "ideal amount" in his account. The possibility of greater diversification due to the lower original margin requirements is the most important benefit a trader will derive from trading mini-contracts. The disadvantage is that commissions are in general proportionately greater than on the regular exchanges. Added to this financial disadvantage is the often-encountered difficulty of locating a broker who is willing or able to trade these mini-contracts for his clients. Many brokers are able and willing, but when you add the specification of mini-contracts to the problem of finding an excellent broker in the first place, it can complicate matters.

Besides that, there are often technical difficulties about prices, information availability, and lower volume and open interest, that can adversely affect a trader's performance. But if a trader with limited funds can find a top-flight broker who is willing and able to handle mini-contracts, and if the trader's method of selections and his results are not adversely affected by using mini-contracts, then going this route can prove to be a very wise decision.

Once you have established what your risk capital is and have made the four necessary decisions (1) who your broker will be, (2) whether or not your own situation requires a full-service broker or a discount firm, (3) whether or not a managed account or a broker with discretionary powers is suitable for you, and (4) whether or not trading mini-contracts is appropriate for you, then you need to get into the mechanics of handling your money after you begin actual trading, and, of course, the matter of drawing down profit from your account. We shall examine each of these subjects in turn.

The first area to consider is the maximum amount of original margin per contract that you are willing to assume. That is, should you consider taking positions in any commodity if your method of selection indicates it will make a good trade, or should you put limitations on which trades to initiate, based upon the amount of margin being tied up? It is true that you can risk more money with a smaller-margin commodity than with a larger-margin commodity. For example, by the selective placement of your initial protective stops, you may risk more initially on Oats than you would on Coffee, but that is not the point here.

In trading the higher-margin commodities, you may be committing or tying up more of your account from a percentage standpoint in any given trade, thereby reducing the remaining amount available for initiating other trades as they come along. Many writers advise never tying up more than a certain percentage of your trading capital in trades at any one time. We do not hold this view as long as certain precautions are taken. These precautions will be examined in more detail later.

Right now the important thing to consider is how much of your capital to tie up at any one time in relation to the margin requirements for the commodities you are trading. For all practical purposes, the total number of commodities available to invest in that do not regularly move in tandem with one another, is bet-

288

ween 12 and 15. This is not a universal truth, but is a generali-
zation of what usually happens. The Soy Complex usually moves in
tandem, that is, in the same direction with the other members of
the complex. Gold and Silver generally do the same thing, as do
Lumber and Plywood, Feeder and Live Cattle, and the Financial
Instruments. Many of the Foreign Currencies also move simultaneously in the same direction.

By looking at it from this standpoint, if the recent technical
and fundamental information is relatively the same for say,
Soybeans and Soy Meal, and if the margin requirements for Beans is
$3,000 and for Meal is only $1,000, and if your methods of selection or your advisory service indicate both are going to move in
the same direction, and you can find no reason why either trade has
a better chance than the other to succeed, then good money management would indicate that you go with the Meal trade. If your total
trading capital is $30,000, a trade in Soybeans would tie up 10% of
your total trading account, and a trade in Meal only 3.3%. The
trade in Meal would leave you more reserve to initiate other trades
than if you had gone with the Soybean trade.

An examination of past price charts will show you the similarities between complimentary price moves that exist in addition
to the ones mentioned above. One must be especially careful in
using this approach to make certain there is no important fundamental consideration that would cause a divergence in the price
movement of the two (or more) commodities under consideration.
For example, if the West German Mark and the Swiss Franc both have
a similar recent chart pattern, and your method of selection indicates that both are due to go up on the futures market, it would
be important to know if the interest rates in Germany are due to
go down, which might be a bearish factor, or if an election is
coming up in one of the countries, the results of which could
adversely affect that country's economic policies and therefore
adversely affect your position in the market. Admittedly, fun-

damental information is one of the most difficult areas to use, since it is far more of an art than a science of technical evaluation.

While there are many ways of looking at the question, it is usually best to devote as little of your total capital to any given trade as possible, if the chances for success appear to be equal either way. On the other hand, how much of your total capital to commit at any one time depends largely on the individual.

We see nothing wrong with committing 100% of your total available capital at any one time, providing appropriate precautions are observed. The only disadvantage we can see is that in doing so, there is no more capital available to initiate a new trade that looks especially promising. This should be of little consequence if your method of selection, or that of your advisory service, is a good one, because new recommendations that are also promising will constantly be coming along.

It seems ridiculous to us, if you have $20,000 in your account, and a total of 10 good recommendations, with each requiring $2,000, not to take advantage of all ten trades; assuming of course, that the basic precautions are taken. The two precautions mentioned so far are first that the $20,000 is genuine risk money, and second that you have total faith in your broker. Further precautions to be discussed later are of equal importance.

It is only by risking your money in trades that money can be made. If you have a $20,000 account and are willing to commit only $10,000 at any given time, you might as well have a $10,000 account, and spend or invest the other $10,000 in some other way. It does make sense however, when you are willing to invest all of your capital at any given time and the recommendations you see either are few in number or not to your liking for some reason, to have your broker invest your idle funds in purchasing T-Bills so that you may at least be earning interest on them while you are waiting for the right selections to come along.

It makes no sense at all, however, in a case like the one just discussed, to increase the number of contracts traded. For example, if you have $20,000 to invest and the only good recommendations available to you have margin requirements totalling $4,000, you might reason that to put all of your capital to work, it would make good sense to buy 5 times the original number of contracts on each, in order to fully utilize the $20,000. This is bad money management, for two major reasons. First, it commits a higher percentage of your total capital to each trade, which is a bad idea in and of itself. Second, it removes available capital from your account so you can't take advantage of other trading opportunities if they become available before the conclusion of the trades you are already in.

It is far better to invest such extra funds in some vehicle, such as Treasury Bills, that are instantly convertible back into cash in your trading account when you need it to initiate new positions. Few things are more frustrating than to have all of your capital tied up when a good-looking trade appears, and then have to pass it up. If you do go the fully-committed route, however, this will inevitably occur from time to time.

This brings up another subject that is related to how much of your total account should be risked at any one time, and that is the trading of multiple contracts. The question of trading multiple contracts is one to consider well from the standpoint of money management. It gets back to the problem of putting all of your eggs in one basket, or at most, in only a few baskets. In accepting the figure of $30,000 as being an ideal amount for a trading account, we must also realize that this figure is based on trading single contracts of each trade.

It follows, then, that you should have more than $30,000 in order to trade more than one contract of a commodity in each trade. Beyond that point, when your capital increases to 40 or 50 or 60 thousand dollars or more, there are two ways to approach the

situation of trading multiple contracts. You can choose to trade
variable amounts, say, three contracts in one trade, one contract
in another, two in another, and so forth, depending upon how you
feel about each trade's chance for success.

Or, you can set a fixed amount, and when your equity reaches
$60,000, you automatically go to 2 contracts on each trade. When
your equity reaches $90,000 you go to three contracts, and so
forth. If a trader has a method (whether it is technical, fundamental, or simply hunches and gut feelings) to differentiate
between the relative profitability of trades, then we prefer the
first choice, that of allocating the number of contracts depending
upon the chances of profitability.

It is important here to differentiate between chances of profitability and chances of success. By chances of profitability, we
mean being able to look at two potential trades, and to determine
with some degree of reliability, that while both trades are likely
to make money, one should make more money than the other. By
chances of success, we mean being able to look at two potential
trades and to determine, again with some degree of reliability,
that one of the two has a better chance to show a profit or at
least to break even, than the other one does. In the later case,
you should seriously consider not trading the less certain of the
two, depending upon how reliable your past judgment has been in
similar situations.

Once your equity capital has significantly increased above the
$30,000 level, then your decision on whether to follow a mechanical
rule or a flexible rule in going with multiple contracts should be
based entirely on how successful you are in determining the chances
of profitability of different trades as they are initiated.
Another option that might preclude your going to multiple contracts
as your equity increases could be a desire to draw the profits down
and spend them, and that option will be discussed later in this
chapter.

292

Since $30,000 will usually be sufficient to handle trading
all of the recommendations you wish to follow, in single
contracts, there is really no reason to go to multiple contracts
unless you are interested in building up more substantial profits
to draw down at a later date; and this, as we shall see later,
also has its disadvantages.

The next item to consider is what percentage of your total
account capital should be committed to any one trade. Some advisors recommend no more than 5% of your total capital being committed to a single trade. The reasoning here is that you can
withstand 20 consecutive losses this way before being out of the
game. Other writers advise no more than 10% per trade, giving you
10 consecutive losses before retiring. We feel that any approach
along these lines is inherently self-defeating, especially from an
unconscious psychological standpoint.

All the discussions we have read invariably rest on the premise that you may <u>very well</u> have 10 or 20 or more losses con-
secutively, and that it is necessary for a trader to guard himself
from being forced out of trading by taking this approach. A <u>part</u>
of this idea is valid in that <u>any</u> method of selection inevitably
will go through its strings of losers, and the <u>validity</u> of this
approach is that it <u>does</u> insulate and protect one during such a
period.

For this reason we recommend a flexible approach along these
lines. If you have a $30,000 account, taking a position in Coffee
which has an $8,000 original margin requirement, would tie up
approximately 27% of your total capital. But, if your other positions are mainly in commodities requiring, say, $1,500 or less in
original margin requirements (which is a maximum commitment of 5%),
then we see nothing wrong in initiating the Coffee Position.

An important differentiation needs to be made here between
the terms <u>committing</u> and <u>risking</u> a certain percentage of your
total capital. <u>Committing</u> means to tie it up in a trade. <u>Risking</u>

refers to how much money stands to be lost if your original stop-
loss point is hit. There is quite a difference. The importance
of not committing more than 5 to 10% of your total capital to any
given trade's margin requirements, is that it permits diversification in trading and does not tie up an inordinate percentage
of your capital in any one position. By putting such a limitation
on your trading, you assure that there will be sufficient capital
available later to initiate additional positions in different commodities. Without a limitation, many opportunities for trades
will come along and will simply have to be passed by due to insufficient capital in your account.

We knew of one trader, some time back, who had all of his
available funds committed to various positions. His account was
in the neighborhood of $40,000, and he had about one-fourth of it
committed to each of four different trades. As it turned out, all
four trades were successful, in amounts varying from a 20% return
on original margin to 158% return on original margin, the average
being about 100%. In the time frame of these trades, he doubled
his equity from $40,000 to approximately $80,000, something that
no trader would be disappointed in.

But during this time, there was a recommendation made by the
service he was using for initiation of a Coffee trade. This trade
ultimately returned 400% to those who participated in it. If he
had not had all of his available capital tied up, so he could have
invested equally in Coffee as he had in other trades (meaning 5
trades of $8 K each instead of 4 trades of $10 K), he would have
made $32,000 from the Coffee trade alone, for a total yield of
$96,000 instead of $80,000 during the same time period. He missed
out on $16,000 only because of having all of his capital committed.

The amount of your capital to risk on any one trade is
another, and equally important aspect of your money management.
Here, some far firmer guidelines can be given. The most important
consideration in this area is to determine the average number of

294

winning trades for whatever trading method you are using. If your selection method has a 50% batting average, that is, if it picks a winner for every loser, and if the return on winning trades averages at least 20 percent of original margin, then you would probably not want to commit more than 10% of your total capital to risk in any given trade.

The word risk here means the percentage of original margin that is being risked. For example, if the original margin for one contract of a commodity is $1,500, a 10% risk means having your initial protective stop at a distance away from your original entry point that equals a $150 loss to you should your stop be hit before it can be changed. In the case of Wheat, since each cent move in Wheat equals $50, a 10% risk would involve placing your initial protective stop at a distance of 3¢ away from your entry point into the trade.

Now, that is the percent of risk on an individual contract, or commodity, and must be differentiated from the risk involved of your total trading capital. If your total trading capital in the preceeding example is $15,000 in your account, then with Wheat, a 10% risk of your trading capital would be $1,500, which represents a 30¢ move in Wheat, or 100% of the original margin requirements for a Wheat contract, assuming that the original margin requirements for Wheat at that time are $1,500.

So in speaking of risk percentage, there are two ways of looking at it. The first, which we just discussed, is in terms of the risk to your total account capital. The second, which we discussed earlier, is in terms of the risk as a percentage of the original margin requirements for any individual trade. Guidelines and parameters for the latter are dealt with in more detail in another chapter "Placing Your Stops".

Earlier when we said that a good guideline is not to risk any more than 10% of your total capital in any one trade, we were referring to the first definition of risk, where you consider that it would take 10 losing trades in a row to wipe you out. This percentage figure, 10%, is an arbitrary one based upon a 50% winning selection method that returns at least 20% profit per winning trade. Obviously, if your method of selection results in 30% or 70% winning trades, and if the amount of profit is 10% or 50% or 200% per winning trade, the ideal amount to risk on any one individual trade must be adjusted according to the data.

Once you have definite figures on the percentage of winning trades that your selection method or your advisory service comes up with, as well as the average profits per winning trade, it is relatively easy to compute what would constitute the ideal percentage of risk to withstand 10 losing selections in a row. Since every selection method varies both in the number of its winning trades and in the percentage of profit on its winning trades, you must compute for yourself the percentage to risk on any given trade.

The goal, however, is to allow yourself enough capital to participate in the number of trades that equals one and one-half times the number of the longest sequence of losing trades generated by your selection method or service. What this means is that before calculating what percentage of your capital to risk, and after determining your selection method's winning percentage and its percent of profit returned, you must examine the results of the method to search for strings of losses.

You may find for example, that with a typical method or service, the average number of losing trades in any one sequence is 5, but that a few times there was a string of 10 losing trades in a row. In that case, you must compute what percentage of risk would enable you to "weather" a period of 15 losing selections, then compare that figure with the winning percentage of trades and profit returned, and decide on your strategy.

You may take an aggressive approach of using the latter figures to justify risking as much as 20 or 25% of your total capital on any one trade; or you may take a conservative approach

296

where, using the above example, you would risk no more than 7% on each trade. Or you may choose a middle-of-the-road course and pick a percentage figure somewhere in between; in this example, perhaps 17% risked on each trade.

This percentage-of-risk approach must be reconciled with the prohibition against tying all of your capital up in a few trades so that there is little left to initiate new trades with. If you determine that it is feasible to risk 20% of your total capital on a single trade, based upon the parameters just discussed, you may still find yourself in the situation of being in only a few positions and unable to enter other new recommendations that come along.

A 20% risk in an Oats trade obviously ties up a lot less money than a 20% risk in Coffee, if you mean 20% of the original margin requirements. But if you mean 20% of your total available capital, just as much money is tied up in one trade as in the other, because you would have 20 or so contracts of Oats, depending upon the relative original margin requirements, for everyone of Coffee. Following the guidelines earlier discussed about trading multiple contracts would prevent the later situation from occurring.

Another important area that affects money management is diversification. Diversification implies not only avoiding multiple contracts until your equity is sufficient to handle them, but also (and more importantly) avoiding trading simultaneously in those commodities that move in tandem. If a trader computes that he or she can trade, on the average between 7 to 14 different commodities at any one time, it is very important that the risks be spread through diversification.

Some commodity writers, incidentally, suggest that no one should follow or trade more than 4 to 7 commodities at any one time. We do not accept this position any more than we believe that someone can read only 4 to 7 newspapers per week, or per day for that matter. Physiological research indicates that the human brain can register a maximum of 7 digits simultaneously, but many excellent advisors concentrate every day, although not simultaneously, on more than 30 commodities, each in as many as 6 contract months, and we believe the average trader can do the same thing, assuming that he has the time and the desire to do so.

Diversification is necessary, not because of your supposed inability as a trader to concentrate on more than a limited number of commodities, but because it protects you from locking yourself into a situation where a sudden fundamental change could adversely affect too many of your positions simultaneously.

As an example, let's assume that you have determined the proper amount of percentage risk, using both approaches discussed earlier, and have established long positions in Corn, Oats, Soybeans, Soy Meal, Soy Oil, and Wheat, while still leaving yourself some capital for additional trading opportunities as they arise. One of two unprofitable things can then occur. If your method of selection (or your advisor's method of selection) was basically wrong in all of the Grains, you will simultaneously have a string of 6 losses. That can have a bad effect on your overall trading program due to the amount of your equity that is wiped out, and it also won't do you a lot of good psychologically.

The second possibility, which is less likely but still dangerous, is that some fundamental event, like a government report with an unexpected content, or an embargo might plummet prices limit-down for who knows how many days in a row, possibly wiping you out completely. This latter occurrence would be bad enough in any single commodity, but when it happens to a whole complex at once, as it frequently does, the effects can be truly disastrous.

From our point of view, all of the Grains, with the possible exception at times of Soy Oil, comprise one complex. Feeder and Live Cattle comprise another and sometimes they overlap with Hogs and Bellies, so often it is best to think of all of the Meats as

belonging to one complex. Lumber and Plywood generally can be
thought of as a single complex. Gold, Silver, Platinum, and often
Copper and Palladium can be considered to be a single complex. The
Foreign Currencies often can all be grouped into a single complex,
but there are many times when they segregate themselves into mini-
complexes.

The Financial Instruments almost invariably are a single
complex. That leaves us with Coffee, Cocoa, Cotton, Orange
Juice, Heating Oil, The Stock Indices and Sugar that do not con-
veniently fall into any single complex, and normally they can be
treated individually unless they are being subjected to the same
basic fundamental events, such as war or depression. This gives us
a minimum of 11 complexes or grouping of commodities that generally
track together, and a maximum of generally 13 to 15, depending upon
how Copper, the Meats, and Foreign Currencies are behaving.

If a trader has capital enough to trade 11 commodities, it is
best for him to wait for and assume positions in the previously
mentioned 11 major complexes, based upon percentage risk relative
to original margin and total equity capital. Normally, it would
be strongly unadvisable for a trader to assume two positions
within the same complex that are in differing directions, such as
going long Gold and short Platinum simultaneously, unless there
were some <u>very</u> sound fundamental reasons to do so or an OCO
situation, in which case it might be advisable to contradict the
principle of complex diversification.

Very often Taurus receives phone calls from new subscribers
asking for general advice on how to approach their own money management. Often these calls are from people with very small
accounts that call for very conservative trading approaches until
their equity has increased sufficiently. Our general rule of
thumb when speaking with these people is to recommend that they
never buy more than one contract of a commodity; that they concentrate on commodities with low initial margin requirements, say

$1,500 or less, or that they go to mini-contracts; and that they diversify by never taking more than one position per complex, regardless of the fundamentals.

We would rather see such traders wait patiently for a position in Oats, Plywood, etc. and gradually build up their capital rather than take undue risks. We also tell them to compute the amount of dollar risk and percentage risk for each trade, and to try to invest only in trades with a risk of 33% or less of original margin. Usually, this is their only chance for success, unless they get lucky, and luck is a fickle thing in the commodity markets. We tell them that the commodity markets have been around for a long time, and they probably will be around for a long, long time in the future, and that we know of no sure-fire way to make a fortune quickly in the markets. Basically, we advise <u>conservatism</u>, <u>discretion</u>, and <u>patience</u>.

The average trader, one with a $20,000 to $40,000 account, is better advised to follow the guidelines as given throughout this chapter. The larger trader is also advised to follow them, except that as a larger trader, he may feel more free occasionally to deviate from some of the parameters we have given; but even then it should be with the clear realization that his chances of success are usually diminished by violating these guidelines.

The final area to discuss is that of drawing down one's profits, and here the subject overlaps with "How Your Mind Affects Your Trading", another chapter in which it is also covered, but from a different perspective. Apparently one of the hardest things for a trader to do is to take profits out of his account to go on a vacation, buy a new sports car, pay off his mortgage, establish a college trust fund for his children, buy real estate, or simply to have fun with. The prevailing view seems to be that this money was earned by hard work, sweat, and tears, and maybe some sleepless nights in-between, and that there is something almost immoral about taking it out of one's account to have fun with. We can only say that we most strongly disagree with that approach, because the enjoyment of money is as important as its acquisition; and if that enjoyment is difficult for an investor to experience, then some serious self-examination or therapy is indicated.

The markets have been around for a long time, and may be around forever, but none of us will be. Life is ephemeral and time goes by as quickly as the winking of an eye. I know of many traders who kept building up the capital in their accounts over the years until they truly had astronomical amounts, only to find they were then too old to do the traveling they wanted to, and were unable to have fun any more. The acquiring of money became an end in itself, and that is sad. Money was meant to be spent and enjoyed, and this point of view is exemplified in the book Moneylove by Jerry Gillies, published in paperback by Warner Books. We strongly recommend it to all traders, especially to those who find it difficult to draw down their profits to enjoy.

At what point should a trader start taking his profits? With the ideal account being $30,000, a rule of thumb might be to draw down $5,000 every time the equity builds up to $40,000 or $45,000. This gives a trader an account with a bit more room to maneuver with in his trading, as well as profits to enjoy whenever his equity increases above the $40 to $45,000 figure and is drawn back down. Of course, some exceptions can be made as long as they are healthy and realistic. Ambitious personal projects may carry a price tag close to a quarter of a million dollars.

In such a case, where the "fun" a trader wishes to have requires larger than normal amounts of money, we feel it is justified to let the account grow. Small withdrawals can be made along the way for small enjoyments, like a special vacation, but profits can be left to build up until the goal amount is reached. This procedure is not without its pitfalls, because a war or a declaration of the Emergency Powers Act could wipe out huge amounts of money, but an option here is periodically to draw down a moderate amount of profits and put them in safer investments, such as T-Bills, or preferably Gold Krugerrands and Silver coins, until the total amount is reached. Assuming that the trader has no psychological hang-ups around having fun or spending money, and that he has no obsession with accumulating wealth for wealth's sake, the amounts to draw down and when to do it, become a very personal matter that each investor has to decide for himself.

If you think you may have a psychological problem, connected with profit-taking, you may contact Taurus, in complete confidence, for referral to a competent therapist in your area, no matter where you live. The important concept here that we cannot overemphasize is that money is not an end in itself, but is a means to other ends.

CHAPTER 13

MANAGING MONEY IN LONG-RANGE TRADES

Money Management for the Long-Range trader is similar in many
ways to money management for all commodity traders, and yet at the
same time, money management for a long-range trading program is
different in many key aspects. We will attempt in this chapter
to briefly cover the similarities, and to cover in as much detail
as possible the major differences. As with the concept of
long-range trading itself, and with many other areas of commodity
trading and investing in general, the principles of advanced
long-range money management are neither mysterious or extremely
complex. Rather, at times they may sound rudimentary and
simplistic, but do not let that lull you into discounting the importance of these principles of advanced long-range money management,
for understanding and applying them correctly are critical to
your success in a long-range commodity trading program.

The first consideration regarding money that any long-range
trader should consider, or any trader for that matter, is the
amount available tohim, and the type of money it is. First we'll
look at the aspect of money-"types". We'll assume at this point
that the capital the long-range investor has is investment capital
and not money that is needed for day to day living expenses or for
fixed future requirements such as children's college expenses or
retirement income. This is investment-type monies, and only this
kind of money should be considered for commodity investing.

A step beyond this consideration is the different types of
investment monies. There are a myriad of types of investment

302

monies due to the different needs and temperaments of the individual investors. The only type of investment money we will consider
here is pure RISK CAPITAL. Risk capital is that money that an
investor can AFFORD to LOSE without any disruption in his life.
Afford to lose both financially and psychologically. It's fairly
easy for most investors to determine if the investment money for
commodity trading is of a risk nature simply by going over their
personal balance sheets and determining if losing these funds would
disrupt their overall financial status.

It's sad to say, but a long-range commodity investor MUST look
at these funds as though he is going to the racetrack or to the
casino table. Regardless of how good his long-range commodity
trading program is, and whether he is doing it himself or following
the advice of a respected advisor, there is ALWAYS the possibility
that he will lose all of his capital. Unlike investing in stocks
or real estate where there will almost always be equity remaining
in his investment, the commodity investor is constantly faced with
the possibility of complete depletion of his funds.

Regardless of the sophistication of his money-management
program or the expertise of his trade selection system, whether of
his own formulation or that of an outside advisor, the long-range
commodity trader should be well aware of the risk involved in
trading commodities. We believe the reader is probably well-
acquainted with the numerous horror stories about multiple limit
days against one's position, and this, unfortunately is a very
real, yet thankfully infrequent occurrence. Of more concern to us
is the possibility that if the U.S. or world economy does collapse
due to the international banking situation or for some other
reason, the President of the U.S. whoever he may be at that time,
has the power invested in him by the Emergency Powers Act to close
the stock and commodity exchanges for 6 months without having to
answer to anyone.

Obviously, this is a pretty gloomy assessment, and we've been
known over the years for our optimistically pragmatic views.

We're not trying to scare anyone out of trading commodities, but
we are making these points to try to emphasize to the reader, as we
did in the previous chapter, that if he risks money he cannot
afford to lose, he IS taking one heck of a risk. This viewpoint of
ours is not only reflected in our approach to committing only risk
capital to the commodity marketplace, but also to our belief about
taking profits out of one's account - and positions - without
having either build up to very large amounts. We will discuss
taking profits and keeping one's account equity within a reasonable
range later on in this chapter.

   Now that hopefully we've emphasized the speculative nature of
the commodity marketplace to any of you who were not already aware
of it, let's proceed with our more optimistic view of how best to
manage your money during your long-range trading program. Now
that you've determined that you DO have RISK capital and can, if
necessary, lose it without affecting your lifestyle, HOW MUCH do
you need to adequately or most effectively trade a long-range
trading program? Assuming that you do not have a hundred or two
hundred thousand dollars at your disposal as risk capital - which
would definitely be more than adequate and effective - there are
different ways to answer that question.

   Let's look first at the minimum amount to really have an
effective long-range trading program. Our belief is that approximately $25,000 is more than enough to be both effective and ade-
quate, and while we would prefer seeing an investor begin with that
amount, actually an amount half that large, or approximately
$12,000 can be sufficient given the right criteria and guidelines,
which we will be discussing shortly. Our figure of $25,000 is
based on approximate margin requirement for trading about 12
contracts. We've decided upon the number 12 as an optimum figure
for single-contract trading, two different commodities each, of 6
different commodity complexes.

   What we are looking for here, of course, is diversification of
risk. We count our six complexes for long-range trading as being:

#1. the Grains, #2. the Meats, #3. the Foods, #4 Cotton, Heating Oil, and the Woods, #5. the Metals, and #6. the Currencies, Stock Indices and Financial Instruments. These divisions are of course, arbitrary, and could be done differently such as the stock indices and financial instruments counted as two separate complexes, but for our purposes, we feel that looking at the marketplace as 6, or at most 7, complexes makes the most sense.

The best approach, we believe, is to attempt to have 1 or 2 positions in each complex, in different commodities. By far the best way to do this is to take a position in one complex, say the Grains, in Corn, and to not immediately take another position in this complex in another Grain unless the other position looks extremely strong. We prefer this approach so as to not commit all of our funds in one complex immediately. By holding enough equity in "reserve" to trade another commodity in each complex, it allows us to be prepared for those special situations that come up and not be over-extended.

Fortunately or unfortunately, this is not always the way it works in real time. Frequently, we will find that several if not most of the commodities within a single complex will be qualifying for long-range trades at approximately the same time, generally because they have somewhat similar cycles, are subject to the same fundamental considerations, or for other reasons. The temptation, of course, is to take a position in each of these commodities, and in the case of Grains, that would entail 5 or 6 positions, depending upon whether or not one was willing to trade a thin market like Oats. This approach, of trading every commodity that looks like a potentially rewarding long range trade candidate, is the best one IF one's equity will permit it.

In order to be able to do so comfortably, one should have an account balance of $50,000 or $60,000 in order to be able to handle the maximum situation that might present itself, that is, if all of

306

the commodities being analyzed were to be entered at the same time.
The SAME TIME here means somewhere over a period of 3 to 12 months.
That's because you may get potential positions and fills in say the
entire Grain complex tomorrow, and while those positions are in
place and working for you, next month you may get signals in all of
the Meats, and the following month in all of the Metals.
Meanwhile, you still have your earlier positions and do not
necessarily have available additional equity with which to initiate
new positions unless you have an account of the 50 to 60 thousand
dollar magnitude to begin with.

It's been our experience that this maximum case of having
long-range recommendations for virtually every commodity is not a
common occurrence, but that it does happen often enough so that an
investor who plans on acting on every good long-range signal,
should be prepared to have the capital for that case when there
will be positions in virtually everything.

What we've been talking about, of course, is the investor who
is willing to and wants to "PRESS" the markets, that is, work them
to their hilt. We don't believe this is necessarily the best
approach, but we do know that many investors are in such a hurry
to make money or like to be so involved in the markets, that this
is the approach they will take: to trade every potentially good
long-range situation. This approach does have its merit of
speeding up the process of accumulating profits, assuming of
course, that one's long range analysis is accurate and that there
are no unforeseen fundamental changes in the marketplace that
adversely affect an entire complex simultaneously.

Now that we've looked at the maximum amount required in order
to press the markets on a long-range basis, we'll turn to the bare
minimum amounts. While it's true that an investor COULD start long-
range trading with only enough equity in his account to initiate
one trade, the first one, and given the high probabilities of success in long-range trading, he could wait until that trade closed

out, assuming it was a profitable one, and then take his profits from that successful trade to increase his equity to begin trading more than one commodity on a long-range basis at one time.

The difficulty, as we see it, with this approach is that due to the sometimes long periods of time before a long-range resting order is filled plus the time involved in the actual position itself, the trader may well have an entire year tied up in getting a position filled, letting it complete itself, and getting his profits out of it. This is an extremely long period of time for most investors to be able to handle psychologically, even if they are doubling or tripling their investment capital.

While it's true that they may be hard-pressed to find any other investment in which they can increase their capital to such a large percentage over a one-year time span, since most commodity traders are interested in getting rich as quickly as possible, they must have an enormous amount of patience if they are going to use this approach. If they do possess this patience, and their capital is so severely limited, then we can find no fault going this way, since it is about the only viable alternative open to them.

Since every investor's situation is different in at least some way from everyone else's, it is difficult to propound ONE best way to initiate a long-range commodity trading program. However, since MOST investors will have an initial equity amount of from $10 to $25,000, the approaches previously discussed about allocating it among the different complexes, whether one commodity or two per complex, will be the approach that will fit the largest number of readers of this chapter.

For those readers, however, who are unable to handle the margin requirements for even trading one commodity per complex, thankfully there is an alternative course of action. While this approach does not provide as much diversification as might be liked, it is a viable way for the small investor to approach the market until his equity has been built up sufficiently to follow the approaches already outlined in this chapter.

308

The alternative is to trade Mini-Contracts on the Mid-American exchange. While at the time of writing this chapter, there are only 9 commodities being traded as Mini Contracts, there are 3 Grains, 2 Meats, 2 Metals, and 2 Financial Instruments, which do provide a rather broad kind of diversification between complexes, and do eliminate the higher-risk commodities. Soybeans, Wheat, Corn and Silver only require one-fifth the amount of margin on the Mid-American as they do on their standard exchanges. Of course, while your original margin requirements are reduced by one-fifth, so are your profits on each trade, as the point value for each commodity is reduced proportionately. Hogs, Live Cattle, Treasury Bonds and Treasury Bills all require one-half the standard margin, and Gold requires one-third the standard margin.

Hence, all 9 commodities could be traded with about $8,000 margin, which isn't bad when you consider that Gold, Silver, and the Financial Instruments are typically higher margin requirement commodities. By further diversifying, that is, taking just one of the Grains, one Meat, one Metal, and one Financial Instrument you could further reduce your total equity requirements to around $3,500 at today's margin requirement figures. So, it IS possible to start long-range trading, even with a reasonable amount of diversification, with less than $4,000!

Admittedly, it will be slow going this way, using the mini-contracts, but it does provide you with an option if your funds are severely limited. You would simply follow the procedures as if you were trading full contracts and demand of yourself a lot of patience, as this approach will take a lot of time to build your equity up to where you will be able to trade full contracts.

If your amount of risk capital is severely limited, we suggest you seriously consider going the route of Mini-Contracts, even though it may take some extra added effort to locate a broker who is familiar with them and/or willing to work with you on using them.

Once you've determined how much you can start with and whether you will begin with full contracts or Mini-Contracts, it is helpful to have some criteria as to whether or not any one particular potential trade is worthwhile, from a financial standpoint, to enter in the first place. We will now look at some of the ways you can use to evaluate individual trades and whether or not you should enter them.

The first way of looking at any potential trade is the amount of dollar risk. As proponents of always using protective stops on every position, this gives you a concrete way of seeing what your dollar risk is. You just take your initial entry point and your initial protective stop point and calculate the difference between the two and then multiply by the point value. Hence, if your entry point in Soy Oil is going to be 19¢ and your initial protective stops are going to be at 17¢, that's a difference of 2¢ and since each cent in Soy Oil is worth $600, 2 times $600 would make your initial risk $1,200.

To this you should realistically add another 5% of whatever this figure is to compensate for "slippage" or not getting filled at exactly where you have placed your order, so 5% of $1,200 is $60, so your initial risk is now up to $1,260. To be completely accurate, you should also add your round-turn commission, and let's say that is another $70, so your true initial risk on this position is $1,330, or almost 11% above the originally calculated risk of the difference between initial entry and protective stop points.

If your trade goes against you from the start and you do not get the chance to trail your protective stops, barring limit days through your protective stop, the $1,330 figure is the amount you stand to lose if everything goes wrong. Realistically, if you have done your original analysis properly in selecting the Long-Range trade, very seldom will this happen, but it will occur from time to time, so it is important for you to know that it is, in this case $1,330 and not say $13,000, which in some markets like Silver and Coffee you may occasionally run across a risk as high as this.

We realize that every investor's situation is unique, so as a result it is virtually impossible to issue specific guidelines that will fit everyone, so we will attempt to state some guidelines that may be of help for long-range trading programs. It's our belief that as good a rule of thumb as any for judging these initial dollar risks is to not risk more than 10% of one's total account on any individual trade. Of course, if your funds are limited or you are a particularly aggressive trader, you may want to increase that figure to 20%, but in no case would we go beyond 20%. Conversely, if you are a particularly conservative investor, 5% would be appropriate. So we have a "range" here of from 5 to 20% with 10% being just about optimum. Of course, if you're trading Mini-Contracts, you have to take into account the fact that the point value is much less than with regular contracts, though the percentage for slippage will be about the same, the percentage of commissions will be disproportionately large for Mini-Contracts.

The second parameter to use when analyzing individual potential trades is to look at your dollar risk as a percentage of margin requirements. In other words, what is your absolute dollar risk as we've just determined, as a percentage of the amount of your equity you have to commit to an individual trade? Here the lower the figure, the more appealing the potential trade. In the example just cited where the Initial Dollar Risk for Soy Oil was computed to be $1,330, and with Soy Oil requiring a margin of $1,000, the Risk % of Margin is 133%, or $1,330 divided by $1,000. If the risk was say $2,330, then our Risk % of Margin would be 233%.

Computing this figure enables you to judge what percentage of your equity for a particular trade is being risked. As with all criteria, there is no hard and fast rule here either as to what constitutes the optimum Risk % of Margin. Obviously, the lower the %, the better, but it has been our experience that somewhere between 50 and 100% is probably the best % to hope for, and we believe that anything above 160% should probably be avoided unless the potential reward is sufficiently great. Even if the Risk % of Margin is very low, unless the potential reward is sufficient, then the trade basically doesn't qualify for a long-range trade since your potential profits just aren't there. This is the reason it is so important to have some idea, even a rough one, of what your potential profit may be on any given trade.

While we've covered in another chapter the methodology of determining approximate target areas, and for sure all targets are AREAS and are APPROXIMATE ones at best, we'll now briefly summarize how to come up with a potential target zone. Probably the quickest way to do so is to look at your monthly charts from which you've selected the potential trade in the first place. Your target zone should be in the area, plus or minus 10% of the point at which your trade would reach the major monthly trendline in about six months. Of course, if you've determined from your cyclical or seasonal analysis that it will take 4 or 10 months, or whatever, to reach that point, you would use that time frame to see where prices will be when that time intersects with the monthly trendline.

There are other methods for determining target zones, and there are special instances when using the monthly trendline and time frame is not the best method. But for our discussion here, this method is as good as any. Going back to our example of Soy Oil, where our initial risk was $1,330 and our entry point was 19¢, let's say the monthly trendline and time frame method projects a price move up to 28¢. Statistically then the chances are very high that if your analysis is correct and a big bull move takes place, AND if there are no unforeseen fundamental changes in the marketplace to stifle it, then prices should run up to 28¢ plus or minus 10% and top out somewhere between 25¢ and 31¢. This plus or minus 10% is more useful for calculating when to move your stops in closer than it is for risk/reward analysis, so for our analysis here, we will use the 28¢ figure.

312

So, if you enter at 19¢ and exit at 28¢, you have a profit of
9¢, and since each cent move in Soy Oil translates into $600, you
have 9 times $600 or a potential profit of $5,400 when prices reach
your target. Of course, prices may stall at substantially less
than your target of 28¢ or zoom way beyond it. There is no way to
absolutely predict where a price move will climax, so the only
approach we can use is to take the target figure that statistically
has the best chance of being hit and base all of our calculations
on it. So using this method, albeit imperfect, at least gives us
as sound a figure as we can come up with, to base our Risk/Reward
analysis on.

Risk/Reward analysis is used by many industries, the government, the military, and unfortunately by too few investors. It
quite simply is a number derived from dividing the Risk by the
potential Reward. Since for our purposes the Risk part of this
ratio is a relatively absolute number, that is, we know it pretty
concretely since only limit days against us can affect it, and the
Reward figure is our best estimate, and thus NOT an absolute number
like the potential Risk, our Risk/Reward ratio is an imperfect one.

Unfortunately, this imperfectness seems to be the rule rather
than the exception when dealing with commodities, or for that
matter, most investments. Since our potential initial Risk goes on
the top of the equation, and we divide it by our potential profit,
then the smaller the number we get from our Risk/Reward
Calculation, the better the investment, at least generally
speaking. It's our belief that the majority of the time no
long-range trade should be entered if the Risk/Reward ratio is
over 0.90. This is a rule of thumb, and the only time we would
consider going against that is when we want a particular trade in
a complex to achieve the diversification we require or if our
capital is such that the Risk/Reward Ratio for any individual
trade just doesn't mean all that much to us, though we believe it
SHOULD mean something to us at all times.

For our example of Soy Oil, with potential profits estimated
at $5,400 and initial margin requirements being $1,000, dividing
the $1,000 by $5,400, we get a Risk/reward ratio of 0.185 a very
satisfactory Risk/Reward figure. One other way of looking at the
Risk/Reward Ratio, in general, is to try and achieve an AVERAGE
figure for all of your trades within a certain boundary. Hence, if
you have five potential positions and 4 of the 5 have Risk/Reward
Ratios of 0.20 each, and one has a risk/reward ratio of 1.50, the
overall average may be around 0.46. For this calculation, we came
up with the average of the risk/reward ratios themselves, which in
actual practice is NOT what you would do. You WOULD take the sum
of all the dollar risks and divide it by the sum of all the potential dollar profits, which, depending upon the actual amounts,
might be more or less than the 0.46 figure we've just quoted.

In any case, by coming up with the average Risk/Reward Ratio,
it gives us a broad picture of how our overall Risk compared to our
overall potential Rewards stacks up. Probably anytime you start
getting an average Risk/Reward Ratio in excess of 0.50 you should
start looking at your methods to calculate initial protective
stops, initial entry points, and target points, because if you
begin running an Overall Risk/Reward ratio in excess of 0.50, it is
a signal that something in your calculation methods may be very
wrong or that you need to make some adjustments. You should also
keep a running figure for all of your completed successful trades
to see what the real figure is compared to your initial Risk/Reward
Ratio calculations. This is one concrete way of seeing how
accurate your target projections are.

Many long-range traders prefer also to make another calculation for all of their potential long-range trades, though we do not
specifically make this calculation, we shall examine it here
briefly. That is, they calculate the potential profit or return on
any given trade as a percent return on equity as a function of
time, to come up with, if you will, an "annual return rate", based

314

on their time frame projections for the length of time from their
entry into a trade until they project their targets zones will stop
them out.

Since we've come up with an average idea of when most long-
range trades will be stopped out, and since the potential profits,
even spread out over a 4 to 6 month period, are so relatively large
compared to other investments, we doubt the value of making such a
calculation unless the investor simply likes doing it to reassure
himself that the potential percentage return on his investment
justifies the high risk of trading in commodities in the first
place, in which case we would have no objections to taking the few
minutes extra time to do the necessary calculations.

We'd now like to examine a situation that at first may seem
like an unlikely one, but in reality occurs much more frequently
than you might expect. That is when you have a number of potential trades within one complex, all of a long-range nature, and you
feel you must narrow them down or even limit them to one. This
most typically will occur when an entire complex is bottoming or
topping, which in the case of most of them will happen somewhat
simultaneously unless there is some special case for one of the
members of that complex.

Despite our desire to be as diversified as possible, our preference in such cases is to trade ALL of the members of the complex
IF our capital is sufficient to do so and still permit us to hold
existing positions or to initiate new positions in other complexes
should they come up unexpectedly - though, seriously, given the
long-range nature of our analysis, how many long-range potential
recommendations can come up UNEXPECTEDLY?

Given that our preference is to trade ALL potential long-range
trades if they meet our trade selection criteria AND if they are
satisfactory from a potential Reward, satisfactory initial Risk,
Risk % of Margin, and Risk/Reward Ratio, are there any guidelines
to use when one must pick and choose between the different poten-

tial trades within a complex if one insists upon diversification, or if one's capital just isn't sufficient to make all of the trades?

Well, of course, Mini-Contracts are one answer, despite the relatively higher percentage of commissions involved in each trade, IF there is a Mini-Contract available for that complex so that you can pick one commodity in that manner. Of course, there are a number of commodities in which there are no Mini-Contracts available to the investor, so in such a case other guidelines must be utilized.

Any of the earlier figures we have discussed, that is, the Potential Profit, the Initial Risk, the Risk % of Margin, or the Risk/Reward Ratio may be used. Since every investor will have different requirements for his long-range program, it is not possible to state which figure will be best for any one investor, but we do suggest that when you must "pick and choose" between different commodities in one complex, or for that matter, between different commodities in different complexes, that you make up a table showing these figures for all of your potential trades between which you must choose and then study that table carefully. Generally from such a study, you will get a "feel" as to which potential trade is best for your particular program.

We've mentioned diversification before in this chapter, and we'd like to approach this subject again. We've always believed that given the nature of the commodity markets in general, it IS important to diversify one's positions between different complexes as a protective approach to trading. Even if you can afford to trade all of the potential long-range recommendations you may come across, it is seldom a sound idea to NOT SPREAD them across as many different complexes or individual commodities as possible.

Let's say you have in excess of $100,000 in your account and you decide to trade 50 contracts all of one commodity. For whatever reason if the fundamentals in that commodity change unexpectedly overnight, you are in a lot of trouble. To concentrate your funds in such a manner is sort of like shooting dice, in that you are staking everything on one roll. True, you may win, given the high percentage of long-range trades that are profitable, but it makes no sense to concentrate your money in this fashion in one single position - too many things could go wrong, and generally this is the time when they WILL go wrong.

Far better, we believe, to allocate the $100,000 between 5, 6 or 7 complexes, and then further sub-divide or allocate these funds to have say 2 different positions within each complex. If you have taken the other approach in the past, that is, concentrated all or most of your funds for "one big killing" or if that idea intrigues you or turns you on, then we respectfully suggest you look inside yourself, because most of the time such an approach is indirectly self-destructive and is indicative of some deep-seated psychological issue that needs to be resolved.

We are often asked for information about pyramiding, so we would like to examine it as it applies specifically to long-range trading. Most investors and analysts take either the position that it is best to start with multiple contracts or to start with a single contract and pyramid. Like everything else we've discussed, there is no black and white with this issue. A good case can be made for using either approach. Assuming an investor has sufficient funds to begin with, the assumption of multiple contracts at the initiation of a position as opposed to pyramiding makes a lot of sense from the standpoint that by so doing your total profits are substantially increased as opposed to adding additional contracts later on, or pyramiding.

However, with pyramiding, adding more contracts as the move progresses, you are working with a position that has "proven itself" so far from the standpoint that the move you've predicted IS taking place, or at least looks like it is. In our example of Soy Oil, if you decide in advance to take your first contract at 19¢

and then add 1 additional contract at each quarter-cent until you have five contracts, at the 20¢ level, you've acquired all of your contracts at an average price of 19½¢ apiece.

What we believe you must do for yourself is decide which is more important to you: buying 5 contracts outright initially at 19¢, reducing your initial risk, in this case, by $1,500, and increasing your potential profit by a like amount, or pyramiding, using the rudimentary method we outlined or any other pyramiding method in order to trade with some paper profits, and more importantly we feel, to get a confirmation of the move by your various entry points.

This entire issue seems to us to be one of individual preference for the investor, since such a good case can be made for either approach. If the concept of pyramiding appeals to you, we suggest you read the chapter on pyramiding where all of the pros and cons of pyramiding are discussed as are the various methods you can use to build your pyramids.

Another frequently asked question is about reserve risk capital. In essence, people ask, "How much should I keep in reserve in case everything goes wrong?" One way of looking at this is to keep in mind that we are talking about RISK CAPITAL in the first place, money you are prepared to lose completely. Also given the relatively high percentage of success with Long-Range trading, our initial answer to such a question is that you should keep NO RESERVES.

This is based on the assumption, of course, that you are following an intelligent trade selection program, and that you are using the money management guidelines outlined in this chapter, such as diversification, Risk/Reward analysis, etc. If you are following sound selection and money management approaches AND if the money you have committed is GENUINELY risk capital, then we are hard pressed to make a good case for not committing all of it to your long-range investment program.

318

A related and frequently-asked question is what to do with excess risk capital funds until they are committed to actual trades as margin. Surprisingly, many investors just leave them in their margin account until they are needed, where they are drawing no interest at all. Many others keep them in money market funds, CD's, or other investment media to earn interest until needed. This latter approach sounds like a good idea, and while it is at least earning interest for the investor, probably sufficient to make up for slippage and brokerage commissions, in many cases it does not permit you as ready access to your funds as you might need.

Of course, with long-range trading, you normally have plenty of time to act on any given trade, which typically would give you sufficient time to liquidate your investments and get them into your margin account. Probably a better approach, and far safer one, is to let your broker handle that for you by investing all of your account's funds that are not being required for margin into T-Bills. Unfortunately, some brokers are reluctant to take on this additional burden of paperwork and supervision. If such is the case, we suggest you consider changing brokers or brokerage houses to facilitate this approach. By having your money invested in Treasury Bills by the brokerage firm, your money is ALREADY there at the brokerage house, you have an insured investment of reasonable yield, and you do not have to give these excess unused funds any of your attention.

We're often asked about taking profits for a long-range trading program, and while we believe this subject more properly falls into the area of technical analysis, which we've covered in another chapter, we will briefly touch on it here since the subject of taking profits does come up so often. From a money management standpoint, the most important aspect of profit-taking shows up when you are able to have multiple contracts in a single commodity. When you are able to do this, we recommend that if you have two contracts in a single position that you plan on taking profits when either the lower end of your target zone is hit, that is, your target less 10%, or when the target itself is hit, and let the other contract ride with ever-increasingly close stop placement. Another approach is to take profits on the first contract at the target itself and profits on the second contract when the upper boundary of the target zone, that is, the target plus 10% is hit.

Obviously, the possibilities are virtually endless for varying when you will take profits, such as if you have 3 contracts in a position or a multiple of three. For single contract positions, we believe the best money management approach is to use the technical one of moving one's stops in close when the lower boundary of the target zone is reached, then closer as the target itself is reached, etc. For multiple contracts, however, you have an enormous amount of additional flexibility for taking your profits, as well as for varying your methods of initial stop placement and for also varying your techniques of trailing stop placement. So, being able to trade multiple contracts is very advantageous whenever you find it possible to use this approach, but in NO case let this advantage prevent you from the DIVERSIFICATION we've discussed.

Most readers will be aware of our interest in the psychological aspects of any kind of investing, and long-range investing has its own peculiar aspects of the psychology involved. Long-range commodity trading TENDS to draw those commodity investors who ARE more inclined to be psychologically able to win and achieve success. Typically, otherwise they would be drawn to day-trading or short-term trading as the fastest way, subconsciously, to lose their money. This is NOT to say, however, that EVERYONE who gets involved in long-range trading is TOTALLY free of subconscious issues that may be self-defeating.

If you have any doubts as to whether long-range trading is for you or not, and you CONSCIOUSLY want to make money in the markets,

OR if the thought of making a lot of money evokes an uncomfortable mental or physical reaction within you, then there is almost a 100% probability that there is some subconscious issue within you which will prevent you from making money regardless of how good your analysis and/or money management is. This is true even if you are successful in your profession or other more conservative investments.

Rather than getting into a detailed analysis here of what may be happening, we strongly and respectfully urge you to take some action if anything we've been mentioning rings true to you. Your courses of action are manyfold, but the best two are to read one or more GOOD books on the subject, do some introspection and self-analysis, and see if that resolves the uncomfortability for you. The next course would be to see a good therapist to seek further assistance. All of these courses of action are thoroughly discussed in the following chapter.

CHAPTER 14

HOW YOUR MIND AFFECTS YOUR TRADING

With the exception of a couple recent books, and a few
articles and chapters in other books written in the past, very
little has been written about the psychology involved in successful
speculation, whether it is in commodities, stocks, or any other
investment medium. What has been written to date is based primarily on conventional psychological theory, modified somewhat to
fit commodity traders. This chapter will take on the whole area of
what differentiates psychologically the winning traders from the
losing traders, a different viewpoint and perspective.

Transactional Analysis, or "T.A." for short, was developed by
a distinguished psychoanalyst, Dr. Eric Berne in San Francisco in
the 1960's and has continued to evolve and improve over the years.
It is, in the opinion of your author, the most comprehensible and
effective method of psychotherapy available at this time. Hence,
this discussion will be from a fresh viewpoint, and will cast a new
light on what really makes a winner in any type of speculative
activity.

It has always been a fairly well-known fact that throughout
history, some individuals have seemed to be "born winners", while
the great majority of people have been either "non-winners" or
"born losers". Philosophers have debated for years whether these
life tendencies have been due to genetic factors, astrological
predispositions, or just plain luck or the lack of it. While we
believe that all of these factors, as well as numerous other ones,
undoubtedly play <u>some</u> role in the degree of success achieved by

any individual throughout his life, we firmly believe that they are minor factors that only play subsidiary and modifying roles to the most important element of success: which is an individual's psychological make-up.

To many observers, each person's personality has a fatalistic cast, in that they feel we are the way we are, and cannot change ourselves. Nothing could be further from the truth. The truth is that all of us have the power to change, alter, and modify our personalities, but sad to say, very few people either know or believe that they have the power to change themselves, and therefore they go through life repeating the same mistakes and follies time after time in a repetitive cycle.

Before we can pinpoint those personality traits that make a winner in commodity trading or any other type of speculation, we must analyze exactly how and why each of us has become the way we are today.

All of us come into this world initially feeling accepting of ourselves and accepting of other people. In T.A. terminology, this is called having the life position that "I'm OK, You're OK". We are born as princes and princesses, but within a period of time, either hours in tragic cases, or years in average circumstances, we gradually change our view of ourselves and of the world around us.

This change in our life position usually is set fairly firmly in place by age 5 to 7, and then we spend our lives to about age 14 confirming that position. From age 14 on, we unconsciously plan and run our lives around the framework of that life position. The very few and very fortunate children decide that they were initially correct about the world, and that they really are okay, and that other people are too. Unfortunately, the children are definitely in the minority, probably comprising less than 5 percent of the population. The rest of us allow ourselves to turn into "frogs" either by coming to decide that we're not okay and other people aren't either; or that we're not okay and other people are; or that we are okay and no one else is.

There are then these four basic existential life positions. The position that "I'm not okay and no one else is", is a tragic one that is held by the "born losers" in life. These people rarely accomplish anything positive, and when they do, they invariably find a way, subconsciously, to ruin it. More common are the other two life positions; and a great percentage of the population has the belief that they are not okay but other people are, a position held by a great number of speculators. The position that believes "I'm okay but other people aren't" is often found in successful lives, that is, lives that are successful on the surface, but are not genuinely happy. This describes the bully, the overbearing businessman, or the tyrannical parent or spouse, who rarely, if ever, can admit to a mistake. Here too, we find a large number of speculators. People in this life position will win in the markets very often, but when they do, it is a hollow victory in that the winnings bring them no pleasure. When they lose they think it is not because of anything they have done, but rather they believe it is due to crooked brokers, manipulation of the market by insiders, or to anything except themselves.

The only consistent, happy, and big winners in any kind of speculation are those that hold the belief that they are okay and so are other people. They are not pollyannas who think a Hitler or a Stalin did permissible things, but instead they believe that everyone is _inherently_ alright, even though their actions may not be morally alright. The winners judge actions and not people.

If so very few people decide when they are little on keeping the life position that they and everyone else is basically okay, why is it that there are any winners, other than these precious few, in the marketplace? The answer to this question is that through self-awareness, tragedy, or therapy, the non-winners and some of the born losers have managed to change their life posi-

324

tions. We will try in this chapter to convey the information
necessary for you to acquire this self-awareness and if this
information is still not sufficient, to recommend other courses
of action the trader may take if he genuinely wants to win. We
say "if" the trader wants to win <u>with caution</u>, because it would seem
that whoever reads this <u>must</u> want to win, otherwise he wouldn't be
spending the time reading this book.

We agree, insofar as you have reached the point where you are
examining on a conscious level <u>why</u> you are not winning, or not
enjoying your winnings, then you <u>do</u> want to be a winner. However,
all but the successful, happy winners, have an unconscious routine
going on within them that really either doesn't want them to be
winners or doesn't believe it is possible. This unconscious
routine is in the form of recordings, similar to tape recordings,
that we implanted in the circuitry of our brains during our early
formative years.

Many people, upon learning this, decide to blame their parents
for these recordings. The truth, however, is that, with the rare
exceptions of psychotic or psychopathic households, parents did the
best they could, at the time, given the circumstances that
existed. The truth also is that, as little children, we ourselves
made the recordings in our brain based upon our own perceptions
of what we believed reality to be. Often an important goal of
therapy is to get the client to realize that his parents did the
best they could, under the circumstances, for the client to admit
his own responsibility for where he is, and for him to forgive the
parents if there is any remaining animosity.

These recordings we have been referring to are automatic, in
that they play on their own, without our consciously having to
press a "button" in order to get them started. There are perhaps
an infinite number of such recordings in the circuitry of our
brains, but they inevitably seem to divide themselves into two
categories, those that we recorded in relation to our mother and

those we recorded in relation to our father. This accounts to
some degree how most of us seem to have two distinct sides to our
personalities, with a number of variations of each of these two
sides.

However, there are times when we feel free and unencumbered by
the past or our subconscious. Those are the times that the recordings are not playing in our subconscious, and we are in what is
called "the here-and-now" or "up-time". The average person spends
only between 10 and 20% of his or her waking hours in this uptime,
and the remainder under the influence of these subconscious recordings.

Winners, on the other hand, those people who believe themselves to be okay and other people to be intrinsically okay too,
spend a far greater proportion of their waking hours in this
uptime, possibly as much as 50 to 60%. They do not spend all of
their time in this ideal state, possibly because the art of
psychology has not reached this degree of human perfection or
possibly because it is just beyond our own human limitations.

No matter how good our mental health is, it is not yet feasible
to control all of these early recordings. Notice that we say
"control" and not "erase" these recordings, because research on the
human brain has shown that these recordings are never erased, but
we can achieve a degree of control over them so that they do not
play automatically or with as great a degree of frequency or intensity as before. They are always there in our brain, whether
playing or turned off, and this accounts for those occasions when
people in apparently perfect mental health go into depressions, or
periods of anger and sadness that do not seem to be justified by
what is actually going on in their external lives: the recordings
have started to play again, at least temporarily.

What do some of these recordings consist of? Are there certain ones that are fairly common and universal, and if so, are some
of those more predominant among speculators? A lot of these recor-

dings have their origins in what T.A. calls "Injunctions". An injunction is a message or an instruction that the child was either given or believes that he or she was given by his parents or significant other people in his early life.

All the injunctions begin with the word: "Don't". A child with a "Don't Be Healthy" injunction will grow up to be unhealthy. A child who perceives he was given a "Don't Be Sane" injunction will grow up crazy. It is important to notice that parents do not intentionally give their children these messages; except for parents who are themselves crazy. It is the child's interpretation of verbal and non-verbal messages from the parents (and other people) that gives force to the injunctions.

For example, children whose parents really wanted them to be of the opposite sex, may not verbally communicate this message to the child, but their actions, whether treating the little girl as a tomboy and praising her for her boyish traits, or continuing to dress the little boy in girl's clothes for the first three to five years of his life, are both giving non-verbal messages to the child of "Don't Be You". This injunction loosely translates into "Don't Be The Sex You Are". At the extreme, these children will have great difficulties with sexual identity as they grow up, and they will also have a great deal of difficulty in actually realizing who they are. They have a recording in their brains that it is not okay to be either who they are or the sex that they are.

A child who perceives a "Don't Be" or "Don't Exist" injunction will engage in life-endangering pursuits, often including motorcycle racing, car racing, sky diving, heavy drinking, obesity, and cigarette smoking. Is this to say that everyone who smokes cigarettes has a "Don't Be" injunction tape in his brain? Yes, as long as he is aware of the dangers involved with cigarette smoking and continues to smoke.

Injunctions vary in degree, and to use this last example, a person with a heavy, or Third-Degree "Don't Be" injunction will end up killing himself, either consciously by committing suicide, or subconsciously by drinking himself to death. With a milder form of this injunction, a First or Second-Degree type, he will engage in pursuits that either have the potential for harming him or that actually do harm him, short of death.

There are 14 major injunctions that have been identified, and a number of less common ones. The ones that most seriously affect speculators of any type appear to be three: "Don't Be Successful", "Don't Make It", and "Don't Think".

The "Don't Be Successful" is the most paradoxical, in that few people trade commodities unless they have achieved some measure of financial success in life; otherwise they would not have the funds available, however small, to speculate. But, the "Don't Be Successful" injunction, or message, includes an element of "Don't Feel Successful", so that no matter how successful a person is in the eyes of the world, he still does not feel successful to himself.

From an existential standpoint, he feels not-okay about himself. You can determine if you have this injunction by asking yourself two questions, and answering them with complete honesty. The first answer that pops into your mind is most likely the correct one. First, ask yourself: "Do I really feel that I am successful?" And secondly, ask yourself, "When I was small, did I believe it was alright to feel proud of myself?" If your honest answer to either of these is "No", it is indicative of your having a "Don't Be Successful" injunction.

To determine if you have a "Don't Make It" injunction, first ask yourself: "Do I have trouble finishing things I've begun?", then ask yourself: "When I was small, did I often have trouble finishing my homework?". If the answer to either or both of these questions is "Yes", then you have a "Don't Make It" injunction to some degree.

To determine if you have a "Don't Think" injunction, first ask yourself: "Do I have trouble concentrating?", and then

328

ask yourself: "Did I often have trouble answering questions or taking tests in school?". Again, one or both questions answered "Yes" is indicative of a "Don't Think" injunction.

Let's assume you and many other traders find that they have these injunctions or recordings in their brain. What does all of this mean? Well, if you have the "Don't Be Successful" recording, it means either that no matter how much money you make trading you still do not feel it is enough; or that when you start making money, for some reason you can't explain, all of a sudden you lose it again.

Having a "Don't Make It" recording works in much the same way, except you are assured of not making money in trading or of losing it back after you've "almost made it". A "Don't Think" recording makes it so difficult for you to make trading decisions that the opportunities have already passed by the time you have made your mind up on establishing a position.

Many people have all three of these injunctions, and many more injunctions too which only increases the difficulties they experience both in their trading as well as their personal and professional lives. Having insight into realizing one has these automatic, subconscious recordings is half the battle. Sometimes, just knowing that they are there, playing out of one's awareness, is enough to overcome them and turn them off. Sometimes they are intense or severe enough that it takes a competent therapist to help the trader deal with them. It is important to remember that all of us have these recordings or injunctions, whether just a couple or a dozen of them, in varying degrees of intensity. Having them is nothing to be ashamed of; but knowing that one has them and not doing anything about them puts into serious question the trader's conscious desire to change his pattern of losing.

Closely related to these injunctions is a phenomenon known as "racket feelings and behavior" because they too are recordings. Again, they divide up into two, one for our relationship with our

father and father-figures, and the other for our mother and
mother-figures in our life. Our spouse and close friends normally
fit into both categories. A racket feeling is almost an identity
feeling, without which we would not feel like ourselves. When we
are not in "up-time", the chances are we are feeling one of our
two individual racket feelings, or alternating between them.

Some of the most common racket feelings are scare, anger, sadness, depression, confusion, and hurt, though there are many others
that are not as common. Each of us has two and only two racket
feelings, and these are feelings we experience every day of our
lives, since they are recordings, and run quite automatically.
Based upon our examination of traders, there does not seem to be
any "favorite" racket feelings that predominate though scare and
anger are frequently found.

Racket feelings,while they can never be erased, can be dealt
with quite effectively, and it is necessary to do so, because they
are so closely linked to your identity, that your subconscious will
go to great lengths in order to get you to feel them, including
failing at your trading efforts. Since these racket feelings are
used by the recordings to cover up genuine feelings, either positive or negative, that were not permitted in childhood (or that the
child believed were not permitted), by one or both of the parents,
in order to keep these racket feelings from interfering with
trading, it is necessary first, to identify them and then to learn
how to deal with them.

If you have not already gotten in touch with the two negative
feelings that seem to predominate in your life, you can find them
by asking yourself a few simple questions. First, ask yourself,
"When you wanted something from your mother, how did you feel?"
Then ask yourself, "When you wanted something from your father, how
did you feel?"

Next, ask yourself "Think of a time in the past few weeks when
things went badly for you. How did you feel?" From these

questions you should come up with two major feelings, and they should seem to you like they are a part of your identity. For example, if your situation for the last question was that of a losing trade, perhaps you felt angry, or scared, or sad. The chances are that what you felt was one of your racket feelings.

In order to keep from setting yourself up to get these recordings going that are such an integral part of you, it takes a bit of practice. Once you have identified your two racket feelings, the best way to bring them under control is always to be on the alert for their appearing. Let's say anger is one of them. Then, every time you realize that you are angry, ask yourself "Is this anger real? That is, is it appropriate and genuine?" If there is any doubt whatsoever in your mind as to its genuineness, think back to what was going on with you a minute or two before the anger first appeared. The chances are it was another, different feeling.

Let's say in the example just given, you were feeling proud of yourself that your stop was as close as it was in order to minimize your loss. Then the real feeling, the one that was forbidden, or at least seemed to you to be forbidden by one or both of your parents, was pride. The way to conquer the negative racket feeling is to close your eyes, remember the proud feeling, either the one that just occured or another time in the past that you felt proud, really get into it and experience, re-live and feel it; then open your eyes and look around at the people and things in your surrounding right then that are pleasant to you. You will have gotten rid of the negative or racket feeling and continue to experience the real or forbidden feeling.

It really isn't as difficult as it sounds, it just takes some awareness and practice, and the more you practice this skill, the easier it becomes, and the less frequent and less intense these recordings of negative feelings will play. You may find when you do this, that on occasion, the feeling you were feeling just before the anger in this example, is also a negative feeling, but that will be a genuine, real, negative feeling, possibly scare over the loss of money. This is alright, since what you are experiencing is a genuine feeling and one that you can use to motivate yourself to action, whether the real negative feeling is scare or anger or sadness or hurt. The only way to deal with a real feeling is to "go with it" and experience it.

If the real feeling over the losing trade is scare, as we just mentioned, use the scare to take action to figure out what to do next. If the real feeling you find is anger, go with the anger and find a secluded or private place that you can rant and rave until you feel the emotion subsiding. If the real feeling is hurt or sadness, have a good cry and get all the emotions out.

A trader who is operating out of non-genuine or racket feelings is in one of his recordings and cannot succeed as long as he is in the recording.

Closely related to all of this is what we do while we are in our recordings, and that usually is to play psychological games. The concept of psychological game-playing was popularized by the late Dr. Eric Berne in his book Games People Play, and all of us do play them. Basically, a psychological game is much like a game we play on a board. There are players themselves, certain moves that have to be made, and a predictable outcome (though the outcome does not seem predictable to the players, at least not on a conscious level).

Dr. Berne identified a number of games people play, and subsequent authors and researchers have further refined his work by categorizing even more games. All of these games are structured, subconsciously, in such a way, that the players end the game feeling one of their negative, racket feelings. In fact, the whole purpose of psychological games is the generation of negative feelings. Games are a way of spending time and they serve to reinforce our basic identity feelings that are intimately tied up with our racket feelings and existential life position.

The best way to stay out of games, and the corresponding racket feelings and life position that go along with them, is to identify the games you play, and by this insight decide you don't want to play these games any more. We will identify what seem to be the most prevalent games that unsuccessful traders play, so you can see which ones you find yourself getting into. There are many others, and anyone who is interested in pursuing the matter further is advised to read the before-mentioned book by Eric Berne, Games People Play.

The first game losing traders play is called "Wooden Leg", and in it, the person who is "it" invariable finds all sorts of personal handicaps to explain why this or that trade went sour. The excuses can include a lack of education, insufficient capital, eyesight too poor to read the charts, or a nagging wife. The message this trader hears runs like: "What can anyone expect of me since I have such a handicap? How can I possibly succeed?" He is, of course, referring to his invisible wooden leg. The other players in this game, whether his family, his friends, or his broker normally feel sorry for him, because they couldn't expect him ever to succeed anyway with such a handicap. The Wooden Leg player will secretly feel satisfied, but he will also feel angry, or sad, or scared due to his imaginary handicap. The game also reinforces his basic life position that he isn't okay and other people are. (After all, they don't have wooden legs).

Another popular trader game is acronymed "NIGYSOB", which stands for "Now I've Got You, You Son Of A Bitch", and is evidenced when the trader saves up bad feelings toward his broker, spouse, or friends until he has a whole list of real and/or imagined wrongs. When this list reaches a certain point, the trader attacks the guilty party, usually verbally, and though the trader has lost in the market, there is a sense of justification for his anger that coincides with his racket anger and his life position of "I'm okay but no one else is".

     "Yes, But . . ." is still another popular game with traders,
in which the broker or friends make suggestions to the trader on
how to win in the markets, to which each suggestion, no matter
how valid an idea, the trader responds with "Yes, but . . .". The
end of this game is when the other player or players become
exasperated with the trader's constant refusal to try any of their
suggestions and either attack the trader or withdraw from him.
The trader can then feel either angry at their lack of
understanding, or hurt or sad, and in any case, the trader again
reinforces his belief about his own and others' okayness.

     While there are many other games, the last we'll examine is
called "Schlemiel" and is a mess-making game in which the trader
makes messes of one sort or another, such as entering incorrect
stops or initial orders, spilling coffee on his important charts
or data, or a similar so-called "mistake". Normally the trader
feels angry at himself, as do the others in the game, or guilty or
sad, thereby proving to himself that he really isn't okay.

     All of these games get in the way of a trader's success, and
usually are carry-overs from the games he plays in his personal
life. An examination of these games, and others will give you a
good insight into those counterproductive and failing ways you
spend your trading time.

     By now, you should be able to see that when we are in our
recordings, which again is probably between 80% to 90% of the
time, it is very difficult to make intelligent investing decisions. Either our old internal recordings are broadcasting harmful old injunctions to us subconsciously, or they are helping to
create negative racket feelings in us, or they have us enmeshed in
harmful psychological games; or a combination of all three.

     It is difficult enough as it is for an investor to succeed in
the commodity markets without having subconscious tapes constantly
telling him that he cannot make it; or feeling angry or scared
without having a good reason to be so; or starting a psychological

334

game that will end up bringing about bad feelings for him and confirming a negative life position he believes to be true about himself.

Interestingly enough, you can easily check out for yourself what
your own life position is. That is, the decision you made when
you were little about how you would view yourself and the rest of
the world when you were in your recordings. By now you should have
identified your racket feelings. Remember a time when you felt one
of those feelings quite strongly and when it was not a genuine or
real feeling (and you can recognize a real feeling by its being
caused by good reasons), close your eyes, and ask yourself: When I
felt this way, did I feel I was ok or not-ok?

You're OK

I'm Not OK You're OK - + Get Away From	I'm OK You're OK + + Get On With
I'm Not OK You're Not OK - - Get Nowhere	I'm OK You're Not OK + - Get rid of

THE OK CORRAL
(Dr. Franklin H. Ernst, Jr.)

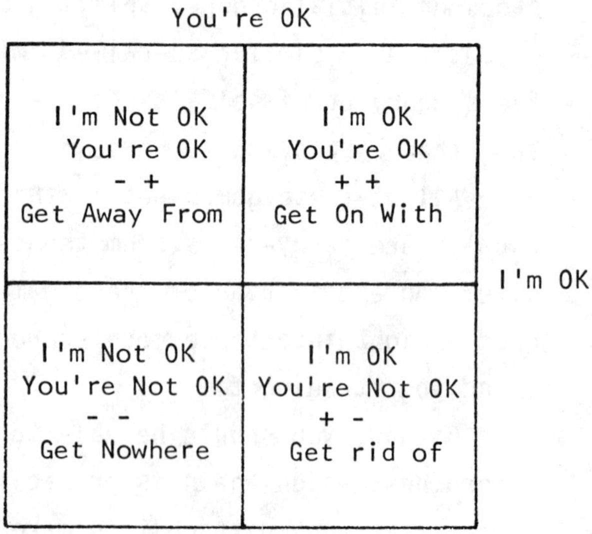

I'm OK

Figure 61

Then pause and wait for an answer in your head. The first
answer that comes will be the correct one. That will tell you when
you are in your recordings whether you are coming from an I'm-OK or
an I'm-Not-OK life position. Then re-create the other racket
feeling and experience, and ask yourself the same question about

others: "When I felt that way, did I feel other people in general
were ok or not-OK?" That will tell you when you are in your recordings whether you view others, or the world, as being OK or Not-OK
as seen in Figure 61.

You may get two different answers, such as in one case it
might be: I'M Not-OK, They're-OK, or I'm-OK, they're Not-OK. This
is normal; since we have two different major sets of recordings,
we often have a life position that is different for each; but in
every case, where there are two different ones, one will be the
more favored of the two.

Another interesting psychological facet that affects traders,
is that of the Karpman Triangle, or a Drama Triangle, as developed
by Steven Karpman. Picture a triangle, with the three corners
labeled "Victim", "Rescuer" and "Persecutor". All of us, when we
are in our recordings, spend our time at one of the corners,
whether we are in a game or not. The different racket feelings a
person experiences coincide with these three corners, and as we
move through our recordings or through our games, we switch positions around the triangle, going from being a Victim who is suf-
fering losing trades, to a Persecutor who berates his broker or
advisor or spouse, to a Rescuer who is apologizing to his victims
and rescuing them from their own guilty feelings.

All through this, the other parties in the drama are switching
sides too to carry the drama through smoothly. When the trader is
in the Victim position, his broker may be the Rescuer and his
spouse the Persecutor. When the trader is in the Persecutor role,
the broker and spouse may take either the Victim or Rescuer roles.
And when the trader is in the Rescuer role, possibly rescuing his
wife from her depression and guilt over having berated the trader,
the broker will persecute the trader for his foolish trades. One
can, upon examination, see how these different roles the trader
goes through fit into his psychological games, racket feelings, and
life positions.

336

Everyone experiences these phenomena to varying degrees every
day. Again, insight and practice are the best ways to stay out of
these recordings and patterns that are so self-defeating to successful trading. A personal example may be helpful. Your author
is a therapist who has spent years analyzing his own life script,
injunctions, life positions, racket feelings, etc. Earlier on in
the preparation of this chapter, when a certain, especially difficult portion came into place for him, he felt very proud and
excited, two feelings that as a child he believed were not okay for
him to feel. Before he was aware of it, (because these recordings
come on so instantaneously at times, even to those experienced in
dealing with them) subconsciously a "Don't Feel Successful" injunction played; he began to feel angry without any real reason, pro-
ceeded to spill his coffee on some of this chapter manuscript,
thereby playing Schlemiel, again unconsciously, and he started to
become a persecutor by blaming the person who had set his coffee
down too close to the manuscript.

Fortunately, due to being aware of his own patterns, he was able
to recognize the recordings that had just played within a minute
or two and he was able to stop them and return to feeling good
about himself and the work he had just accomplished. This is a
very small example, but it is so indicative of how most of us
spend the greater part of our lives going from one recording to
another without even being aware of it.

It cannot be emphasized too strongly that everyone has his
own set of albums of recordings, and that this is nothing to feel
bad about or ashamed of. The important thing is to learn to
recognize them when they start, at least as often as possible, and
then to turn them off. If a trader is into unjustified feelings
of scare or anger or whatever, that are racket feelings, or if he
is into any of his games, or is at some point on the Karpman
Triangle, then his chances of success are virtually doomed.

All of these recordings combined, form what we call a
person's Life Script; and for those of you who wish to study this
area in more detail, we can recommend an excellent book by Claude
M. Steiner called Scripts People Live. Basically, scripts mean
that each of us when we are very young, while we are still
deciding about our own and other people's OKness, and starting
to develop our racket feelings, and beginning to practice the games
we will play throughout life, then also decide, usually
unconsciously, what our life is going to be like. In effect, we
write the script for our own lives, and we then proceed over the
years to marry spouses, choose careers, take jobs, make investments, etc. that will fulfill and carry forward the life script or
life plan we have unconsciously written for ourselves.

There are two ways of categorizing life scripts. The first
is by their intensity. Normally people's life scripts, assuming
that they are not winning scripts, and not many people's are, are
either of the "garden-variety" type or of the tragic type. Most
of us fit into the "garden-variety type" in that nothing ever happens in our life that is extremely dramatic; or if it does, it is
very rare. It is more of a plain, banal existence. The tragic
type, sometimes called the hamartic type, is much more dramatic.
In the hamartic script, people commit suicide, commit homicide, go
crazy and are institutionalized, kill themselves indirectly, or
are constantly involved in one major crisis after another.

Upon reflection, the reader can probably identify many of his
friends as falling into one of these two categories. Commodity
traders can fall into either category. They are into garden-
variety scripts if they lose a little bit of money, make a little
bit of money, lose a little bit of money, and so forth. They are
in a tragic script if they do such things as go bankrupt, lose
their life savings, develop ulcers, or commit suicide.

It is important for each trader to give some thought to these
types of scripts in order to get an idea of where he is heading in

the script he wrote unconsciously so many years ago. It may be frightening, (and that would be real fear, not racket fear) if the trader realizes he is caught up in a tragic script. but it need not end tragically since the scripts we wrote so many years ago CAN be broken and re-written, either through insight, self-awareness, or therapy.

The other way of categorizing life scripts is by their nature, instead of by degree. This way, life scripts, fall into the categories of "Winning Scripts", "Non-Winning Scripts" and "Losing Scripts". A commodity trader with a losing script will probably not be reading this chapter, not if he has already started trading, because he would by now have lost all of his money and be bankrupt and destitute. A trader with a Winning Script may be reading to this chapter to gather more knowledge about himself, but he has it made financially and takes profits out of the market on a consistent basis. This is not to say he doesn't have his losses, but on balance, he wins.

The trader with the "Non-Winning" Script could just as well be categorized as having a "Non-Losing" Script, for he neither wins nor loses. This script is usually of the garden variety type, and this trader, when he does win, ends up losing it back, and normally he muddles along for years until he has eventually lost his money or decided to give up trading. Sometimes the "non-winner" could have an hamartic script where he loses all of his money quickly, but this would be followed by depression or anger instead of suicide or institutionalization.

There is one last way to look at scripts that we would like to touch on, that is developed very well in the previously mentioned book by Claude Steiner. Steiner breaks scripts down further, into three major types: the Mindless Script, the Joyless Script, and the Loveless Script. With the Mindless Script the person who has it believes that he cannot think, and has no control of his mind. With the Joyless Script, the person believes that he can never be happy. And with the Loveless Script the person feels that he is unworthy of being loved and can never achieve intimacy. As far as we can tell at this point, these three types of scripts are divided among commodity traders in about the same proportion as among the general public, and we mention them here only to give you additional information about Life Script types.

Regardless of the script type a trader has, his Life Script follows a predictable pattern or repetitive sequence. If you stop to think about it, you will probably realize that many times in your life events have seemed to repeat themselves in a way similar to occurrences in the past. A typical sequence for the commodity trader is that in Act One, he works long and hard to acquire the money necessary for trading, investigating methods of selecting commodities, and deciding how he is going to trade. In Act Two, the trader starts trading, begins to have some successes, becomes confident, and begins to plan how he will spend the fortune he is amassing. In Act Three, a surprise occurs, which might be a string of losses, drinking too heavily, getting fired from his job, losing all of his money, a lawsuit or some other suitable dramatic tragedy. In Act Four we see our hero, the trader, in the "pits", despairing, possibly alone or rejected or abandoned, whether in reality or in his imagination, by his family, friends, and broker.

That is the end of the play, but not the end of the sequence of plays, for at some time, after the curtain comes down on Act Four, off-stage, the trader "pulls himself up by his bootstraps" and begins working long and hard again as Act One starts all over. There are, of course, an infinite number of variations in this script, as there are a near-infinite number of plays that have been written over the centuries, but all scripts have certain elements in common. They are all repetitive and predictable and move from the hero working hard in some way, to his beginning to succeed, to a supposedly unexpected surprise, to a tragedy of some sort, to his

340

payoff of negative feelings. Throughout all of this, the trader is playing his games that are most appropriate to each Act, choosing the positions in the Drama Triangle that fit best for the Scene, maintaining his one or two favorite life positions, and feeling his racket feelings throughout the entire drama.

If this sounds familiar to you , don't be surprised, because it happens to all of us, unless we are one of the fortunate few who started life with a Winner's script or who re-wrote his script along the way. Winners have scripts too, with a sequence of Acts that repeat themselves, but instead of the play's being a tragedy or melodrama, the Winner's script calls for an uplifting play, which contains drama, but has a happy ending. In Act One, the hero again would be working hard, but he would enjoy doing so. In Act Two, the trader would start trading and becoming successful, just as in Act Two of our former drama. Act Three also has a surprise but instead of losing all his money, the winner makes the big trade. In act four the winner enjoys the fruits of success, and we have the happy ending. After the curtain has come down, our hero, the winning trader, either gets ready to go back to Act One and start working the markets again, or he decides to move on to some other venture or pursuit or return to his beach house in Florida.

There are degrees of failure or success in both the Winner's and Loser's scripts or dramas. The magnitude of the win or loss varies with the individual and usually becomes more intense as the cycle repeats itself over the years. There is no standard time frame for the four acts to take place in. For one person Act One, the working hard, with or without pleasure, may last for a period of months or for years; and so may the other acts in the play.

You may ask at this point how it is that in a Losing or Non-Winning script, the trader gets from the disaster of Act Four back up into Act One. We mentioned that this was done by his pulling himself up by his bootstraps, and this is done in one of five ways that all traders, and non-traders too for that matter, use every day, throughout their lives, and which seriously affect their trading and success if not recognized. These five ways are called "Drivers", a concept developed by Taibi Kahler, a psychologist in Little Rock, Arkansas.

Drivers are a different type of recording that we all have, and the only difference between each of us is which of the drivers are most influential in our lives. The drivers are belief recordings in our heads that tell us: <u>we are okay if</u> . . . , The five drivers are: "Please Others", "Try Hard", "Hurry Up", "Be Strong", and "Be Perfect". We all have them, and at appropriate times, they can initiate appropriate behavior in us. There are times when it is best to please other people, to try hard at a task to be perfect in what one is doing, to hurry something up, and to be strong in a difficult situation.

It is when these drivers act in an automatic, recording kind of way that the trader gets into trouble. The trader who is in a Please Others recording agrees with all the suggestions of his brokers and advisors so as not to displease them. In effect, the recording playing in his head, is "I'm okay if I agree with them and don't hurt their feelings by disagreeing". The trader who is in a Try Hard driver really does try hard to make his mind up about when to enter or exit a trade, but he never really does decide until it is too late. In effect, he is okay if he tries hard; and trying implicitly means <u>not finishing</u>. The trader with a Hurry Up driver in action will rush through his selections, calculations, broker phone calls, and so forth, and hurry to the point where the likelihood of mistakes is increased tremendously. The trader in a Be Strong shows no joy over his wins nor pain over his losses even though the latter is eating him up inside and affecting his judgment. The trader with a Be Perfect driver recording playing is so careful in his selections and calculations, and so afraid of making a mistake, that he seldom if ever, acts until it is too late.

342

Everyone has all five drivers in their brain, but we all have two that are favorites. If you haven't already figured out what your favorites are, the drivers which affect your trading most, you can identify them by asking yourself first "When I was small, I felt I was okay around my father if I --------(blank)" and fill the blank in with one of the five drivers just listed. Then repeat the question "When I was small, I felt I was okay with my mother if I (blank)". There you have your two dominant drivers, the ones that most adversely affect your trading, even though the other three may pop their heads up from time to time. By being aware of your dominant drivers and of how the other ones work too, it is possible for you to bring them under control so that they do not adversely affect your trading.

As we said, there are times when it is quite appropriate to use these drivers, when they can be of use to you. Can you imagine wanting to be operated on by a surgeon who was in a Hurry Up driver instead of a Be Perfect? It is good for the trader to Be Perfect, but only to a reasonable degree in making his selections and picking his stops. The same is true of the Hurry Up driver when time is of the essence and speed is essential, even if the hurrying up results in a decision to postpone action because not enough time is available.

It's important too for the trader to Be Strong at times when the markets are running against him, and to Please Others, and possibly more importantly to please himself, by enjoying his successes and spending his profits. It's important too to Try Hard when it is necessary to persevere, as long as the trying ends up in action. These recordings, the drivers, differ from the other recordings in that they can be turned to good use by our becoming aware of them; whereas becoming aware of the other recordings, the injunctions, rackets, life positions, and drama triangle positions can be useful only for getting out of them.

All of this brings us to an important question that has been asked repeatedly by writers in the field of speculation. Why can two traders, with identical capital, with identical information, both technical and fundamental, both place the same trade at the same entry point, possibly even with the same stop-loss point, and yet one consistently wins while the other consistently loses? The answer lies in their scripts, whether they are Winning ones or Non-Winning ones, and in the other factors that we have discussed that go along with their scripts.

We mentioned before that people can and do re-write their scripts. Your author personally knows literally dozens and dozens of people who have done so. You may ask, if it is that easy, why doesn't everyone do it, and why aren't all commodity traders successful? Well, in the first place, it usually isn't that easy. The average trader has spent anywhere between 20 and 60 years developing, writing, and acting and re-acting his script, so it is very much an integral part of him, just as his injunctions, life positions, rackets and games are. Change is seldom easy, but it need not be difficult.

That statement sounds like a contradiction, but it is not. Change is seldom easy because neither the average trader or the average person in general, is aware that he has the power to change his life, that is, to change his script. Or they may believe it in some sort of vague way, that they have the power to do so, but the recordings in the brain circuitry are so deeply embedded that they seem unable to move off dead center and do anything about their lives. This resulting frustration, especially after spending periods of time in Acts One and Two when things look like they are getting better, only to repeat themselves in disaster, eventually leads to the fatalistic attitude that it really is impossible to change their lives.

Change need not be difficult once the trader believes it is possible and acts on that belief, taking responsibility for what he

is and what he has done with his life up to that point. This is
the reason that the ratio of winning traders, year in and year out,
is at most only 1 of them to every 10 non-winners. The losers or
non-winners either do not know they can change, do not believe they
can change, or do not know how to go about changing. One of the
primary goals of this chapter has been to try to give you enough
information to explain how and why your life works the way it does,
why you have the same feelings over and over, and run into the same
roadblocks, and why your life seems to be cyclical or repetitive in
nature. This knowledge, especially if the trader seriously thinks
about it and how it may apply to his own life, will lead to
insight.

And this insight should be enough for the trader who does not
win consistently to know he can change his life, to believe he can
change his life, and to feel he can change his life. Hopefully,
this chapter has given you some of the tools to get in touch with
what is going on in your life that keeps putting up roadblocks to
your trading success.

A word of caution is in order in that it is very easy for a
person to believe he understands the psychology of his life, and
well he may on an intellectual level, only to end up in disaster
again. This is simply caused by over-confidence and not a not-
thorough-enough understanding of himself. What happens here is
that the trader temporarily assumes the life position that he is
OK, and that other people aren't. After all, how could they be,
when they're mired in all their own muck and he at least
understands himself now, and is ready to move ahead and show all
of them how successful he has now become.

This is a big pitfall to avoid and is commonly seen in clients
who are not yet through therapy but who think that they are, and
terminate therapy too quickly. The only real check for this, is if
you are feeling confident and successful, to ask yourself, with
complete honesty, whether or not you are feeling superior to the

other traders in the marketplace. It is true that if you have re-written your script to a winning one, then in that respect, and in that respect only, you are superior to them, but you are not superior to them as human beings. If you notice a chuckle or a smile of one-upsmanship or cockiness, beware. You are still in your script, and it is just a re-write, not a new one.

What is one to do then in such a situation? Or what can you do if you find that you do not yet have the tools, the understanding, or the insight to feel the confidence and glow of a winner? There are several steps you can take but before you take any of them, you must stop trading. You can continue paper trading if you wish, as that will give you some practice in not beating yourself or in not getting angry at the winning trades you have no money in, a condition which is remarkably similar to not beating yourself when you do have money in losing trades.

The three courses of action available to a trader who reali-zes he cannot yet re-write his script into a winning one are: reading, practice, and therapy. From the standpoint of reading, we would recommend these books, taken in the following order: First, Games Investors Play by your author, first, I'm OK, You're OK by Dr. Tom Harris, Born to Win by Muriel James, Success Through T.A. by Jut Meininger, and Scripts People Live by Claude Steiner. You will notice that none of Dr. Eric Berne's books are mentioned, and that is not meant as a discount to Dr. Berne. We believe you would enjoy all of his books, but the ones listed above have more recent information in them and more practical applications, whereas those by Berne, while very enjoyable to read, are sometimes a bit theoretical instead of practical. If we had only one book to recommend, it would be our own Games Investors Play because the theory in it is easy to understand and the book has exercises at the end of each chapter to help the reader learn more about him-self.

The best option is probably the quickest and most effective, and that is to see a good therapist. This option is best only if

the trader sees a <u>good</u> therapist, as therapists are like brokers
and advisors, in that they come in all shades of quality and com-
petence. Not too many years ago there was a stigma attached to
someone's going to see a therapist, and in some parts of the
country and in some quarters, a bit of that attitude still
remains. Fortunately, the public has become better-educated about
mental health, and most people realize there is nothing wrong with
someone seeing a therapist nor does it mean that the person is
"crazy".

If you still feel uncertain about your winning abilities
after reading this book, and thinking it over, and after
reading some of the recommended books, please, do not feel
discouraged nor hesitate to see a competent therapist. The cost
involved is small in terms of the benefits you can reap in your
trading as well as in your personal life. Even if you are a
winner in the markets from the standpoint of making money consistently but you find that you either cannot enjoy it or do not
seem to be able to derive the pleasure from it that you would
expect, this too calls for action.

The therapist does not have to be one who specializes in T.A.
psychology, as long as he is well-referred. Taurus Corporation
maintains a directory of what we believe to be excellent therapists
in all states of the union, and Canada and Mexico, in virtually
every major city and many small ones. We will be happy to forward
to you the names and phone numbers of some in your area, in
complete confidence, if you request us to do so.

Again, let us emphasize that this is a condensation of basic
T.A. and Life Script Theory and how it applies to winning in commodity trading or in any other area of life. Transactional
Analysis, or T.A., is not the only type of therapy nor is it
necessarily the most effective. In your author's belief it is the
most readily understandable, the quickest, and the most practical.

CHAPTER 15

WHERE TO GO FROM HERE

The reader may well ask now, "If I want more information about some of the subjects in this book, where do I go from here?" We sincerely hope that we've included enough information in this book to satisfy most reader's needs, but we also know that many, many of you will want to pursue some areas of commodity analysis or psychology in greater detail.

As a result, we're including the following "Suggested Reading List" for those of you who do want to go further and to read and study more. Many of the books in this list are ones we've purchased many copies of to give to friends and associates, and all of them are in our Taurus library, most in well-worn condition.

While this list could have been expanded to include many, many additional titles of considerable merit, we feel this list as it is contains the key books in the fields of commodity analysis and self-help psychology. Any person who reads and understands the content of these books can justifiably consider himself an "expert" in either or both fields.

We are providing as much information in terms of date of publication, publisher, and ISBN number as is available to us in order to facilitate your locating and purchasing these books. We have also included a brief description of our own impressions of the content of the book we are talking about in order to let you "pick and choose" among those that seem most important to you, in case time limitations prevent your being able to read all of the books. We have included none in this list that we consider to be marginal or only partially beneficial, but instead all of the following books in our opinion are truly outstanding ones.

348

As other, newer books, are published in these fields, we will review them in _Taurus_, but it is difficult for us to believe that the books in this list can be much improved upon.

SUGGESTED READING LIST

Born To Win, Muriel James & Dorothy Jongeward, Addison-Wesley Publishing Co., 1973. ISBN 0-201-03278-3

Born To Win is probably the most comprehensive and clearest book on self-help psychology that combines Transactional Analysis and Gestalt. It is very readable and stimulating. Perhaps it's only shortcoming is a lack of a sufficiently in-depth exploration of script analysis and people's individual life scripts. However, this deficiency is more than compensated for from its approach in examining the different facets of one's psychological make-up to determine what constitutes winners and losers.

Bulls, Bears and Dr. Freud, Albert Haas, Jr. and Don D. Jackson, The World Publishing Co., 1967. No ESBN No. available.

A thoroughly delightful little book written with a great deal of humor and insight. Though directed specifically at the mass and individual psychology of the stock market, the incisive comments about bull markets, bear markets, brokers, computers, and investor psychology make this book well worth reading if you can locate it.

Charting Commodity Market Price Behavior, L. Dee Belveal, Commodities Press Division of Belveal & Company, Inc., Wilmette, IL 60091, 1969. No ISBN No. available.

Though possibly difficult to obtain a copy of this book, it is one of the two very best books on technical analysis and chart interpretation. Mr. Belveal not only explains chart interpretation, but demonstrates the principles with a multitude of illustrations. Though the book is oriented around technical analysis, the style of writing is anything but that, being very easy

to read and straightforward. He defines what he believes to be
the four major areas of technical chart analysis and describes in
infinite detail the subtleties of each. A careful study of this
book will open totally new avenues of understanding and profit to
the novice market speculator as well as the most experienced
market practitioner, both from commodity and stock chart analysis.

The Commodity Futures Market Guide, Stanley Kroll and Irwin
Shishko, Harper & Row, 1973. ISBN No. 06-033397-9.

This book reviews technical and fundamental methods of price
and analysis, the logic and rationale of changing price differences as they affect both speculators and hedgers, government regu-
lation of both domestic and international markets, the uses of put
and call options, including a complete section of actual trade
hedging examples. This is an entirely positive, systematic analysis of the diverse facets of commodity trading, and a practical
approach to making profits.

The Commodity Futures Trading Guide, Richard J. Teweles, Charles
V. Harlow, and Herbert L. Stone, McGraw-Hill, Inc. 1969, No. ISBN
No. available.

This book is really a complete guide to trading commodity
futures, and while it is a bit dated due to when it was published,
the information in it is just as valuable today as it was when it
was written. It goes over in great detail the role of the speculator in the markets as compared with other types of speculation,
the operation of the exchanges, how to open accounts, place
orders, understand monthly statements. The authors also outline
how the reader can formulate a trading plan, and they discuss with
disturbing honesty the "random walk" theory.

COMMODITIES Magazine, published monthly by COMMODITIES Magazine,
219 Parkade, Cedar Falls, IA 50613. Unquestionable a must to
subscribe to this publication for anyone who is in the commodities
markets or thinking about getting into them. It's impossible for

350

us to speak too highly of the editorial content, breadth of
articles, graphics and illustration of this magazine. If you're
not subscribing now, you should be.

<u>Commodity</u> <u>Trading</u> <u>Systems</u> <u>and</u> <u>Methods,</u> P. J. Kaugman, John Wiley &
Sons, Inc., 1978. ISBN No. 0-471-03569-6.

A really complete guidebook to a fuller understanding of
technical analysis systems as applied to the commodity markets.
This is a somewhat technical book, and probably would not be of a
lot of use to the beginning analyst. However, for the more
advanced student of the market who is looking for an in-depth
discussion of a multitude of technical systems, this
mathematically-oriented text will fill the bill.

<u>Economics</u> <u>of</u> <u>Futures</u> <u>Trading,</u> Thomas A. Hieronymus, Commodity
Research Bureau, Inc., 1971. Library of Congress No. 75-181523.

This is a college-level textbook for a course in commodity
futures markets and trading. It's also a "how it's done" and
"how to do it" book to guide commercial people in the commodity
trades and those who want to speculate in the commodity markets.
A bit weighty at times, nonetheless this book presents a lot of
material not otherwise available in most commodity books, and a
different viewpoint on the markets.

<u>Elliott</u> <u>Wave</u> <u>Principle,</u> Robert Prechter and A. J. Frost, New
Classics Library, 1981. ISBN No. 0-932750-02-8.

This volume details how to successfully use the Eliott Wave
in your own trading program. It includes coverage of the use of
ratio analysis to forecast highs and lows in the marketplace.
Also covered is how to predict the time frames between bull and
bear markets.

<u>Fastest</u> <u>Game</u> <u>In</u> <u>Town:</u> <u>Trading</u> <u>Commodity</u> <u>Futures,</u> Anthony M.
Reinach, Commodity Research Bureau, Inc., 1973. ISBN
0-910418-04-7.

This is definitely one of the two most entertaining as well as informative books on commodity trading that is available at this time. It is the kind of book that most professional speculators and advisors, after having read it, wish they had written themselves. In addition to the entertaining aspects of the book, there are excellent techniques outlined and explained thoroughly and in great detail.

Forecasting Commodity Prices, edited by Harry Juler, Commodity Resarch Bureau, Inc., 1975. ISBN No. 0-910418-05-5.

A unique work that provides technical and fundamental background in separate studies by different experts in each commodity to help the reader forecast price movements in twenty different markets. Also included is a separate study, not devoted to any particular commodity, on price forecasting with the aid of charts. Identified are the really important market factors that influence price movements for each of the specific markets.

Games Investors Play, Michael P. Chisholm, Butterfly & Buttercups Press, 1981. Library of Congress No. 82-70369.

. Written by the author of The Taurus Method, Mr. Chisholm is a practicing psychologist as well as commodity advisor and analyst. This book is based on the premise that investor's psychological problems, generally of a subconscious nature, sabotage their trading decisions and prevent them from succeeding in any type of investing. Basically a do-it-yourself workbook and text, it enables a reader to identify what these problems are for himself, and then gives practical, concrete advice and techniques to use to overcome these problems.

Getting Started in Commodities Futures Trading, Mark J. Powers, Investor Publications, Inc., 1982. ISRN No. 0-914230-01-8.

While this is a basic beginners handbook, it is still worthwhile reading for veteran traders, and makes a wonderful gift for family members or friends who would like to be able to understand what you are talking about. This book covers the pros and cons of commodity investing versus stock investing and delves into how to choose a broker and some aspects of technical analysis.

The Handbook of Commodity Cycles: A Window On Time, Jacob Bernstein, John Wiley & Sons, 1982, ISBN No. 0-471-08197-3.

This is the first really in-depth examination of cyclic analysis for short and long-term trading, giving proven price patterns that lower investment risk while improving profit performance. Over 130 tables of original price data help the reader identify cycles of differing lengths and explain how to read timing signals to determine when a cycle is beginning, peaking, or bottoming.

How to Make Money In Commodities, Bruce G. Gould, Bruce Gould Publications, P. O. Box 16, Seattle, WA 98111, 1980. No ISBN No. available.

Originally published a few years earlier in a spiral-bound, larger format, this book outlines in detail one specific technique for dealing with the markets, and we must admit, a very successful technique when it is followed carefully. Basically it explains "trading ranges" in commodities and how to utilize OCO orders with them. A highly-specialized, but very good volume.

How to Profit from Seasonal Commodity Spreads: A Complete Guide, Jacob Bernstein, John Wiley & Sons, 1983, ISBN No. 0-471-86432-3

This book represents the product of a massive research effort, and is the first working tool for determining profitable seasonal commodity spreads and spread combinations. Using computer analysis of daily price data for up to 14 years for 21 different commodities, the reader is presented with those spreads having the greatest proven profit potential. Also discussed for the first time are two new indexes, Seasonal Run and Percentage Reliability, to judge optimal entry and exit times for trades.

<u>Investor's</u> <u>Quotient,</u> Jake Bernstein, John Wiley & Sons, Inc.,
1981, ISBN No. 0-471-07849-2

Written by one of the best-known and most accurate commodity
analysts in the business, who is also a psychologist. Most
investors lose in trading commodities because of their own psychological hang-ups, and this book helps the reader understand how
his own emotional make-up contributes and limits his successes in
investing in the commodity markets.

<u>Moneylove</u>, Jerry Gillies, Warner Books, 1979. ISBN 0-446-91009-0

Although only available in paperback, this small book can do a
tremendous amount to help a person erase negative programming
messages in their brain around the subject of money. The author
conducts seminars around the country and the principles espoused
in this book basically are that money is <u>not</u> evil, and that money
is good since it provides a means to good ends. The basic message
and principles in this book make it very worthwhile for everyone
to read and study thoroughly.

<u>Money</u> <u>and</u> <u>Energy,</u> C. V. Myers, Soundview Books, Darien, CT. 1980.
ISBN 0-934924-00-7.

This book is filled with good observations written in a
straightforward, commonsense manner. He takes a careful look at
our total U.S. financial picture, covering the areas of money,
debt, inflation, and the energy situation. He tells the reader
how the U.S. got to where it is, and while his conclusions as to
where we are all going are not particularly optimistic, his
suggestions for individual protection in the years to come make a
lot of sense.

<u>Overcoming</u> <u>The</u> <u>Fear</u> <u>of</u> <u>Success,</u> Martha Friedman, Seaview Books,
1980. ISBN 0-87223-594-7

The subtitle of this marvelous book is, "Why and How We Defeat
Ourselves and What to Do About It," and excellently epitomizes the
content of this volume. The author poses the question of why is it

354

so difficult to get what we want out of life and to feel that we
deserve it once we do get it. She addresses herself to the fear of
success, a very common phobia within our society. She tells in
plain language and with concrete examples how people unconsciously
sabotage their chances for success, and shows how to recognize and
overcome these subconscious fears. She describes the roadblocks to
success with real stories of individual clients of hers. This is a
book that is one of those most highly recommended by us.

The Professional Commodity Trader, Stanley Kroll, Harper & Row,
1974. ISBN 0-06-012468-7

Whether one is interested in the commodity markets or any
other form of speculation, Mr. Kroll's book is absolutely the most
enjoyable to read of any account we have ever run across of an
individual trader's rise from small trading to accumulating
literally millions of dollars of profit in a relatively short
time. Mr. Kroll describes and illustrates with graphs his trades,
on a daily and weekly basis, as he progressed towards his millions
of dollars and managed to accumulate migraine headaches, ulcers,
hypertension, and insomnia along with the tension that accompanied
his market moves. One of his basic premises is that his success
was due more to analyzing his bad trades than to rejoicing over
his good ones. Along the way Mr. Kroll reveals to the reader the
techniques that he utilized and refined in order to make his
millions of dollars, thereby giving the reader a lot of avenues to
investigate in his own search for market profits.

The Profit Magic of Stock Transaction Timing, J.M. Hurst,
Prentice-Hall, Inc., 1970. Library of Congress No. 72-118287.

While this book is directed at the stock market, the techniques for development of one's own cyclical analysis, timing windows, and targets are probably the most detailed ever published.
Anyone who is interested in cyclical analysis, and developing
their own techniques, will find this book invaluable as the methodology is easily converted over into the commodity markets.

Profits Through Seasonal Trading, Jack Gruschcow and Courtney
Smith, John Wiley & Sons, 1980. ISBN No. 0-471-06158-1.

This invaluable sourcebook presents a very complete and
thorough study of the seasonal cycles of commodity prices.
Twenty-four of the most actively traded commodities are investi-
gated in detail. Not only are the cash prices analyzed, but also
studies of the nearest futures contract, and the seasonal tendencies of each of the individual contract months.

Rules for Financial Survival in the 1980's, Julian M. Snyder,
International Moneyline Press, 25 Broad St., New York, NY 10004,
1980.

A privately published book by one of the most astute
newsletter writers in the country. He examines carefully the economic situation in this country, and the world, explaining his
views as to how we got where we are, and where we are going from
here. More important are his suggestions for suviving the upcoming
economic upheaval as he foresees it.

The Silva Mind Control Method, Jose Silva, Simon & Shuster, 1977,
ISBN 0-671-22427-1

A more advanced method of self-hypnosis, self-psychotherapy,
and psycho-cybernetics, this is a detailed do-it-yourself explanation of how to use Silva self-visualization methods that are taught
by Silva Mind Control Centers around the country. The techniques
outlined in this book will definitely help the reader, if he prac-
tices them faithfully, to overcome stress, resolve bad habits, and
become much more creative.

Technical Analysis in Commodities, edited by P. J. Kaufman, John
Wiley & Sons, Inc. 1980. ISBN No. 0-471-05627-8.

A sophisticated, and very mathematical book that discusses in
great detail the newest, most sophisticated concepts and techniques
in price forecasting, hedging, and speculation. It is written by a

356

number of experts in the different areas being covered. There are some really interesting insights into price distortions, moving averages, and computer testing.

Techniques of a Professional Commodity Chart Analyst, Arthur Skiarew, Commodity Research Bureau, 1980. ISBN No. 0-910418-10-1.

A very practical book that presents in amazingly simple terms a number of different technical chart techniques. A lot of good information on oscillator techniques, moving averages, long-range charting, and targeting is presented. Extremely well-illustrated to make it even easier for the reader to follow, we highly recommend this book to anyone who wants to learn more about charting techniques, their interpretation, and relative merits.

Trading In Commodity Futures, Frederick F. Horn & Victor W. Farah, New York Institute of Finance, 70 Pine St., New York, NY 10005, 1979. ISBN 0-13-925941-4.

If available to you, by all means get the second edition and not the first edition of this book, as the revisions are substantial and have led to a greatly improved work. This book would make an excellent textbook for teaching a course in commodity future trading, though it is not written in the heavy handed manner of so many textbooks, but is instead quite readable even when covering such areas as customers' opening accounts, order placement, and fundamentals, some subjects that are very difficult for most authors to write about in a less-than-esoteric manner. This book serves a double function of presenting trading in commodity futures from both a trader's viewpoint as well as the broker's point of view, and presents complex regulatory and analytical material in a straightforward language of todays business world. There are numerous examples and illustrations to enable the reader to comprehend more rapidly the points the authors are making. Both neophytes and experienced traders alike will benefit from reading this edition, whether from cover to cover or simply a chapter at a time to suit their individual needs.

<u>TNT</u> <u>The</u> <u>Power</u> <u>Within</u> <u>You,</u> Claude M. Bristol & Harold Sherman, Prentice-Hall, Inc. 1971. No ISBN No. available.

From the standpoint of positive thinking, it is an early classic that is, despite its age, very readable and quite stimulating. It's definitely one of the forerunners of mental visualization techniques, and if one can approach it without letting it's somewhat pollyanish terminology bother them, then we find it highly useful. It has some specific techniques of getting your subconscious mind to assist you in your projects, most of which are not seen in subsequent books.

<u>View</u> <u>Points</u> <u>of</u> <u>a</u> <u>Commodity</u> <u>Trader,</u> Roy W. Longstreet, Frederick Fell Publishers, 1973. No. ISBN No. available.

Mr. Longstreet who is or was Chairman of the Board of Clayton Commodity Service is one of the legendary figures in commodity investing, and this book is a behind-the-scenes look at the techniques and methods he used in trading in order to achieve his financial success. Since his approach to trading is more fundamental than technical, and since he believes that psychology plays such an important role in the movement of prices, this book is a refreshing change of view from all the stodgy books available on the fundamentals of trading.

APPENDIX A

SEASONAL PATTERN CHARTS

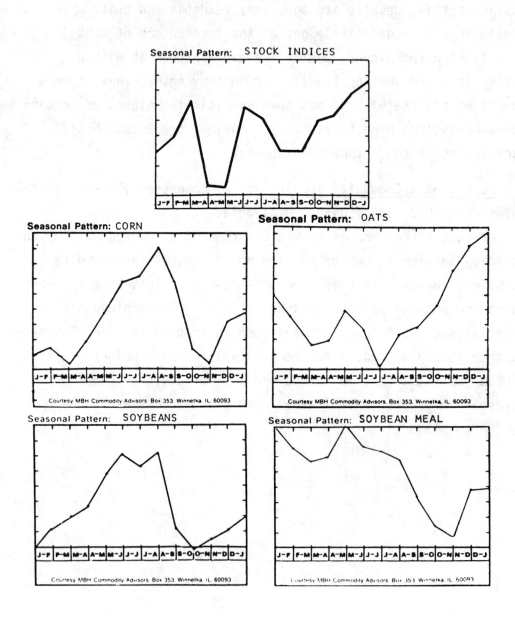

Seasonal Pattern: STOCK INDICES

J-F F-M M-A A-M M-J J-J J-A A-S S-O O-N N-D D-J

Seasonal Pattern: CORN

J-F F-M M-A A-M M-J J-J J-A A-S S-O O-N N-D D-J

Courtesy MBH Commodity Advisors, Box 353, Winnetka, IL. 60093

Seasonal Pattern: OATS

J-F F-M M-A A-M M-J J-J J-A A-S S-O O-N N-D D-J

Courtesy MBH Commodity Advisors, Box 353, Winnetka, IL. 60093

Seasonal Pattern: SOYBEANS

J-F F-M M-A A-M M-J J-J J-A A-S S-O O-N N-D D-J

Courtesy MBH Commodity Advisors, Box 353, Winnetka, IL. 60093

Seasonal Pattern: SOYBEAN MEAL

J-F F-M M-A A-M M-J J-J J-A A-S S-O O-N N-D D-J

Courtesy MBH Commodity Advisors, Box 353, Winnetka, IL. 60093

Seasonal Pattern: SOYBEAN OIL

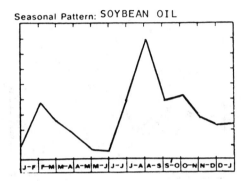

Seasonal Pattern: WHEAT

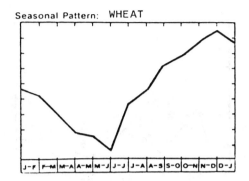

Seasonal pattern: LIVE CATTLE

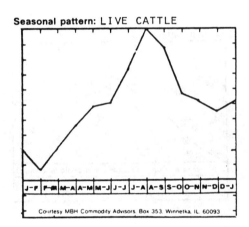

Courtesy MBH Commodity Advisors, Box 353, Winnetka, IL. 60093

Seasonal Pattern: HOGS

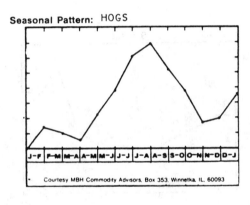

Courtesy MBH Commodity Advisors, Box 353, Winnetka, IL. 60093

Seasonal Pattern: PORK BELLIES

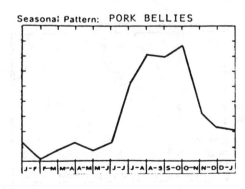

Seasonal Pattern COCOA

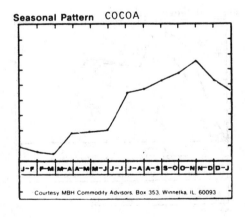

Courtesy MBH Commodity Advisors, Box 353, Winnetka, IL. 60093

A-3

Seasonal pattern: COFFEE

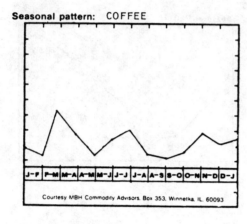

Courtesy MBH Commodity Advisors, Box 353, Winnetka, IL. 60093

Seasonal Pattern: ORANGE JUICE

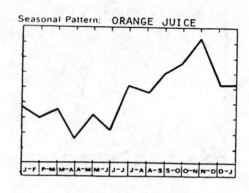

Seasonal Pattern: SUGAR

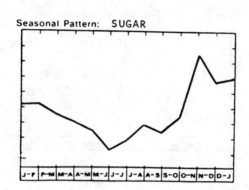

Seasonal Pattern: COTTON

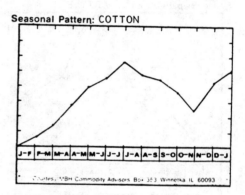

Courtesy MBH Commodity Advisors Box 353 Winnetka IL 60093

Seasonal Pattern: LUMBER

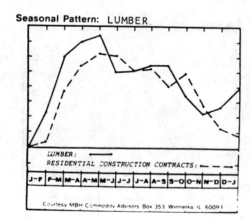

LUMBER:
RESIDENTIAL CONSTRUCTION CONTRACTS: ─ ─ ─

Courtesy MBH Commodity Advisors Box 353 Winnetka IL 60093

Seasonal Pattern: COPPER

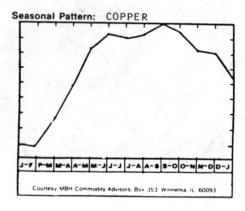

Courtesy MBH Commodity Advisors, Box 353, Winnetka, IL. 60093

Seasonal Pattern: GOLD

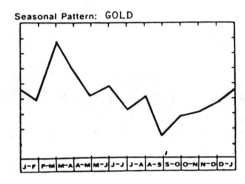

Seasonal Pattern: PLATINUM

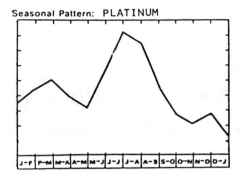

Seasonal Pattern: SILVER

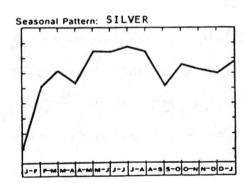

Seasonal Pattern: DEUTSCHE MARK

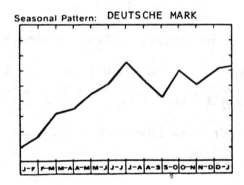

Seasonal Pattern: SWISS FRANC

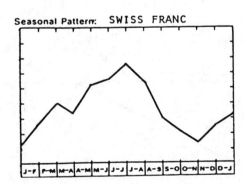

Seasonal Pattern: TREASURY BILLS

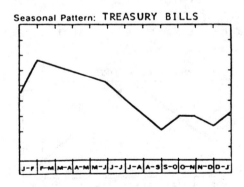

APPENDIX B

LONG-RANGE CYCLE GRAPHS

On this and the following three pages are Long-Range Cycle Graphs to assist the reader in visually determining the Long-Range Cycle in Prices for twenty-six commodities. Most of the data from which these graphs were constructed was obtained courtesy of Mr. Jake Bernstein of MBH Commodity Advisors.

The usage of these graphs is explained in the text of this volume, but we would like to caution the reader that these Long-Range Cycles, like all technical commodity data, are subject to distortions caused by other, perhaps unknown, longer-range cycles, fundamental occurrences, and other factors. These graphs are, as a result, guides to following the Major Trend, and not absolute predictors of price motion. Given those caveats, these graphs should be immensely useful to all traders.

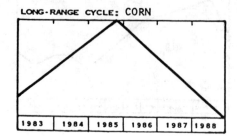

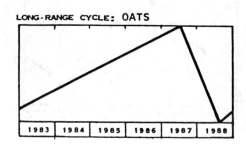

A-5

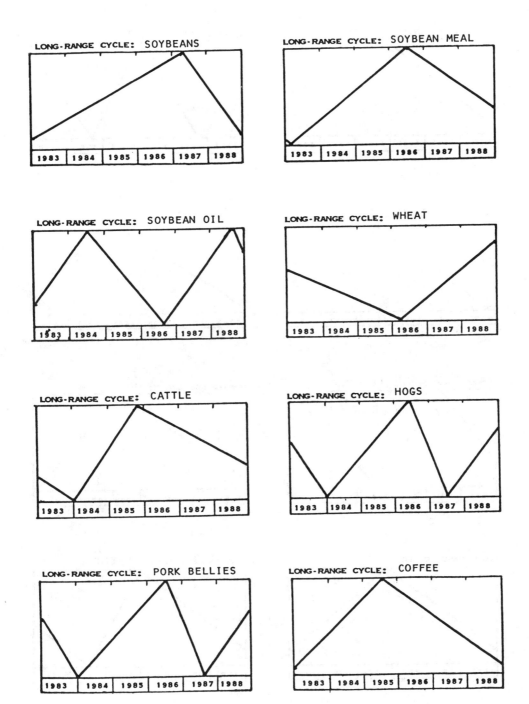

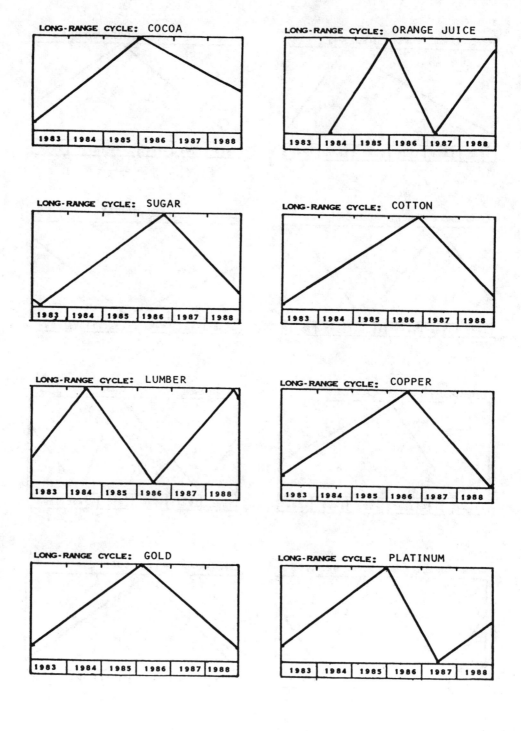